LOOK WHERE WE'RE GOING

ESCAPING THE PRISM OF PAST POLITICS

By the same author

Freedom and Capital, Blackwell 1961

Blind Victory, Hamish Hamilton 1986

The Edge of Now, Macmillan 2001

Out of the Energy Labyrinth
(with Carole Nakhle). I.B. Tauris 2007

Old Links and New Ties, I.B. Tauris 2013

Energy Empires in Collision, Gilgamesh 2016

The Mother of All Networks, Gilgamesh 2018

LOOK WHERE WE'RE GOING

ESCAPING THE PRISM OF PAST POLITICS

DAVID HOWELL

FOREWORD BY
THE LORD SPEAKER, NORMAN FOWLER

UNICORN

This edition first published by Unicorn in 2019
an imprint of Unicorn Publishing Group

Unicorn Publishing Group
5 Newburgh Street
London W1F 7RG

www.unicornpublishing.org

ISBN 978-1-912690-54-1

Printed and bound in Great Britain

Cover design by Unicorn

Book design by Graham Hales

Contents

Dedication

To Davina for living with an author
To Shiva, the god of paradoxes, in which
all opposites are reconciled
And, to the next lot and the lot after that

Author Acknowledgements

THE bibliography on page 257 of this book is my main thank you list, although by no means all the authors there will thank me for being included, or for the comments I offer on many of their works.

Other thanks must go to countless colleagues who in conversation or by correspondence have shed a new ray of light across the turmoil of our times as we all wonder how we came to the present atmosphere of deep uncertainty and apprehension, and where it may lead us from here.

I owe a special debt of gratitude to my assistant (and daughter), Kate Bain, who has worked through numerous drafts and amendments, and to those at Unicorn who have both encouraged me and coped with an author's endless changes, additions and inefficiencies – Ian Strathcarron, Ann Donald and Louise Campbell in particular.

My warmest thanks are reserved for my wife Davina for putting up with the hell of an author in the home.

Needless to say, the words , thoughts and views which follow are my own and no one else is to blame.

David Howell. July 2019, London

Foreword

by Norman Fowler, The Right Honourable Lord Fowler, Lord Speaker

DAVID Howell has been at the centre of British politics for over half a century. He was a speech writer with Edward Heath, later one of his ministers and a vigorous defender of his old boss. He wrote speeches for Margaret Thatcher in opposition then was a member of her first Cabinet. Later he was a Foreign Office minister in David Cameron's government. Throughout his political career he has maintained a close interest in world affairs, stretching way beyond Europe, which is unusual for a British politician. Today he chairs the House of Lords International Affairs Committee, for which he campaigned.

His skilful and invigorating new book draws on that experience and is what he describes as a hybrid. In one part it is the recollections of a senior and respected politician of a rich and varied career; in another part it looks forward and poses some of the major issues that politicians will have to grapple with in the age of social media, the iPhone and the blog.

I first worked with Howell in 1979 (as the title page photograph in the book shows), when we sat around the Cabinet table of Margaret Thatcher. For both of us it was it was the first time there with the risk of being overawed by the seniority of some of the company. There was Quintin Hogg, the irascible Lord Chancellor, who had been a power in the party for as long as I could remember. There was Peter

Carrington who gave amusing and world-weary reports each week on the major international developments and near him the bulky figure of Christopher Soames, the son-in-law of Winston Churchill, whose experience included the plum diplomatic job of ambassador in Paris. There was Keith Joseph demonised by Labour as an extreme free-market apostle but, in fact, one of the gentlest members of the Cabinet. Then of course, there was Willie Whitelaw the bluff ex-Guards officer who was quite indispensable for the successful running of the Government.

Added to this there were the openly ambitious like Michael Heseltine and the resident doubters like Jim Prior, Peter Walker and Francis Pym, who had already spent five long years of opposition becoming accustomed – or not – to the new leader. Howell and I were the most junior members of the Thatcher Cabinet which, over the years and through frequent changes of cast, was credited or blamed in presiding over a revolution in British politics. According to the legend it was a period in which monetarist theory, deregulation and a scepticism about social policy held sway. So how accurate was such a picture? Howell argues that it was not quite like that; I agree.

From the beginning it was clear for entirely pragmatic reasons that certain steps needed to be taken. Industrial relations law had to be reformed, particularly after the disaster of the Winter of Discontent. Equally it was clear that public spending had to be sensibly controlled unless we wanted to see increasing taxes on the public and businesses. There was no need to be a disciple of Milton Friedman to recognise these truths – though I suspect there were quite a number of the Cabinet who had never read the great man's theories on money supply. Then there was privatisation, still characterised in the public mind as the essence of the Thatcher administration – but, emphatically, it was not at all how we started.

If you look at the Conservative manifesto for the 1979 election you will find only two new privatisation pledges, both in my area of transport. The first was to denationalise the vast state-run conglomerate, the National Freight Corporation, which ran everything from road haulage to Pickford's removal services. Does anyone still argue that we need a state-run removals business? The second was to privatise the

British Transport Docks Board, which ran a series of ports around the country like Southampton and Hull. The resulting Associated British Ports is one of the most successful of all privatisations.

In pursuing these policies, I was not being pressed forward by Chris Patten and Angus Maude, the authors of the manifesto. Quite the opposite. The order had come down from the top. We were not to frighten the electoral horses. There were strong fears that such a policy was not of proven popularity with the party, let alone the public.

Howell argues that many of the signature policies of the new government evolved from past experience and past failures. The Winter of Discontent marked the long-delayed end of the belief that only Labour could manage the trade unions. It became clear that Ted Heath, far from being the discredited figure of lore, had laid the foundations for proper reform. The anti-inflation policies became popular with large numbers of the public, although not with union leaders – nor, as Mrs Thatcher once added gratuitously, with farmers. Margaret Thatcher was in the right place at the right time for these reforms, just as Ted Heath had been in the wrong place at the wrong time.

Heath also faced one obstacle which we were able to do something about in the Thatcher years: the opposition and obstructiveness of some of the senior figures in the Civil Service. Howell, a former Civil Service minister is outspoken on this. It would be nice to say that we eliminated such opposition; nice but not quite true. I remember when I was leading a four-day departmental meeting on the reform of social security, I was contradicted publicly by the Second Permanent Secretary in charge of the policy area, who made it quite clear that he rejected reform. I should have had him moved – no one would dream of sacking such a top official – but instead I simply drove around him. To be fair, such open disloyalty was almost unknown in my dealings with the Civil Service and most worked beyond normal hours to make our policies work. When I abolished the dock labour scheme in 1989, I remember one civil servant telling me that taking off the regulations and allowing the ports' areas to flourish had made his career worthwhile. I had more trouble – as did David Howell – with the chairmen of nationalised industries who regarded the public companies as 'theirs'.

* * * * *

So much for the history; what of the future? Here Howell proves himself a totally original thinker. Indeed, had we listened to him in the past we might have avoided some undoubted errors and omissions. He argues strongly for an extension of popular ownership – in particular that everyone working for a company should have a stake in it; this was how the National Freight Corporation started in the private sector, with remarkable success. Annual general meetings had to be held at Wembley or in some convenient theatre to accommodate all the new shareholders who wanted to attend. The chairman needed to field questions from the floor on drivers' hours and not just the prospects for the year. Sadly, by the time I joined the board ten years later the position had already changed, leading one chairman to refer to what had once been his shareholding staff, as 'hungry mouths to feed'.

However, it is in international policy that Howell makes his really distinctive contribution. He goes back to the early 1970s when the choice between Europe and the Commonwealth was portrayed as distinct alternatives. 'Far away' Commonwealth nations like Australia and Canada were swept to one side as not having the same relevance as the neighbouring countries of Europe. The same argument also told against the countries of Asia. But, as Howell points out, the world today has changed almost out of recognition. The communications revolution has seen to that. It is a far cry from the days before the internet, the mobile phone and relatively easy international travel.

Happily, Howell does not get bogged down in the politics of Brussels. He proposes instead that Britain should look outward to the Commonwealth, very much including the developing economies of African countries like Nigeria, and to Asia, but at the same time developing our links with Europe. They are not alternatives. It may well be that this new way forward will be put to the test in the next decade. Certainly, there will be problems, but this book contains the hope that Britain can move forward from the sterile political arguments on the European Union and open a genuinely new chapter. It is a book that all politicians should read.

Being on the Purpose and Nature of This Book

*'If you really want to face the future without fear, make
sure you're carrying a bit of the past with you.'*
—Rabbi Jonathan Sacks[1]

*'The farther backward you can look, the farther
forward you are likely to see.'*
—Winston S. Churchill[2]

*'The web of history is wearing dangerously thin. If
the web breaks civilisation breaks. Such a break with
the past is the most fearful of the calamities that can
fall upon humankind.'*
—Herbert Agar in A Time for Greatness[3]

ABOVE my desk hangs a picture. It is a copy, a very good
one, brush stroke by brush stroke, of Turner's *The Fighting
Temeraire*, voted at one time Britain's favourite picture. It
shows the magnificent old HMS *Temeraire*, a ninety-two-gun ship-
of-the-line, being towed by a steam tug to the breaker's yard, the
age of sail being pulled to its end by the age of steam power, new

technology about to open up limitless new worlds, and new politics, as the old order fades.

There are similarities here with the underlying theme and messages of this book. What the chapters ahead seek to illustrate, through a mixture of memoir, anecdote and explanation, is how the grand political and philosophical debates and struggles of the last century have been largely overtaken by new technologies which have changed everything: our lives, our concerns, our politics and parties, our behaviour and our national direction and destiny.

Over the period of roughly half a century, British politics have been transformed. Gone, so it seems, are the time-honoured stability, pragmatism and mannered debates which the world saw as the hallmarks of the Westminster model. Maybe this picture was rose-tinted, but it was widely believed.

In its place we have miracles of connection and glittering opportunities. But we also have angry and polarised discourse, a society divided, a political system distrusted and a kingdom threatened with disunity. The democracy which was taken for granted fifty years ago now seems to have a missing half – as the pages ahead will explore.

How has this happened? What are the lessons to be learnt? Where do the roots of discord lie? How do we escape the myths of the past which continue to distort our views, but retain and build on the best of the past which served us well? And how far do the upheavals of the outside world account for our changed circumstances?

The book divides roughly into two periods although with a good deal of overlap. The first period examines the twenty-five years or so from the late '60s to the early '90s. This period marked the slow retreat of collectivism and state ascendancy of the kind which had dominated the Western world for the previous half century, in war and peace, and the gradual acceptance of economic liberalism and market power from the mid-1950s to what was seen to be its apogee, roughly in the early 1990s.

The second period covers the next twenty-five years or so, from the mid-'90s, perhaps the high point of free-market fervour, to the present twenty-first century times of turmoil, with revolutionary technology entering every sphere of existence, public and private. This is a time when the old ideological arguments seem to have slipped out of focus, when the simplicities of the Western liberal case have turned into bewildering paradoxes, and entirely new forces, powers, dangers and debates – and in some cases, new stories, which distort the very democratic process itself – begin to shape the future.

At the hinge of these two very different periods, more or less midway, sits the premiership of Margaret Thatcher, whose very first Cabinet is the first picture in this book.

The British Cabinet of 1979, of which I was a member for four years and of which I have acute memories, is a good staging post in my story because it marks both an end and a beginning. What truly went on within it reflects the clashes and confluence of two eras. It was the end in British politics of the era of collectivism – the consensual doctrine of interventionist governance which had reigned widely, in one form or another, for most of the twentieth century until that date. It was also the beginning, the first dawning – and warning – of a quite different era of splintered views, shattered certainties and disparate and divided powers and forces which have come to colour the world today.

By going back to the two governments of the last century in which I served, I hope to identify the tremendous contrast in economic, social and surrounding political circumstances between that era and the present one, despite the tendency for public debate to cling to old shibboleths, old struggles and the old political lexicon. The Book of Thatcher is now closed, or so it will be argued. There is a need to escape past assumptions and modes of thought and debate, and the hall of mirrors which successive interpretations have bequeathed to us. But the need also remains to pick out those principles of that era which remain valid, enduring and essential to preserve.

Myths cloud the story at every point. For example, the Heath period of government is more or less written off by historians and condemned in some Conservative circles by the decision to join the European Community.[4]

Meanwhile, the Thatcher era is still seen by some as a free-market nirvana to which they long to return, a more certain world of values and verities that they believe have been lost. For others that period represents a destruction of collective and community values and a surrender to narrow doctrines of self-interest and winner-takes-all capitalism. Some observers and analysts have depicted it as the burial of social democracy which had governed post-war Europe.

Yet, instead of dying away, in the course of my writing, the virulence of these different attitudes has intensified. The hankering for a return to the apparent simplicities of free-market economics has increased while, on the other side, the rejection of the liberalising approach has been elevated into a moral crusade against the Thatcher legacy. In the words of Rabbi Jonathan Sacks 'morality had been outsourced to the market'.[5] Or take a statement by Justin Welby, the Archbishop of Canterbury, that a form of capitalism has been growing which has 'lost any contact with moral foundation'.[6] Today's confusions are squarely blamed on the alleged excesses of the past.

A powerful feeling of resentment has grown up – not just in Britain (although especially here) but in advanced societies generally. People have come to believe that their identities and worth are not getting a fair share of recognition or adequate respect – that, most emphatically, the economy does not work for everyone, that capital ownership, and the dignity and security that go with it, is over-concentrated in the hands of those who already own more than they can use. This is the message that the new connectivity spreads with increasing vividness and speed. In doing so it leads almost seamlessly to a suspicion of supranational institutions and rules, and a demand for the reassertion of the place and role of nation states in the international order – a call to put 'our own people' first. Echoes of this have rattled through the Brexit debate in the UK and will continue to do so.

It will be argued in the chapters ahead that these feelings are heavily fuelled by parodies of the past, that none of these versions truly portray the political world of forty years ago, or where it has led us to now. Nor do they help us address today's issues in a balanced way.

Nonetheless, the realisation is growing that something is fundamentally and dangerously wrong with the world's economic (and therefore social) structure and Britain's own part of it.

A central contention of the story is that populism is here to stay and grow as massive, all-embracing digital connectivity, identity politics, and migrants on the march guarantee that populist pressures will not go away. The micro-chip inevitably sees to that. When three-quarters of the world's population has access to the World Wide Web; when twelve-billion smart phones, or more, are in use; when most individuals have their own 'echo chamber',[7] this is inescapable. The populist 'box' contains many different types of grievance and protest. It has its own vocabulary of intolerance, denunciation of élites and rage against foreigners – of the kind which engulfed Europe in the twentieth century. Its shadow darkens even more moderate kinds of nationalism, which may amount to no more than proper love of, and loyalty to, one's country. We must guard against a process which, in the words of Parag Khanna, is 'democracy being hijacked by populism'.[8]

The implications for both domestic tranquillity and international stability are vast . They have major significance both for the global re-positioning of Britain (which is a central part of this story) and for those who wonder how and when the Donald Trump phenomenon will end in the United States. It means that virulent antagonism to technocrats, élites, public authorities, 'experts', and that amorphous enemy, 'the other', will grow, that narrower breeds of nationalism will flourish and that the European Union will continue to be a target for populists from all quarters and within every member state.

Two even more basic issues that arise from the populist ferment will also be examined:

First, whether the processes and procedures of business and finance today, with the staggering concentrations of wealth they generate, can any longer be called 'capitalism'. Whether they are described as 'crony capitalism', or 'plutocracy' or 'hyper-capitalism', do these transactional patterns and extraordinary outcomes merit the capitalist epithet at all ? Do they match the wealth-spreading, free-market democratic capitalism of the textbooks at any point? Or are we now living with a new cosmos, that certainly still has strong capitalist features but also deep differences – a process whose course and behaviour is not fully understood and to which the old analysis and the political battle-lines, no longer relate?

Secondly, we ask whether, in an age of revolutionary communications technology, it is any longer possible to distil mass opinion in the way which the traditional institutions of democracy require.

In his powerful book *The Future of Capitalism*,[9] Sir Paul Collier sums up the imbroglio of misapprehensions. Today's anxieties, he writes:

> have promptly been answered by the old ideologies, returning us to the stale and abusive confrontation of Left and Right. An ideology offers the seductive combination of easy moral certainties and an all-purpose analysis, providing a confident reply to any problem. The revived ideologies of nineteenth-century Marxism, twentieth-century fascism and seventeenth-century religious fundamentalism have all already lured societies into tragedy. Because the ideologies failed, they lost most of their adherents, and so few ideologue politicians were available to lead this revival. Those that were belonged to tiny residue organisations: people with a taste for the paranoid psychology of the cult, and too blinkered to face the reality of past failure.

As the chapters ahead will show in detail, current thinking is dominated by exaggerated generalisation (that fatal intellectual *déformation*) that must be dismantled if we are to see or move ahead clearly and safely.

Thus, we are surrounded with versions of the political past which have been coloured and overstated to the point of falsehood. We have allowed these fables to narrow our views of the challenges before us. Adding to this, new forces are at work which distort the interpretation of events and opinions almost beyond recognition, driven by technological manipulation and opinion-bending, and by algorithms which can even read an individual's moods and half-expressed concerns with a scale and precision inconceivable a few decades ago.

* * * * *

One of the more significant of past political myths, at least in the British context, is the insistent claim that the arrival of the first Thatcher administration marked a massive swing away from the state and the collective interests of society to narrow individual interests and motivations: from social cohesion to market greed; from ethics to profits – and much more besides. When Margaret Thatcher observed that there was 'no such thing as society' – meaning of course that society, far from being a solid lump, was a complex mosaic of interests and lives, and is now becoming even more so – it was pounced upon as evidence that the community spirit was under assault and that social democracy had collapsed.

Was this anything like what occurred? Or is it, as I shall argue with evidence, bunkum? Memories are fading about the Thatcher and Reagan years and the rhetorical high profile they and their supporters gave to free-market doctrines and capitalism as it was then perceived. What happened was quite different and much more limited than the revolutionary rhetoric implied. A line will be traced in the pages ahead between the political world of 1979, with its issues – which in retrospect look so clear cut – and today's maelstrom of doubts. However, there has been more than enough distortion to give these false pictures of the past a life of their own.

For example, it will be shown that the swing to free-market capitalism was very limited, a far cry from the unbridled free-market fiesta the critics feared and the most zealous free-marketeers hoped for. Moreover, consideration will be given to how much of this swing was simply a natural resurgence of markets.

Ownership may have moved from the state to private enterprise. But throughout the Thatcher period the degree of close regulation, if anything, intensified as new regulatory authorities spread their wings. Ironically, major utilities found themselves under more exposure and control in the private sector than in their state-owned days, when 'control' had often been little more than a private dialogue with nervous civil servants and uncomprehending ministers.

Without it being ordained by legislators or blessed by philosophers or doctrines, the world has been compelled to accept the truth that markets cannot work without the state and the state needs markets in order to function – more so than ever in the digital era. The issue is one of balance between the state, the market economy and the communities within society.

The author Raghuram Rajan likens the three domains to three pillars – state, markets and community – which must have equal importance to sustain a functioning society, and to anchor the individual in the disorienting swirl of change.[10] No state can survive now by dominating or trying to eliminate markets and private property, or without ceding power to vibrant communities within it, and to free and liberated markets. The mixed and managed economy, in some form or other, is all prevailing. As maintained by Francis Fukuyama in *The End of History*,[11] the Right's liberalised market systems have triumphed almost everywhere, consigning detailed centralised planning and control to the dustbin.

But here is the paradox: Using the old language ,if the Right has won, so has the Left. Élites and established hierarchies of the pre-digital age are now under attack as never before. By enabling and transmitting almost total transparency, the revolution of instant communication has seized power away from governing structures, ruling classes and cabals, and from central planners. Outraged charges of unfairness and lack of social justice now clog the media. In this sense it is the Left that has 'won', in diluting and weakening the ruling order and reducing its authority to an inchoate mess. Through social media and the global reach of smart phones and their successors, protest against authority is now empowered with a speed, organizational force and mass never before available; it is governments, rather than *les misèrables*, who find themselves behind barricades as they struggle to maintain legitimacy. Far from being the end of history, this has been the unfolding prologue to a new phase of disarray in human affairs.

In truth the old Left–Right vocabulary of politics is incapable of explaining or conveying what has occurred in the redistribution and interplay of modern power. Political parties based on the old language have lost coherence. Technology pulls leftward and rightward simultaneously. It is attached to no 'isms'. It can neither be conserved nor socialised. On one side, power goes to the market, to business and to the new giant oligopolies controlling the master algorithms of the planet; on the other side, it splinters away to the people in their myriad cells, units, groupings, tribes, families and factions – and, indeed, to the empowered individual, who is connected to every corner of the world and to every source of knowledge and information.

[handwritten margin note: and lost]

BEING ON THE PURPOSE AND NATURE OF THIS BOOK

The Meek Have Inherited the iPad

When nearly every member of a society has his or her own echo chamber and is able to transmit opinions instantly to millions, we have taken the power of the masses – just about as far as it can go. The meek have inherited the iPad and the oppressed have their eyes on their iPhones.[12] Although in ways unforeseen by Karl Marx, it seems that the triumph of the proletariat, the all-conquering march of the masses and the classless society, has arrived.

But has it? Again, the question is: What are we really seeing? In early days the internet was going to be the great instrument of citizens' empowerment, breaking down the centres of privilege and influence. In latter days it has become the agent and enabler of global networks of unprecedented size, monopoly power and influence, soaring above nation states and opening the way to targeted persuasion of the subtlest, and often most poisonous, kind.

Like the earlier dream of all-conquering markets in Thatcher's days, the subsequent dream of the internet as the great instrument of citizens' liberation has evolved into something else, which the conventional political debate has been unable to connect with or even describe. The grammar of the political past has become redundant. The phrase 'the masses' sounds antiquated, like the old language of class distinction. But there is now a new kind of mass, far more connected by technology than ever before, more opinion-fired and much more fragmented, resentful and disputatious. The triumph belongs to nobody. Everyone or no-one has won.

Empires without Power

Preoccupation with the controversies of the past would matter less if it were not for the way they blind us to what is happening now. Discussion continues as though the power of cabinets and national leaders to shape events today is just the same as it was forty years ago, and as though the democratic, free-market, capitalist process is exactly what it was in previous decades. However, the reality is quite different. In today's democracies, our own in Britain very much included, power at every level has seeped away from the central governments and elected authorities of the past. That power and legitimacy, which we

23

in the '79 Cabinet team assumed so confidently we possessed, is no longer there. That world has gone forever.

On the global scale power has also obviously shifted, but not in the historically 'normal' way from West to East, or from one empire to another, as many commentators like to maintain in apocalyptic style. Instead we are witnessing central power and authority drain away in two directions: first, in countless rivulets to open sites outside the administrative order, to non-state actors and agencies, some open and good, some dark and evil; secondly, to the tech Leviathans which now preside over nations, transforming the lives of every citizen in ways of which we are barely conscious.

The mantras and clichés of the twentieth-century Left–Right political debate, largely economic in flavour, but with deep philosophical roots, have few answers to questions raised by current global forces: algorithmic power; transparent inequality; the fragmentation of identities; terrorism and rising gang crime; pockets of moral wilderness in our great cities; global ecological challenges; or the rise of non-liberal China. Technology is centre-stage, where it was already moving when Margaret Thatcher formed her first Cabinet and has left many of the philosophical wranglings of that era far behind. The intellectual giants of the twentieth century have not prepared us *in any way* for the hyper-capitalism or social disorder and rancour of the digital age, as completely distinct from an earlier era of democratic capitalist behaviour rooted in trust, civility and obligation and in clear principles, going far back into the history of civilisation.

Furthermore, as chapters ahead will explain, nothing has prepared us in the West for the rising power and influence of Asia, and its fundamental challenge to Western hegemony, values and systems. In 1979 the USA was entering its unipolar moment, with enthusiastic British encouragement. A century ahead that would prove Asian rather than American, was inconceivable; a world order shaped by superior Asian influence and principles entered no-one's calculations for a single second.

In contradiction to past 'absolute truths', the practicalities of modern economic life mean that, with or without conditions of political freedom and genuine democratic governance, economic success can be delivered — at least for a time, as China demonstrates. The Chinese model, with its confusing and often obscured mix between illiberal state involvement and capitalist enterprise — on a colossal scale — fits neither the rhetoric nor the realities of the twentieth-century past.

* * * * *

We are stuck with the remnants — the philosophical leftovers of the political collectivists from Marx onwards. But we go on fighting about laissez-faire and Marxian capitalism, long since dead and their coffins sealed, so it was thought, by the digital age of popular empowerment. (In one minor sense only may the old ideological head-to-head still be truly relevant, given the back-to-Marx theme song in Britain of the Labour leader, Jeremy Corbyn and some of his party.)

Meanwhile, the time-honoured polar argument, still prevalent among some Conservative thinkers, between those who still believe in the power of the state and those who think individuals should be left to run their own lives, has become redundant, reduced to a marginal issue of adjustment. Columnists may still like to dilate on it, but it now belongs in the sidelines.

This new reality is a lesson which has been learnt by both authoritarians and democrats alike, if not by theorists.

The digital age now tells every ruler what even the demagogue dictators of the twentieth century did not understand, or ignored — that markets *must* be allowed to operate freely to a very large degree and that the attempt to govern and control the total state from the centre will not work even in the short term, let alone for the decades the totalitarian leaders of the twentieth century hoped for, with their visions of new orders and all-knowing state plans.

Perhaps even the last country on earth in the twenty-first century to defy this reality — the 'hermit nation' of North Korea — is reaching its moment of truth. Already some market sectors under Kim Jong-Un's regime have been cautiously allowed to thrive. Now comes disruption, not just by the decentralising pull of information and communications technology, but by Donald Trump's wheeler-dealer offers to transform a frozen state-run economy into a new Vietnam (itself one of the new species which doesn't conform with past templates or philosophies of state or free-market economies).

Instead, we see today the mushrooming of a new genus in the evolutionary pattern of governance. Enter illiberal democracies which go through the elaborate charade of elections and, through force majeure, are compelled to permit enterprise and markets to flourish within limits, in the knowledge that there is now no choice. The 'choice' between markets and the state is now irrelevant or even unavailable. In these blurred worlds there is law, but not the universal rule of law; law for the people but not for the government; elected leaders but not removable leaders; rights by permission but not by lawful entitlement.

Profound thinkers like Fareed Zakaria[13] and David Runciman[14] have warned us strongly about these threats to our cosy democracies and Left–Right political squabbles, which carry on while the democratic ground is slipping away beneath our feet and, with it, the norms-based Western patterns of behaviour between nations and peoples. There will be a return to their views and others towards the end of this story. Here, the conclusion is simply that the economy-centred debates which raged through the twentieth century do not equip us for today's problems, or for understanding how government is to be carried on and social order upheld, nor for adjusting to the fundamental changes in the international order, with its rising Asian preponderance, or for calming today's churn of economic and social discontent. Nor do these past philosophic battles equip us to address today's existential threats of uncontrollable new infections or approaching climactic upheaval and environmental destruction. The issues are not addressed, not explained, not linked, not understood. Something very big is missing.

The Theoretical Fog

As these familiar debates and thought patterns become sidelined, we are left with a theoretical fog swirling around us, hindering us from seeing our new conditions clearly.

Take as our a case in point the Thatcher legacy. Was it a stripped-down state with markets triumphant? No, her legacy after thirteen years in office was a still huge UK state sector, with public spending still at 40 per cent at the end of her premiership, having risen in real terms by about 1.3 per cent every year between 1979 and 1990. The legacy was still a massive National Health Service – one of the world's largest employers – plus pages of laws and statutes pouring out faster at the end of her premiership than at the outset[15] – more rights and freedoms in theory but more laws and controls in practice.

Despite many public commitments to deregulation, notably in the financial sector, the regulatory environment grew more extensive than ever, while welfare spending remained at record levels, with government intrusion and involvement (good and supportive but also tiresome and disincentivising) on an unprecedented scale. Whatever else this could be called, it was certainly not the world of the weak state, small government, market greed and lost community spirit the critics keep portraying.

As I shall show, the legend of the Thatcher era of rampaging free markets, of blind faith in untrammelled market forces, is distracting us from real and truly dangerous forces now transforming the patterns of society. These forces are creating evolving capitalist processes different from anything that went before, shifting the global power balance, promoting new kinds and perceptions of inequality and injustice, and leaving the moral compass spinning. We remain stuck in a quagmire of false antitheses – between the state and the individual, between ethics and profits, between the community and self-interest, between the common good and market forces – the pitched philosophical battles of the past which are completely superseded by other more real and relevant issues today.

Plainly the last thing modern democrats want is reversion to the kind of powerful and coercive state fashioned by Stalin or Hitler or envisaged by Hegel. The twentieth century saw that idea off, with all its horrors. But nor can we welcome a state so weak and challenged that democratic government becomes unstable, constantly pushed this way and that by volatile and incoherent public opinion, and unable to inspire loyalty or provide a governing framework of standards and conduct. That is not democracy, and never was.

Instead, the new Asia, which is becoming the determining influence in all our lives, East and West, and about which I shall have much to say in later chapters, is settling for a kind of technocratic yet accountable government which conforms to no Western principles and cannot be explained in the language of Western politics and philosophy.

The old dogmas of ideological battlelines between state legitimacy and individual freedom, which continue to trouble the body politic in the ways described above, are all essentially Western topics, addressed through Western thinking and historical experience.

But surrounding and overlaying them is a global contextual shift of fundamental and all-embracing significance.

Our Western future and the key strategic issues facing us are going to be shaped as much by Asia as by America. The twentieth-century transatlantic relationship is becoming like 'driving forwards while looking in the rear-view mirror'.[16]

There is a tendency in London and Washington, and in other capitals, to attribute the transatlantic deterioration to Donald Trump. The nightmare, we are assured, of American self-centredness will pass and we will be back to good old Uncle Sam and Pax Americana, the world which Ronald Reagan and Margaret Thatcher lived in and worked together to uphold.

As will be explained in Chapter Fifteen, no view could be more wrong.

* * * * *

To lift thinking out of the old polarities, many myths about the political past must be put aside and new methods of governance accepted and fostered. Government, as the humble and trusted instrument of the people, must be reborn in a new setting. The escape from the dichotomies of the past must somehow be engineered. This book will attempt to help in doing just that by describing some of what really went on inside the Thatcher administration and by tracing the lessons from those times for today's world, with its very different challenges and hazards.

Possible Side Effects of Reading on from Here

An early warning for those who read on from here, and especially for those who have an understandable aversion to political memoirs, is that this book is a hybrid. Nowadays, a genre called 'autofiction' is said to blur the line between autobiography and fiction; here I am blurring the line between history and memories, between accounts of events and evolving ideas, and some of my personal journey through the ideological thickets in quite extraordinary times.

These are dangerous days for moderates. The middle ground of political debate and discussion has become a perilous no-man's line, dotted with mines and swept by snipers and machine gun-fire.

By 'moderates' I do not mean those poised half way between the old Left and Right positions, traditional centrists caught in the old debate between socialist state planning versus free markets. We have left all that behind as the pages ahead will show. I mean moderate against ideological and dogmatic certainty of any backward-looking variety in relation to the issues of our times.

So, if you are convinced you are right and have clear-cut solutions to hand, put this book down at once. It is not for you.

If, for instance, you either *know* that Britain is on the certain path to liberation and greatness – the stairway to heaven,[17] or, on the other hand, *know* that leaving the European Union is the greatest disaster for Britain since 1940, then read no further.

If you think, looking back, that everything Margaret Thatcher did as Prime Minister was perfect and that good government began in 1979, or, at the other extreme, that she and her policies inflicted catastrophic damage on Britain, that her premiership was a disaster and of no relevance to today's issues, then stop here. You are in a world out of which this book steps.

(Or for that matter, if you are looking for a truly detailed and deep account of the Thatcher years in particular, then go straight to Charles Moore's magisterial, authorised biography[18] or to Jonathan Aitken's *Margaret Thatcher: Power and Personality*.[19])

If you believe that democracy is just about majorities and that those minorities who disagree with you are therefore anti-democratic, or that democracy is about obeying something called 'the will of the people' and that the power of mass opinion justifies vitriolic and personal attacks on opponents as acceptable, then turn away. What lies ahead will not please you.

If you believe even half of what you read in the daily newspapers, especially the negative, shock-horror stuff, or the phantasmagoria of Left–Right party politics, or that governments are in charge of everything, or completely 'in control' (and therefore to blame for everything that goes wrong), or that the 'answer' is a strong leader possessed of clear-cut convictions to see us through, then here you will be disappointed.

However, if you hope that the current divisions in our society can be bridged (and may not be nearly as deep as depicted), that the forces at work pulling us together are mostly stronger than the forces pulling us apart, that the paradoxes and disruptions of globalisation are survivable, that the bewildering momentum of technology and the massive growth of communications are manageable without dragging us into anarchy, that the bitter polarisation of debate should and can be challenged and some civility restored to it, that new battles can and must be fought to uphold new kinds of democracy, then there just might be something here for you.

If you care for serious argument, put forward with some sense of accountability (unlike the venomous one-liners that flow through Twitter), if you believe that a careful reappraisal of the last fifty years of political thinking and ideas and their consequences can help to better explain where we have got to and what might come next, then I hope you enjoy reading on.

Read selectively. Chapters are essays. Not every one of them connects, but then nor does every part of life. If you think, as Margaret Thatcher thought, that looking back is pointless, then start where the new world started, at Chapter Fourteen.

But if you believe, as I do, that an understanding of roots is the beginning of wisdom, never more so than in this age of turmoil, then start here.

PART ONE
ORIGINS

Chapter One

The Crossroads Cabinet

V ENICE, 19 June 1980, the Group of Seven Summit. Looking around the table at the eight leaders of the Western world, I was seized by the extraordinary emptiness of the occasion. This was truly the Wizard of Oz moment when, behind the giant machinery and awesome panels of power, there turns out to be, as in the story and the movie, just one elderly blinking gentleman, not intending much and not knowing much either. The trappings were there but not the power. Much larger forces were sweeping the world, turning leaders into followers who were neither shaping nor fully understanding what was happening, or the direction in which they were being pulled.

Earlier in the day I had been late for the motor launch. Margaret Thatcher was asking, slightly impatiently, where I was. I had a filthy cold and had had no breakfast. We were on our way along the Grand Canal and out across the lagoon to visit the Isola Torcello where exciting new Byzantine frescoes had just been uncovered. This was considered to be a suitable dawn pastime for the British Prime Minister and her delegation before the day of summit meetings ahead. I was the only other Cabinet minister in her entourage; I was there because the world was having an oil shock and this summit was intended to be all about oil.

Jimmy Carter was still in the White House and had arrived in an oversized US warship parked somehow in the lagoon. He was said to be accompanied by 800 staff, although a nought may have been added, or the crew thrown in. We, on the other hand, had just our launch.

We arrived at the island as the sun rose and, sure enough, a magnificent breakfast feast had been laid out. However, the Prime Minister swept the party on to the nearby church in search of culture. Culture involved a ladder climb up several levels of scaffolding to view the recently uncovered walls. Most of us were tired and hungry by this time, but Mrs Thatcher was up on the high viewing platform in a trice. Then she was down, and it was time to return to the launch the Grand Canal, sweeping again past the croissants, to be in time for the first round-table meeting of G7 leaders later that morning, in the vast monastery library on Isola San Giorgio Maggiore. I was kept tightly in tow and told I would be summoned to attend the library meeting shortly, to brief the leaders on oil and energy.

This I did, at a circular table around which sat the then leaders of the free world: the Prime Minister of Canada, the President of France, the Prime Minister of Italy, The Chancellor of West Germany, the Prime Minister of the UK, the President of the United States and the President of the European Commission.[20]

Otto Lambsdorff[21] and I, the two Energy ministers called in to brief the mighty ones, waited outside, along with the Foreign Minister of Japan, Saburō Ōkita. Although Mr Ōkita was the head of the Japanese delegation and although Japan was already then the second largest economy in the world (and a giant consumer of oil and gas), the wonders of protocol and bureaucracy meant he did not qualify for the inner meeting of the lofty and had to wait with us to be summoned. He did not say much but his silences were friendly. Perhaps he thought we were a ship of fools.

Otto Lambsdorff was also the West German Industry minister, which included energy, so he was there with a rather wider brief than mine. Using a stick (he lost a leg at the end of the war), he moved with amazing speed through conference rooms and onto platforms. He was a gloriously non-interventionist, free-market politician who believed that the immediate 'great world oil crisis' was no such thing and would be solved by market forces. I believed him to be right (although on broader issues we were both wrong – see Chapter Four).

However, on the specific issue, with oil markets self-adjusting and with prices already falling from the sky-high levels of only a few months earlier, it was clear that the immediate 'crisis' was over, and we briefed accordingly.

We were out of line with the thinking of most of the leaders around the table, all of whom had clearly been supplied with crisis-strewn briefs. With the exception of Margaret Thatcher, they were fired up to 'do something'. Was not that why the world's leaders had been brought together? Was not every media headline filled with warnings of catastrophe and demands for action?

For the leaders, it was very confusing – the crisis was not running according to script or in line with opinion columns. As a result, the conversation around the table became desultory and disconnected. They wanted to lead somewhere: Surely there was a need for action, for coordination, for strategic plans? Which levers should be pulled and what would happen if they were? There was vague talk of the need to build more nuclear power stations – to get out from under the oil sheikhs. The truth which could not be uttered, the communiqué which could not be issued was, as Otto Lambsdorff and I believed, that the situation was not fully understood and there was nothing much to be done.

I never did get my breakfast but I had learnt that wherever the sources of power now lay, they were not around the table in the San Giorgio library in Venice that morning.

May 1979 – Thirteen Months Earlier

Of the twenty-two full-time members of the Thatcher Cabinet (and two more there 'by invitation')[22] who first assembled that May morning in 1979, nineteen are now – forty years later – dead, leaving Michael Heseltine, John Nott and this author, plus Michael Jopling and Norman Fowler.

In the picture of the first Thatcher Cabinet – see first image, first plate section – we stare out confidently at the camera. 'A battle-hardened and seasoned team' Michael Heseltine called us. But the old battles were already being replaced by new ones while we sat and stood there. Unimaginable upheavals lay ahead, terrible errors

35

were waiting to be made, glaring lessons to be tragically ignored. Of course, there were triumphs too. And there was a decade to go before the collapse of the Soviet Union and the definitive end of the Cold War.

It was another world. Not one individual in the picture carried a mobile phone. Nor had we the slightest inkling about social media, Facebook and Twitter. Charles Moore tells us that at that time there was not a single computer in No.10 Downing Street.[23]

On the left of the picture[1] are Michael Jopling, one of the most formidable of chief whips, and Norman Fowler, first as Minister of Transport and later, for six years, Social Services Secretary, a role which had sunk and would continue to sink many less able occupants. Today he is Lord Speaker, greatly to the good fortune of the House of Lords as it struggles to shake off its museum status and views and adjusts to the digital age.

Michael Heseltine, the old lion, remains in his palatial Northamptonshire lair letting loose the occasional roar, especially against Brexit. I backed him for the leadership in 1990 but when he asked me to be formal seconder of his candidacy, I ducked out. It seemed to me that we were already too far apart on where the European Union was heading and our different viewpoints would not look good in the campaign. Also, less honourably but more prudently, my constituents were livid with me for publicly supporting him at all. I need not have worried. Michael got Peter Tapsell[24] to second him — ironically a real proto-Brexiteer and far more outspoken against the EU than I ever was.

The third survivor, John Nott, resigned after the Falklands saga, chaired a venerable city banking house and went down to his Cornwall arcadia to look on the world with beautiful cynicism and write sometimes waspish books.

As this is not a conventional memoir — more an unearthing of the past to explain the present — it starts not at the beginning but somewhere in the middle of the fifty-year period preceding the present hour (which is slightly less than the time I have served in Parliament).

---

1 And theoretically 'in attendance', although in fact regular Cabinet members'

We begin with a group of individuals – the first Thatcher Cabinet in 1979 – at a strange moment in history. What impact did they really have? What follies did they inherit with which they had to struggle, and what follies did they go on to commit? Where did they succeed and why is there so much unfinished business? I shall trace where their ideas came from, which way the forces around them were taking them, what bubbles of illusion misled them and, above all, how a thread runs from their actions and beliefs to the current mood of uncertainty.

Camera Unity

In that first photograph we look united. It had not been so in the months and years before and was not to last long afterwards. Our story will show how, by the chances of politics, random events and the interplay of individuals and ideas, this disparate group came to be assembled at the crossroads of political history.

We had very high hopes. We sensed the world was at a turning point, almost a new Enlightenment and that, despite pressing problems, we could play our part in setting the new direction. What had been labelled the 'neo-liberal agenda' now had its moment, a political apotheosis with leaders (shortly) in the White House and 10 Downing Street who believed deeply in the power of markets and in the inadequacies of the state to run economic and industrial matters.

In the minds of at least some of us, there was a feeling that we had reached a watershed. From here on we could encourage and release new trends and forces which would change not just Britain but maybe the world. 'Bliss it was in that dawn to be alive,' and so on.

Some of us, especially the newcomers to Cabinet membership, felt an exhilaration which comes around rarely in life and very rarely at all in politics. This seemed a coming together after years of struggle, a consilience not just of political ideas but of changes running from deep in the national psyche to the surface of everyday life, and hence to behaviour, work and attitudes.

Of course, we were right and we were wrong. There were indeed tides moving across the planet which were washing away almost a century of thinking about centralism, collectivism and the power of the state. Although we could not foresee it, these tides were about

37

to get much more powerful. A decade of recovery in the national mood and performance lay ahead and with it, recovery in Britain's international standing. Beyond that we could not see, and in particular how differently it would end politically.

The Labour landslide of 1997 may have first looked like a continuum of the Thatcher era but it was the beginning of the end. Free markets were set to explode financially. Internationally, liberalisation, the melting of the Cold War permafrost, the break-up of decades of state dominance, and the warm feeling that the hour of worldwide democracy had come, would turn to fragmentation, violence and terror in many parts of the world, in the Balkans most immediately, with the Middle East region following on. 'Unassailable' absolutes, such as that economic advance could only work with democracy and freedom, were to be challenged by Chinese proof of the opposite. Rock-solid America was to wobble, the 260-year unity of the United Kingdom to be challenged, the sensation of clear and shared national purpose to be lost. Victories that seemed to be won against statism, Left or Right, would start being unpicked. Even Marxist–Leninism, one of the blood-soaked killer doctrines of the nineteenth and twentieth centuries, which many thought had been staked through the heart, began to be resurrected.

The contrast of the mood in '79 with today could hardly be greater. Then, there was certainty and conviction. Now, there is none. Then, it was clear that a new common ground was struggling to emerge in politics. It was going to be very tough; indeed, it proved to be far tougher than we imagined. However, the vision and the direction were there, a kind of new dispensation which would combine the best of the political Right (enterprise and wealth creation) with the best of the Left (shared wealth flowing down to all), and from both sides, jobs and higher living standards for everyone.

To be sure, our term did not start like that. The inheritance from Jim Callaghan's Labour administration was truly appalling, as many contemporary accounts confirm. However, after a very rocky start, battles began to be won. Over the decade to come, Britain shed its sick-man-of-Europe image and became a pace-setter, the fastest-growing and most dynamic European nation. We were riding high. There was a real sense of achievement, a feeling that we had found new common ground which would be a solid base for British advance, and an example to the world.

Yet the current situation is nothing like the one we hoped and planned for. Traces of the 1979 beliefs and visions survive but they have been overlaid by entirely new structures of concern. How did this come about? What earth-shaking events and transformative powers cut across our ideas, exposed major new problems and changed the trajectory of our reforms?

A big problem here is the labels. The critics of the Thatcher era rapidly seized on the rhetoric about free markets (especially in Keith Joseph's speeches) and painted a picture of a government dedicated to unbridled competition, with rewards for the strongest and the weakest going to the wall. Admirers have gone to the other extreme and painted the era as one of liberated free markets bringing health, strength and untold benefits to a previously stagnating and discontented nation.

Neither picture is accurate. Both are caricatures. Thatcher commentators, historians, authors and opinion-formers would have done far better to begin with Grantham. Alderman Roberts's retail business there was not run on fancy theories or 'isms'. What went on in the Thatcher home was far more important and influential: what values were shared; who did the unpaid work that made daily life and business possible?

Had the commentariat of the Thatcher period listened *less* to the doctrinaire expositions about monetarism, market forces and the like, and *more* to the voice from Grantham they would have discovered in the new Prime Minister an overwhelming interest, not in economic theory, but in the practical details of life – the vast structure of work and organisation, and the disciplines and priorities of family and household life. These elements are largely unpaid and mostly unrecorded in economic statistics, yet they lie at the heart of an economy and a society. This was the social dimension of market economics, and the core – the foundation layer – of our national health, balance and progress which later got lost. Most liberal economic theorists and many free-market economists never gave this aspect the slightest recognition.

At the end of the 1970s, power was already slipping away from governments, not just into markets but into markets unlike those ever known before. These markets were accelerated and globalised to perform and react at speeds well beyond the human mind and control. The world was already tumbling into new networks of international cooperation and new algorithms of control, with giant new communications companies that would come to dominate the global connection system.

Neither we nor our advisers – nor the academic world, the columnists, and the armies of experts in their think-tanks and foundations – could foresee these developments. We were to relearn the truth that the power of commerce and innovation exceeded the ability of any national government, ours included, to keep up. This was the lesson we had not grasped and therein lay the seeds of many trials and tribulations to come.

Chapter Two

The Wind Changes

ABOUT two-thirds of the way through the twentieth century something akin to a paradigm shift occurred in Western political thought. A hundred years of rising veneration for state power and planning began to go into reverse and everywhere minds turned to the unravelling of state dominance and to better ways of meeting people's hopes and goals.

Now it was 'flexible' everything. This was the new music: fluidity, multiplicity, plurality became the new keynotes. Forget rigid hierarchy and the old, clanking, incompetent apparatus of the collectivist state with its monopoly of data and planning power. The private sector could do better and the multi-formed and multi-centred market would be called in to redress the balance and ensure competition kept monopoly at bay.

Whether it was electricity supply, prison management, railway operations, pension provision, goods-vehicle testing, parking controls, health provision, education, road management, map-making, telephony, port operating, waste management, housing provision, licensing, training, standard-setting, or even defence and security – regarded as the core functions of government – state monoliths were 'out' and multi-operator industries and services were 'in'. We were at the genesis of the age of contracting out, hiving off and privatising. At last the state was in retreat.

Of course, it was hard to see then that this new approach, which blossomed with particular vigour in semi-socialised, mixed-economy Britain, would be turbo-charged by the microchip. It was even harder to see that the more globalisation in its new form proceeded – impelled by mass demand – the more contradictions it would create.

We were at the start not just of a major dismantling and dispersal of British state enterprise, but of a planet-wide enthusiasm for privatisation which continues spreading to this day. By the century's end, the privatising trend had permeated areas where the role of the state had been unquestioned since the Middle Ages, such as the dispensing of law, collection of levies and taxes (tax farming), the organisation of armies, and many of the welfare and protection roles the state had assumed over the last two centuries. This shift certainly qualifies as paradigmatic change.

The 'Thatcher' moment was 1979. Are we now, forty years on, with global financial markets forty times larger than in 1979 and with the microchip a thousand times as powerful, at the edge of a fresh and even larger transformation in human behaviour patterns and, therefore, in political thought? Could we be at the point of a further breakthrough of relatively new scientific ideas and attitudes in the domain of politics and the public mood?

Clearly, the answer is yes. However, before hard reasoning, there are impressions to record and a spot of intuition to deploy; some would call it a straightforward return to common sense and the acceptance of obvious new realities.

To consider a straw in the breeze, I notice my desk is piled high with a flurry of 'End of' books: *The End of Science, The End of Economics, The End of History, The End of Geography, The End of the Free Market, The End of the Nation State, The End the Welfare State, The End of Capitalism* (again) and *The End of Democracy* itself.

Almost all of these works note a common phenomenon that is already evident to ordinary members of society, if not to their political leaders. It is that the living of life has become more a matter of self-organisation, of network relationships, than of conformity with hierarchies and superior levels of authority. To an almost frightening degree, most people find that the simplicity of just looking 'upward'

– to 'them', the central authorities, the state – has been replaced by a host of connections and rival points of power, guidance and influence, and to a host of choices about which connections to activate.

This is a hugely democratising and de-concentrating process, increasing accessibility to technology, information, finance and power itself, with implications for existing institutions, whether in the private, corporate, or the public and governmental sectors. As Thomas Friedman reminds us, it is the outer edges of organisations, including governments, which gain this power, in varying degrees, not the centre.[25] However, the price of opening the gates of opinion to all is to substitute cacophony and volatility for authority and decision.

Democratic elections are meant to hand complex matters to elected representatives for a decent period. They, in turn, sustain and oversee executive management and power. To govern is to choose. That is the settlement. That is democracy in its parliamentary mode. However, if technology now allows objection to every government decision and perpetual disagreement on alternatives, with a thousand different and constantly shifting viewpoints, how is orderly government supposed to operate?

In a networked structure the old deference towards authority, whether raised by votes or appointment, fades dramatically. The central question of philosophy and government returns in new guise: Who should rule and who should control? A network has no centre on high, no godhead from which wisdom flows and no need of such an arrangement. If authority remains then it has to govern by different means and cope with quite different attitudes towards itself.

Against this backdrop even the least inquiring mind must be driven to conclude that something tumultuous has occurred across a very wide field of life and learning. If these familiar events and patterns are coming to an end, we can only wonder what is beginning in its stead; how can it be described and who is going to describe it?

Back in the 1960s, long before the word 'privatisation' was thought of, and before it became apparent – at least among political thinkers – that a liberalising, decentralising reaction to the age of the big state was under way, one could sense signs from the frontiers of science that different theories about the way the world worked were coming and would permeate the social sciences, economics (although economists proved a poor filter), politics, business and everyday life.

This is why, the past being prologue, it is necessary to unspin it as far as possible. We need to see what really happened: how the 1960s 'paradigm shift' began – the move away from state collectivism towards a privatised and marketised world; where it came from; how it brought together 'us', the class of '79, as we reacted to it, and the many mistakes we made in the struggle from ideas to policy and to practice; how triumph led to political disaster then to worldwide disruption, then once again to another colossal revision of views which now sweeps us along into the turbulent present and the still more disruptive future.

Triggering the Avalanche

The Thatcher Cabinet of 1979 foresaw none of these changes, nor that it was about to trigger an avalanche of newness far beyond its control. State socialism was giving way to markets everywhere in the world as the failures of central planning clocked up and the centrifugal pull of digital enterprise gathered speed. It seemed the right and sensible thing to follow the trend. Having wished into being new market forces, the Government began chasing after them as they gathered their own momentum. Like the water-carrying brooms empowered by the sorcerer's apprentice, the process could not be stopped.

More immediately, the market-minded Cabinet of '79 had three closely interrelated priorities in mind. The first was to curb the power of over-mighty subjects, namely the trades unions – to close down old and excessive sources of power. The second was to unleash sources of new power – market forces, free enterprise and innovation – and to do this partly by unravelling the giant nationalised sector and opening the path to privatisation, and the spread of wealth which would hopefully follow.

. The third priority was to curb the growth of the money supply which would, in theory, reinforce the first two aims, as many argued:

The first aim largely succeeded, helped by changes in the pattern of industrial production. The third objective half worked as budgets were cut harshly, although to what extent this was a direct cause of tight money, restraints on public spending and higher consumer taxes, is open to debate and will be discussed later. It was the second priority that seemed to work best of all, after initial delay while the Government struggled to get on top of its chaotic inheritance. New kinds of popular capitalism were unleashed and rapidly gathered global momentum, both boosting and turbo-boosted by new technology.

Yet it was increasingly on the international stage that the new Government's success or failure was going to turn. Conventional political wisdom, of course, said otherwise; political strategists and election masterminds have always said otherwise. Opinion polls most definitely claimed otherwise, as they listed familiar domestic concerns like education, crime, inflation, living standards and health as political priorities, and put international issues and foreign affairs way down the list. Who cared about those? 'All politics is local' was the homespun wisdom[2]. It was bread-and-butter issues on which governments should focus and the matters to which parties and vote-seekers should give maximum attention. There were, went the confident and expert assertion, no votes in foreign policy.

I always wondered about that – a slightly patronising view of public opinion, it seemed. Was that right then? And is it even remotely right now? It may be that the domestic priorities are the subjects that people, when asked, say they care about. (The growing inability of opinion pollsters, or anyone else, to elicit people's true feelings from their feedback samples, especially about politics, is a development we shall return to later.)

However, this cosy homespun emphasis means less and less as domestic and outside conditions interweave. The narrower worldview has gone, swept away by the all-connecting microchip. It was already slipping away as we faced the camera that morning in 1979. The coming pages will confirm that the real determinants of almost all domestic issues now lie either below the radar of macro-economists altogether – in the small world from which Margaret Thatcher came – or way above national boundaries, in regions which can only be marginally

---

2 Usually attributed to the late Tip O'Neill, 47th Speaker of the U.S.House of Representatives

shaped by a nation's government and its leaders. The old view of government power and control over national life lies in the same waste bin as today's assertions about taking back sovereign control, making our own laws and acting independently; all nonsensical concepts, unattached to the real, interwoven world.

The handling of almost every matter of public interest, and a good many of private interest as well (or what was once considered private), now transcends domestic political 'issues' and debate, pays little attention to international borders and has zero regard for established and home-grown norms and traditions.

A debate of asinine polarity has risen in modern Britain as to whether we should be rule-takers or rule-makers (mostly in the context of our relations with the rest of the European Union). They are just not alternatives. As a great trading nation, Britain sells into multiple markets. In each, we have to follow the rules and regulations set by others to gain entry and do business. The same applies in reverse to those from whom we buy. In our home market they must be rule-takers and we the rule-makers. And so, we are and should be for everything we create, make, supply, implement, import and consume within our national boundaries.

In all cases demand is the master, supply the obedient and compliant servant. To the consumer, the origin of a product or service matters less and less, the price and quality more and more.

This is the pattern not just for trade, but for almost every aspect of life. In the digital age, in which we are deeply immersed, the definable home or domestic area is shrinking and the area of interconnection, interdependence and outside-driven and outside-compelled behaviour is expanding. The 'sovereign control' we are so eager to regain from the EU becomes more accurately a sovereign 'agility' as we seek to respond to countless laws and regulations made by others and to international norms and bigger-than-any-government forces and procedures which constitute the international market place.

The European Union's mistake, which will force it to reform or die, is to try to take over everything, to demand a set of all-embracing EU-specific rules that lock the whole of a nation's economy and society into a single web of treaty confinement. What the EU panjandrums forgot, or failed to grasp at the outset, was that in the age of the microchip an economy constantly adapts itself to different markets, different customs, different laws and different alliances. Digitalisation permits, indeed requires, endless differentiation and makes central control not only increasingly inefficient but also unnecessary.

The UK Brexit issue, still bogged down in parliamentary paralysis and deadlock at Westminster while this account is being written, is really a global issue – part of a worldwide trend.

We are heading for a Europe of constant bargaining, not unlike the Perpetual Diet of the old Holy Roman Empire; always arguing, always in session. There is no 'solution' or *finalité* ever to be reached about a nation's precise relations with its immediate neighbours in all their changing complexity, and never has been. The balance between collaboration and national sovereign pride will always shift and be in dispute as new issues, challenges and tasks arise.

The immigration issue and its impact on every aspect of interstate relations throughout the European continent is a classic example of such a new factor, unforeseen and unplanned for by governments. There will always be more.

How this new state of being comes about will be explored later. For now, it is critical to understand, as many politicians do not, what cabinets and national governments and political leaders can and cannot achieve in contrast to a previous age, and where the limits lie.

Forty years have passed since the morning of that Cabinet picture. For historians and long-viewers there are two ways of looking at what has occurred. One is to argue that history repeats itself in waves of theory, ideological fashion, action and reaction – up and down, back and forth like a pendulum – every four decades or so. The other is to see history through the lens of evolution. There is evolutionary progression – we are getting smarter. That means there will be no repeats, that next time it will be different.

The pendulum viewpoint would suggest that the Thatcher Cabinet was indeed meeting at a swing moment as the world moved away from decades of collectivism and centrism towards markets and capitalist free enterprise. People had had enough of central planning incompetence, the extreme reaction being the implosion and collapse of the Soviet

Union and its paralysed satellite system. The battle between central planning and decentralised market liberalism at last seemed to be tipping in favour of the latter. It was the Hayek hour, when what had been eccentric became obvious: that market prices contained more and better information than the wisest planning mind could ever contain. There could be no argument. There (was) is no alternative, or TINA, as it came to be known.

Except that there was an alternative. It came not from the Left and the guardians of the old consensus, although they were naturally deeply hostile to what they saw as the new ideology of the Right. It came from capital markets boosted by technology in ways which were beyond imagination in 1979.

Did anyone in 1979 see what was coming? Did anyone foresee the uncontrollable world of high-frequency trading, the ten-fold multiplication of currency market trades, the total globalisation of finance, (as outlined in Edward Luttwak's *Turbo Capitalism,*[26], or Clyde Prestowitz's *Three Billion New Capitalists,*[27]) or the Asian currency turmoil, the mushrooming growth of money markets, the mad, risky sub-prime market for home loans which would never be repaid, the final world-shaking global crisis of capitalism, marked by the spectacular collapse of the venerable Lehman Brothers Bank?

No, of course we did not. It lay decades ahead. However, in a sense, it was inevitable. Open the door, uncork the bottle and there would be an almighty Western world financial bust-up. Those 'unforeseen consequences' which Nigel Lawson wrote about[28] we now live with. And unsurprisingly world sentiment has been drifting back to big government, with the state again playing the chief-saviour role in social and economic affairs.

The pendulum sceptics would argue that it was indeed inevitable, that it was bound to happen and, in a few decades, will swing back again. C'est la vie.

However, the evolutionist might argue differently. He or she might argue that simple calls for a return to the ancient regime, for 'giving the state a more positive role in creating and maintaining wealth and well-being' are not enough.[29] He or she might contend that this thirty to forty-year cycle has been overtaken by bigger forces still. Permanent advances in technology and its exploitation have been so immense that patterns have changed for good and there is no going back.

In this version the revolution has not revolved but has continued ahead in an upward-curving line of progress. Connection and communication are now so advanced that the process of governance has changed, totally and universally. Power has been irreversibly spread by the information explosion, the Web, the digital dominance and the cyber empire. History, this school of thought would maintain, does not repeat itself, even if, in the words of Arthur Balfour, historians repeat each other.

So, was 1979 truly a turning point in both British and international affairs, a permanent shift in the pattern of progress, demanding entirely new mindsets and methods of governance? Or was it just an interlude, a flare up of bright hopes doomed to be snuffed out as it ran out of control – in which case, are we back where we started, resurrecting the past and giving new life to old theories, old doctrines and old ways and measures?

In later chapters this question and the acute dilemmas it continues to pose will be considered. Much now hangs on the answer. However, to start finding the answer, we must go back to that first Thatcher gathering and its origins. What was it really like around the Cabinet table? Exactly how did the people in the photo came to be there, where had we had come from and where did we believe we were going?

Chapter Three

The Seventy-Niners

*'At some point in time the secrets of one period must
become the common learning of another'.*

The Radcliffe Report 1976.

THE Cabinet of '79 assembled at a conjuncture in the
evolutionary route which leads from then to now: from a
world for which a British government could produce (and exert
substantial control over) policies and measures, to a world in which
infinitely more powerful trends and algorithms are sweeping us along
and which political leaders must learn to ride, impossible though the
task may seem to be.

Let us briefly examine who these Seventy-Niners were and how
they came to be there that morning for that picture: what they were
thinking and hoping for; how they were constrained within limits
which they did not fully understand; what then occurred; which
way the forces around them were taking them; and, above all, how
the consequences of their actions, reactions and beliefs affect us today.
Most of all we will trace how their efforts have led inexorably to the
present day, and onwards into a very uncertain future.

To return to the picture, the Prime Minister sits, of course, at the
centre, with Willie Whitelaw on her right and Quintin (Hailsham)
on her left. Wets and Dries all around. Here we are united for a
photographic moment; soon we were to be at loggerheads. Some

would insist that the hour of market forces had come and that nothing should stand in the way; some that, while new global forces were at work, to proceed with caution (especially where jobs and industrial disruption were concerned and the trades unions involved); some that nothing much had changed.

By some quirk of the camera I appear to be a head taller than the rest of the back row. Perhaps I should have been warned about what happens to tall poppies. That I was there at all was in consequence of a tragedy. Three weeks before that day, an explosion had shaken my desk, then in an office just off Westminster Hall. Going out at the end of the hall I could see a plume of black smoke rising from the underground carpark exit ramp, the other side of New Palace Yard. This was the assassination of Airey Neave – the pointless murder of a truly heroic man.

Although it never occurred to me at the time, this horrific event was going to change my life completely. Airey had been shadow secretary of state for Northern Ireland. His death left a gap in the shadow cabinet team as the general election rapidly approached. Some papers began to speculate that I would be named to fill in, presumably because I had been Minister of State in Northern Ireland six years before, in the Whitelaw team.

This surprised me since I had not seen myself as full Cabinet material. I had been very active in Conservative Party policy discussion in Opposition and had also been drafted into the impossible job of heading Mrs Thatcher's speech-writing team.[30] However, I had not envisaged being a member of either the shadow cabinet or the new Cabinet proper.

For better or worse, I was wrong. No successor was named during the remaining part of the election campaign. Although I had been very fond of 'the Province' and had made many good friends there, I did not feel qualified to go back. Instead, on the Saturday morning, twenty-four hours after the Thatcher victory, I was summoned and handed, to my total surprise, what seemed to be the central job in the new government – the one where inflation, industrial relations and the coalminers, North Sea development, the budgets and future of the biggest state industries, the nuclear power industry, Middle

East politics and a dozen other 'hot' issues came together in a massive swirl of immediate politics, a growing sense of crisis and new strategic imperatives – namely, the role of Secretary of State for Energy.

* * * * *

I learnt much later that Michael Heseltine had been offered the post of Energy Secretary but turned it down, insisting that he be given the environment portfolio. Energy was an area about which I also knew very little – and just how little I was to learn painfully and rapidly as the country, and the globe, was plunged into a major OPEC-driven oil crisis almost on the day of my appointment.

Coming downstairs at No.10 after having been handed this assignment, I walked through the connecting doors to No.11 then, as you could in those days, to No.12. The Chief Whip, Michael Jopling, was folding little bits of paper and putting them on a small snooker table. These were the approved candidates for junior office in the new administration and I had three to select: a minister of state and two parliamentary secretaries.

Actually, Michael said, it was only two, because the Minister of State had to be from Scotland and had to be Hamish Gray,[31] given Scotland's proximity to many of the North Sea oil developments and given, as I was to learn, the immense skill and patience required to deal with the determined Shetlanders. So, there were just two juniors to choose.

My hand hovered over the table and I was told to get on with it as others were waiting to make their choices. I chose Norman Lamont whose abilities I knew – he had succeeded me as chairman of the Bow Group – and John Moore, whom I hardly knew but had spoken for at a public meeting in his constituency during the election and who seemed to know more about finance than the rest of us. Thus, are lives and careers shaped in a chance moment. Luck was on my shoulder because both were brilliant and went on to much higher office. Seeing Humphrey Atkins, I blurted out that I was rather glad not to be the new Northern Ireland Secretary. No, said Humphrey tersely, but I am.

However, returning to the murder of Airey Neave: Besides it being an appalling and tragic atrocity, it was also a warning of something else to come. The simple bipolarity of the Cold War, when we knew our enemies, their techniques and their potential, was giving way to a world of highly fragmented and yet closely connected terror; new power in new hands. Power was slipping away into a thousand networks and a million cells, and also into unfamiliar forms: some good, some bad, some wonderfully beneficial, some deeply dangerous.

Defence of the realm, in the basic sense of keeping people safe and alive as they go about their daily business, was widening into a range of complex threats and sources lying far beyond the reach of military manpower and equipment, tanks, missiles, air power, sea power, or civil defence.[32]

At work here, as elsewhere, could we but see it, was the oncoming omnipresent paradox of globalisation which was going to pull societies and nations both ways: simultaneously towards the passions of local identity and populist impulses and, at the same time, towards frameworks of transglobal force and domination far beyond the reach of any national government. This would tear apart cabinets, such as ours in 1979 – and pull apart governments, international institutions, and the twentieth-century global order – and yet deeply, paradoxically, connect us digitally with an intensity never before experienced in the history of humankind.

Little of this was apparent to us as we lined up for the camera that May morning. It was a time of vision and discord, of soaring hopes and of deep unease. There was a sense that the state was too large and the trade unions over-mighty and that we were near the end of an era of big government. However, of what we were about to unleash, of the storms of turbo-boosted capitalism ahead, we had only the barest inkling.

* * * * *

There is a real atmosphere to convey about the early Thatcher Cabinet meetings. It is a story that is understandably absent from many excellent and otherwise authoritative accounts of the period. Norman St John-Stevas[33] remarked to me, on our way back from a particularly sulphurous and rancorous Cabinet meeting, that there was no point in ever writing about such occasions because no-one would ever believe how appalling they really were. At least with Ted, remarked a frustrated Jim Prior, Cabinet meetings were calm, sometimes even quite enjoyable.

In the Cabinet of '79, our immediate troubles – and acrimony – stemmed mostly from the Winter of Discontent left behind by Jim Callaghan's government: the dangerously high inflation rate (combined with low growth to add up to the phenomenon of 'stagflation') and the public sector wages spiral.

A third of the Cabinet believed that 'deals' of some kind with the trade unions or, if not (horror of horrors) some kind of incomes policy, were the only answers. The rest of us did not. Some of us thought that the new policy of squeezing inflation out of the system by pushing down hard on public spending, keeping interest rates high and raising taxation to boot, was going too far too fast, but that the underlying approach would work. All these doctrinal differences were to claim their victims. One of the first to go was Norman St John-Stevas. He was devastated, accused of excessive leaking.

Another early purge victim, whose dismissal surprised me even more, was Lord Soames. Christopher Soames, son-in-law of Winston Churchill, was a key figure in the Churchill entourage in war and peace; Brussels Commissioner; Paris Ambassador; adroit and healing last Governor of Southern Rhodesia (Zimbabwe), jovially presiding over the Zimbabwe Independence ball – unquestionably a major statesman and servant of the state.

However, none of this availed in the Cabinet. His advocacy of a compromise settlement with strike-threatening civil servants (he was Lord Privy Seal and, at least nominally, in charge of the Civil Service) branded him a definite 'Wet' and Mrs Thatcher was having none of it. Wetness in itself was not a capital offence: Others such as Peter Walker and Jim Prior were to last much longer. His real fate (he was sacked in the first reshuffle) became inevitable a few weeks earlier.

At the outset of a Cabinet meeting the Prime Minister complained about leaks. Prime Ministers usually do. 'They must,' she said, 'stop.' Only just audibly Soames muttered that many of them started from No.10 itself. Mrs Thatcher paused, pen in air, as if dumbfounded. 'What did you say?' she demanded. 'Kindly repeat.' Sheepishly the great man uttered a softer version of his view that some leaks might possibly have escaped – of course, very few – from No.10 briefings. 'Never,' said the Prime Minister. He was plainly doomed.

The division between Wets and Dries was not the only or perhaps the most telling variable around the Cabinet table. There was that subtle difference which shapes outlook so often between the economically secure and the not so secure: between those who never think about money and who, indeed, hardly know what is in the bank and those who have to think about the overdraft and know exactly what their limits are. The Thatcher Cabinet had rich and poor in it, landed and bourgeoisie. Very roughly this coincided with the two natures, or two constituencies, of which the modern Conservative Party had come to be formed – the true conservers and the radical free-market reformers (in effect, the descendants of the free-market liberals who had come to rest within the Conservative Party from the 1930s onwards). Victory and bonhomie and a spirit of compromise could keep these differences at bay for a time. But they were bound to surface and contribute to the political turmoil to come.

Looking back, one can be more forgiving and even laugh about it all, at least a little. Everyone, from the Prime Minister downwards, was under the kind of pressure that comes from discovering problems and obstacles about which there had been no warning, from being surprised in the way that can shorten tempers and weaken the discipline of patience.

Margaret Thatcher was not the sort of person to offer collective balm and reassurance in our various struggles. On the contrary, we were suddenly her enemies. For me the transformation was especially acute because, only days before, when we had been sitting in the Crest Hotel, Bolton as election day approached – as the polls looked bad and half her 'advisers' were pouring out criticism and telling her what she was doing wrong – she was a mild, almost vulnerable, person, requiring sympathy and support. Her daughter, Carol, was present and put her arm round her demoralised mother, saying to the rest of us around the table, 'There, look what you've done.' 'Actually', said Margaret, sniffing, 'I thought I was doing quite well.'

Chapter Four

The Tigress Emerges

ONLY weeks before the first gathering of the new Cabinet I had been at the Thatcher dining-room table in Flood Street being fed layer upon layer of excellent smoked salmon at 2 a.m. while we tackled the umpteenth drafts of her campaign speeches. There were a few giggles, some flat jokes and a lot of good asides from Mrs T about the ways of the world.

Now, barely a week after election-day victory, everything was different. The tigress emerged. No-one was safe from the lash of her tongue. That included not just the younger Cabinet members, such as me, but the truly senior and eminent figures such as Quintin Hailsham and Peter Carrington. She even peppered her hero, Keith Joseph, with shrapnel as he wrestled with the dilemmas of the motor and steel industries, and countless other industrial horror stories.

Her particular skill was to divide us against each other. If we had been friends before election day, or at least on friendly terms, we were now foes. Support for any other colleague became dangerous. Back up someone protesting at heavy cuts in their department's budget and one immediately came under challenge to cut one's own budget instead. Better to stay quiet and let the other chap sink. Each for himself. It was not a very friendly round-table atmosphere, nor, it seems, was it intended to be.

My own first department, Energy, was in extreme disfavour from the start. It seemed we could do nothing right. The Permanent

Secretary, Sir Jack Rampton, struck me as a mild and helpful senior official: not someone to set the Thames on fire, but perfectly ready to support ministers as we rode through the furnace of issues. But from the start Sir Jack was persona non grata at Downing Street. Heaven knows why. The department had been through hell under the previous Secretary of State, Tony Benn, who, towards the end of his time, had been so disenchanted with his Cabinet colleagues and their comprehension of energy issues (I was to find the same problem) that he refused to attend Cabinet meetings at all, declaring a sort of departmental UDI. Inevitably, the department was demoralised and disoriented.

Now it had to cope with mighty issues central to the political and economic scene, and to the future of the nation. No support or understanding came from No.10. There was a refusal to engage until poor Sir Jack had been removed and a new Permanent Under-Secretary chosen. To this day I believe he was badly treated, and pointlessly so.

Even then it appeared that we were still in the doghouse. No serious discussion of the huge dilemmas we faced took place and it seemed that all channels were blocked or by-passed by whispers and rumours as to what No.10 was said to want – often more an interpretation of the views of the ebullient press officer at No.10, Bernard Ingham.

Thus, when I came under pressure from the key movers in the ascendant OPEC organisation (Sheik Ahmed Zaki Yamani from Saudi Arabia and Sheikh Ali Khalifa al Sabah from Kuwait) that Britain, as an expanding North Sea oil producer, should join their powerful cartel, I saw no point in reporting their approach to the Prime Minister whose views, I knew, would be not only dismissive, but possibly unfriendly for even having broken bread with such folk.

Bernard I rather admired but he did not seem to be my friend at court. This might have been because, when Angus Maude asked my opinion as to his suitability for the No.10 press job – Bernard being at that time a senior civil servant in the Energy Department, much concerned with conservation – I had replied negatively. I felt he was not suitable and sensed that this had gotten back to him. Anyway, my admiration clearly was not reciprocated and I was conscious of a growing flow of hostile briefings from his direction.

Within the Cabinet, the one safe figure never criticised to his face or behind his back, as several others were, was Willie Whitelaw. Willie had made a simple decision: Mrs Thatcher was the Prime Minister and Prime Ministers always, but always, had to be supported. Willie was the man who had told me some eighteen months earlier, in Opposition days, that I had to accept the invitation from the leader's office to head her speech-writing team. I had not been at all keen but Willie explained that it was not an invitation, it was an order. And in party politics one had to do as instructed. Now he was the Cabinet's rock, the soother when Mrs Thatcher was too sharp or impatient, the calmer-downer when there were inevitable remonstrances against the Prime Minister's more outrageous and unfair remarks.

Willie had lived through the dramas and divisions which marked the fall of Ted Heath six years before. In that sense he was indeed battle-hardened, although not at all involved in, or much interested in, the policy shifts and debates that had brought the new government into being.

He was determined there should be no repeat. He had seen from the heart of the Heath Cabinet how it went wrong, as we had seen from junior posts outside the Cabinet (in my case in the Civil Service Department, the Northern Ireland Department and the Department of Energy – in each case newly created). He had seen what, looking back, we can now all see as the false dawn at the beginning of the Heath administration,[34] where many of the ideas in 1979 had been incubated, but then put aside as, in the favourite words of Ernest Marples,[35] the urgent had once again crowded out the important.

Now the Whitelaw role was again central, not just in the Cabinet but throughout the Conservative Party. The division was depicted as between Wets and Dries but was, in fact, as old as the party itself, going right back to Sir Robert Peel and the repeal of the Corn Laws. Was the soul of the Conservative Party with the true Conservatives, carefully 'rejecting the inessential while preserving the essential', revering customs and procedures, respecting minorities, eschewing majoritarianism? Or was it with the dedicated adherents to free-market principles, determined to break away from the corporatist/socialist consensus in which they believed Britain had become ensnared?

The Thatcher era is depicted as unequivocally with the latter and it is true that after 1979 she gradually removed some of the old-school Conservatives who were most sceptical of free-market theories and of government being guided by this ideological lodestar. This, as in the title of Ian Gilmour's memoir,[36] was 'dancing with dogma'.

However, as always, the lines were not so clearly drawn in reality. What many media labellers never understood was the deep Thatcher instinct for the values and world of the small shop in Grantham. This is where free-market theory ended and bourgeois values began. Whitelaw may have protected the Cabinet from Mrs Thatcher in some of her more unreasoning moments, such as those which Charles Moore describes so graphically in the run-up to general elections and at more strained moments in Cabinet. But the real binding force that held Conservative Cabinets together through a thirteen-year period of radical change lay in Mrs Thatcher herself. She may have danced with dogma but she was also a conservative. Common sense was greatly preferred to ideology.

Chapter Five

Manoeuvres at Court

THE question now for the new Cabinet team was whether we had the stamina and skill to be a reforming and lasting administration, riding, perhaps even mastering, the waves of world change, or whether we would be swept away like a passing thought. Plenty of key figures, in industry, the press, and academia, were convinced we would not last. Sir Denis Rooke said as much to me when I tried to discuss the longer-term evolution of his colossal gas empire. He and it would be facing bigger issues long after the Thatcher administration was gone, he said.

There was a counterblast from the Prime Minister. When it came to privatisation, Sir Denis would not countenance it at first. The technique from the Treasury in the face of intransigence, which I deplored, was to circle the victim and bite off 'assets' for a quick sale. This seemed to me idiotic short-termism, certain to make the enterprise a less attractive entity when it came to full privatisation. Nevertheless, it was the view from the Treasury, strongly supported by No.10. In the British Gas case, two of the juiciest 'bits' were Sir Denis's networks of gas showrooms, visible on many high streets, and his highly successful oil-well operation at Wytch Farm in Dorset.

So intense was the No.10-plus-Treasury fury with Sir Denis, for what was seen as general obstruction to strategic government privatisation aims, that the PM took a personal and intense interest in the issue, catching the hapless Secretary of State (me) in the crossfire and drawing opprobrium from both sides. Cecil Parkinson told me that Mrs Thatcher had taken to carrying press cuttings about gas showrooms in her handbag, to be produced and flourished in meetings, a cameo at which we all laughed – in my case with a sort of gallows humour – because Cecil had an amazing skill to make political situations amusing, even when they were really rough and unpleasant.

Eventually the showrooms were rung out of Sir Denis, as was Wytch Farm – the substantial on-shore oil concession, owned and operated by British Gas on the Dorset coast. From the Treasury came whispers that I had been much too weak with the mighty Sir Denis and certainly should not have supported his reappointment at the end of his chairmanship term, which came up at about this time. Actually, I admired him and the way in which the huge British Gas empire had been managed. The conversion of the entire supply system from coal to North Sea gas sources, with millions of home appliances being adjusted to receive and burn the slightly different gas quality, had been undertaken with enormous but quite unsung skill – a major triumph of engineering and managerial organisation. Unfortunately, Sir Denis had a habit of talking about the fourteen-million household consumers he had to look after – a bigger army than any political party by a long chalk – as 'my' customers. The move towards privatisation needed, in my view, the most careful handling – which it was not getting.

Peter Walker,[37] a consummate political operator and two Energy Secretaries of State on from me, manoeuvred the gas enterprise into the private sector as one entity, satisfying many of Sir Denis's conditions, albeit in the face of a stream of Treasury protests. The time for privatisation had become ripe and Sir Denis had become convinced, after years of having his investment programme and strategy messed about by ministers, that he would do better with private investors.

As my differences on energy issues with No.10, and with the Treasury over its short-termism, widened, my move to Transport lay shortly ahead. The transition from being a sort-of court favourite to being almost outcast was swift. One minute one was among the saffron-robed, as *The Times* described us, the next minute the robes were gone. No doubt life was like this in Tudor courts, so perhaps this was nothing new.

The Transport world was a much smaller parish. At Energy, it seemed that I was at the epicentre of both domestic and world events. In a pre-privatisation world, the Energy Secretary was responsible for a gigantic chunk of British industry: either under direct state ownership (electricity, gas, coal, nuclear power); or under extensive government influence (North Sea oil, the oil industry, including 51 per cent ownership of BP); all energy aspects of foreign policy; OPEC at its high noon, with a roaring world oil shock; Arthur Scargill and the coalminers' union; with energy conservation; and with much else besides. All elements of government strategy seemed to run through the department, then housed in the old ICI offices on Millbank with vast, ugly rooms, rattling windows and draughts – and no sign whatever of the energy efficiency and conservation of which we were supposed to be the leading advocates. Hugh Fraser[38] described Energy as the biggest ministerial empire since the height of World War II.

Transport was quite different: fascinating, vital for the future, but far less central to the strategic preoccupations of the day. Politically it was also a no-win, nightmare portfolio since everyone was (and is) a transport 'expert', as successive battered Transport Secretaries have discovered. The wisest ones get out as soon as they can.

The key players in the transport world of the 1980s were Peter Parker at British Rail, Peter Masefield at London Transport, the freight kings at the National Freight Corporation (NFC) such as Frank Law and Peter Thompson, and the road and bridge builders. Everyone wanted to spend more money – and a lot of it. A positive story emerged with the privatisation of NFC via a management and staff buy-out. This had been mostly set-up by my predecessor, Norman Fowler, but it fell to me to finalise the deal from the government side.

It was the ideal and model privatisation. Even Mrs T gave it a wry nod. Almost the entire 15,000 workforce received shares, which immediately soared in value, trade union restrictions evaporated, productivity climbed and all kinds of property assets were revealed. For example, the unions had insisted on lorry parks to accommodate enormous turning circles for HGV drivers. With privatisation, it emerged that they could turn in much shorter lengths, thus releasing swathes of space in city centres with fantastic development value.

The railways were not so lucky. The legend was that the Prime Minister did not like trains. She may not have seen train travel as the future but she was realistic about its role. She certainly was cool towards Sir Peter Parker, which was regrettable since he was a man of great charm and boundless enthusiasm. Over at the Treasury, the railways were simply regarded as a money sink, an ever-present source of demands for more subsidy.

The cards were stacked against me on this front. Even the newly elected François Mitterand's enthusiasm for a Channel tunnel was cold-shouldered in Whitehall. The Chancellor, Geoffrey Howe, said he had just been on a most pleasurable cross-channel ferry crossing to France, so why did we need a tunnel? Naturally, at No.10, the Prime Minister was convinced the taxpayer would end up paying for it, unless we could somehow shift the risk onto private institutions and other countries.

From No.10 came the view that, if there had to be a Channel link, it should be a road. A fantastical scheme from the head of British Steel, blunt-speaking Sir Ian MacGregor, a Thatcher favourite, was advanced. This would involve constructing a four-lane motorway going through gigantic steel tubes resting on the seabed. The tubes would be fabricated in Newcastle and floated around the east coast to be sunk into position. For ventilation, huge rubber snorkels would protrude above the waves in the Channel, one of the world's busiest shipping lanes. If struck in the usual fog they would bend over and bounce back. Cars and trucks would drive down spiral roadways either side, from specially constructed islands at either end to the seabed motorway below. There was more of this, very much from the school of Heath Robinson, all of which had to be politely evaluated before being shown up as utter nonsense.

Secretly I paid a Paris visit to the French Transport Minister, Charles Fiterman[39] (a former Communist) to reassure him that London would come around to a straightforward high-speed rail tunnel – as of course it did – although I am told that, when the ebullient Sir Peter starting enthusing about a second tunnel, a permafrost descended at No.10.

Short-term thinking was further displayed at the Department of Transport when I was given traffic projections, backed by an insistent official, showing that there was no case for ever building a second Severn bridge. Luckily Welsh politics prevailed, the crossing was built – and, still, the traffic projections proved far too low. Other half-baked advice was that it was too expensive and too late to acquire land for building service stations on the newly opened M25 and that widening it to three lanes, let alone four, could not be economically justified.

To better answer the infrastructure question, we have to go back to the Heath era, a decade before Thatcher. Heath's administration is regularly denigrated, mainly because it ended in ignominy (and now by the besmirching Operation Conifer against the character of Ted Heath himself, where, at the time of writing, efforts to remove by independent enquiry the reputational stain of the grossly mishandled police investigation, have been blocked).

However, the years leading up to Ted Heath's unexpected election victory in 1970[40] contained many of the seeds of eventual Thatcherite revolutionary thinking. One was that the private sector, suitably regulated, would make a better fist of long-term investment than the state corporations; in fact, this was the seed from which the privatisation idea grew. Another was that Downing Street needed much stronger resources to knock departmental heads together, overcome short-termism and develop and stick to a consistent strategy. A third was that Britain needed less government and better government and that the collectivist era was over.

These were powerful ideas in their infancy. Yet none of them reached the policy stage during the Heath administration. Distractions overwhelmed them. As quoted earlier, the urgent always trumped the important.

The free-market instincts and philosophies which the Thatcher era adopted were not new, although often depicted as such by the media; rather, they had been pushing forward slowly for years against the preceding dominance of collectivism. Collectivism and the centrality of state action, in varying forms, had prevailed almost unchallenged since its rise at the end of the nineteenth century with the concurrent and almost universal rejection and defeat of laissez-faire capitalism.

From the periods before and immediately after World War I, collectivist economic and social policies had become the orthodoxy accepted by almost every political party and government. As Walter Lippmann wrote, classical liberalism had 'become frozen in its own errors' and 'failed as a coherent progressive philosophy',[41] opening the door for the exercise of every kind of twentieth-century state power from the milder Fabianism and Keynesianism to the ugly tyrannies of Germany, Italy and the Soviet Union. 'Nowadays' wrote H.G. Wells in 1922 in *A Short History of the World*, 'there does seem to be a gradual convergence of reasonable men towards a scientifically studied and planned socialism.'[42]

Historians like to have their theses and antitheses. To challenge state power and argue for markets to work as a balancing and corrective process, as seemed no more than common sense from about 1970 onwards, becomes, under the historian's zealous keyboard fingers, dramatised into a lurch from what is conceived as 'the political Left' to what is conceived as 'the political Right'. The pantomime mentality takes over. The media portrays moderate market liberalisation as a deliberate political campaign to elevate individual greed and selfishness, to downplay the community and public welfare in favour of narrow individualism – in short, to swing from one ideology to another.

As will be shown, this is most emphatically not how we thought or what we believed in 1979 and, more importantly, not what happened. I shall argue that this kind of thinking comes from the tired remnants of ideologies which, even in 1979, were beginning to be overtaken by the new realities, dangers and opportunities of the digital age. This process has advanced infinitely further under the pervasive influence of technology. In consequence, the real and worthwhile legacies and lessons from those far-off days are quite different from those which, with maddening persistence, get recited and which continue to warp and distort our politics, our public debates and our daily lives.

A decade earlier, similar ideas had been developed in some quarters and inside certain think-tanks such as the Public Sector Research Unit under Ernest Marples's patronage, and at more philosophical and less detailed level in the Institute of Economic Affairs. However, there had been scant support from the bulk of the party and its official research divisions. Ted Heath himself, in Opposition in the 1960s, had been keenly interested and supportive of detailed plans to reduce the size and power of the state. But, within weeks of taking office in 1970, this had started to fade as the Civil Service advisers closed around him and pushed him back into their way of thinking – to what was deemed 'on', as opposed to 'just not on'.

At the time of the Thatcher victory in May 1979, five years after the fall of the Heath administration, some members of the Cabinet team felt it was a new dawn, some were nervous of her intended radicalism, some were disappointed that it came too late, or did not go far enough, or lacked strategic underpinnings. However, it was clear to most that a watershed of some kind in government attitudes, at least in Britain and probably elsewhere in the world as well, had been reached.

What are the links or threads between that era and the totally different conditions which now prevail, both domestically and internationally? What have we inherited? Was the Thatcher Revolution really a revolution at all and has it been eclipsed, just as the collectivist era seemed eclipsed before it? And do the ideological debates and theories of the last century still have any relevance to current and future challenges and threats?

Back then, in 1979, our minds were on debilitating inflation and weak economic growth and on what would cure so-called stagflation (high inflation *and* high unemployment). We were focused, with good reason, on the restrictive and over-mighty power of trade unions, on wage inflation, on the inefficiency of a vast state industrial sector, the perennial Irish Question, the oil shock and energy crisis. Abroad, the Cold War Soviet threat continued, with the Atlantic Alliance more than ever our bedrock.

* * * * *

A now forgotten obsession of political commentators of the time was with the so-called doctrine of monetarism. Because at least two members of the '79 Cabinet – Keith Joseph and Geoffrey Howe – had been completely converted to the magic powers of monetarism as a scientific means of crushing inflation, , the political analysts began to depict this as a Thatcher-introduced novelty.

It had, in fact, been the gospel of American economists (most prominently Nobel Prize-winning Milton Friedman) for years before and was the required medicine imposed on the Labour Government when Britain had gone bust in 1976 and had had to call in the IMF for a loan.

The theory that one could squeeze out high inflation by strict limits on the supply of money (where it could be defined), supplemented as necessary on the demand side by higher taxes and tight public-spending controls, had been widely espoused around the world for some time. With inflation running at 18 per cent, the incoming Thatcher team certainly knew that strong medicine was needed. It worked for a while, though many older and less efficient industries could not compete with the strong pound which, as a consequence of high interest rates, was one of the outcomes.

However, to associate this policy with 'unbridled capitalism' and a collapse of the moral order, demonstrates how confused both the history and its interpretation have become. If anything, tight monetarist policies were an attempt to put on the bridle.

We have already noted how 'market forces', hailed in Britain as some revolutionary idea in 1979, had, in varying forms, long been the norm of commercial life; indeed, had been the norm since the 1930s in the United States and in many other countries.

By 1979, the last large state bastions of collectivism, were hanging on only in the Soviet Union and in China — in collapsing Soviet centralism and in Mao's mad remedies. Elsewhere, a handful of retreating emulators around the planet, the former Bandung generation of anti-Western states, were discovering that Marxism–Leninism did not work in practice and that markets needed to be given their proper space.

The Thatcher Cabinets became associated not just with monetarism, but with 'punk monetarism' because the real zealots among them, and some prominent economic advisers such as Alfred Sherman, Sir Alan Walters and Gordon Pepper,[43] all echoing Milton Friedman, talked the talk about the wondrous efficacy of monetary control, and because it seemed to be working. In point of fact, the remarkable fall in inflation between 1982 and 1988 was just as much driven by technology,[44] although that would not be acknowledged until later. Additionally, of course, the communications revolution and the cheap and easy transfer of new technology to low wage economies, notably China, was bringing down the price of most things (except oil). Nevertheless, at the time, the control of money supply gained most of the credit.

The stance of some of the driest Cabinet members (not only Keith Joseph, but also John Biffen and John Nott) on all these fronts helped build up the image of Thatcherite zealotry about monetarism. Cabinet discussions were wracked by issues about the size of the public sector borrowing requirement (PSBR), albeit piddling by today's standards. When Geoffrey Howe put up taxes further in the 1991 Budget, on top of high interest rates, strong sterling and public spending cuts, it sealed the impression of dogma and led an army of so-called expert economists (the famous 364 of them who wrote to *The Times*) to believe that not just the monetarist stance, but the whole monetarist doctrine was wrong-headed and should be abandoned. In their view babies and bathwater should be tipped out.

We were, of course, in a world of Punch-and-Judy make-believe. As Margaret Thatcher told Peter Jay in a TV interview a decade later, monetarism was 'not a doctrine to which I have ever subscribed', repeating, to remove all doubt, that it was not a 'theory' either to which she had ever subscribed.[45]

Later, much later, the other arch-apostle of the arcane workings of monetary policy, Nigel Lawson,[46] became more sceptical about the love affair his colleagues had with the supposedly scientific wonders of money supply control, accepting that the powers of interest rates to squeeze out inflation were 'overstated'.[47] He shared his 'mistakes' frankly and honestly with the House of Commons in his resignation speech.[48] What had been obvious to a few of us from the start we had to keep to ourselves, drowned out by the theological insistences of monetarism's high priests that it had powers and precision beyond our understanding.

We had to watch as it slowly dawned on its chief advocates that monetarism was, at best, an uncertain weapon and that definitions of what constituted the money supply were far from clear and therefore, obviously, far from controllable. In addition, there was the simple fact that 0.5 per cent rise in interest rates, by adding to unemployment, could *raise* public spending, thereby defeating the objective. Later, too, the obvious point dawned on the enthusiasts that the exchange rate played a crucial part in the levels of production and demand and, therefore, in inflationary pressures. Trying to fine-tune a complex and internationally exposed economy by influencing the exchange rate was a fool's errand.

In short, we had to pay a price for the education of minds prone to seizing on simple doctrines and 'answers' to events and trends with far deeper causes, many of them outside political control and certainly outside the control of individual national governments.

As an issue, the monetarism debate barely features in sober financial and economic assessments nowadays. Some control over some aspects of money supply may now be a part of the central banker's toolkit, but it is noticeable how interest rates have taken a seat at the far back of debates about inflation and economic growth. Instead, with confiscatory low levels of interest being maintained, well below the level of inflation, careful savers are defrauded daily.

Today, we have been left with the relics of monetarist thinking in a reverse and perverse form. The new monetarism has taken the form of quantitative easing (QE), pouring a sugar-rush of newly manufactured money into the system in the belief that, this time, it will raise economic growth and head off depression.

Once again there has been the painful discovery that the simplicities of monetarism, whether used to push down or boost up the economy, do not work well in practice. The QE impact on the price of assets, on property prices and on the savings accounts of the well-off has been truly rewarding. But on the economy generally, on the living standards of just-managing middle- and lower-income wage-earners, it has been negligible, as events both sides of the Atlantic have demonstrated.

Bernard Bernanke[49] may have been determined to use monetary expansionism to prevent deflation after the 2008 Lehman debacle but, as he discovered, his conventional economic thinking let him down. Not only did the theory, once again, not work but in digitalised financial markets its results were even more perverse and unexpected. As Lawrence Summers[50] pithily observed, quantitative easing 'boosted supply and destroyed demand', further depressing prices and wages – the exact opposite of what was intended.

This, then, is the miserable legacy of the monetarism debate of the Thatcher era. In its twisted QE version and with all its passions, it is another dismal, if not downright disruptive, visitation on the present era we could well have done without.

* * * * *

The fading subject of monetarism, once at the heart of politics, is a reminder of how far the economic policy debate has moved on. In Britain, all immediate attention has been on Brexit, the unity of the United Kingdom, global networks, environmental and climate concerns, terror on the streets, recycling on land and in the oceans, migration pressures at the borders and a host of unforeseen concerns. Looming over us are the rise of China, the wobbly American alliance courtesy of President Trump, the volatility of people power, the distortions of democracy, the media, and online-delivered perceptions of unfairness and inequality. Running through it all, arguably at the root of it all, lies the ubiquitous impact of digital technology – the communications explosion and the hyper-connectivity which now influences every sphere of existence and has created giant new centres of global power and influence.

Other 'old' issues certainly persist, like the Irish Question in a new form.[51] Russian aggression and disruption, another play from the past, is back with a vengeance. *Plus ça change.* However, of the philosophical and economic debates of yesterday the current commentariat seems to have little new to say except in one respect: The system is not delivering the resources which a caring society now demands. It is not working for everyone. Meanwhile all the rest – the raging monetarist debates, the supply-side arguments, the macro-economic shift – are fading away into irrelevance and live only in the minds of the myth-makers.

The taxi-driver who takes me from Cambridge station to the Churchill Archives Centre on the other side of the city has plenty to say about the past and what is wrong with the present. For him, the finer points about past economic quarrels have long since vanished, if they were ever there; it is clear – we should bring back Margaret Thatcher. It does not concern him too much that this would be from beyond the grave. She was on the side of the people and she would have sorted Brexit out long ago. For him, the remedy from the past is the sense of national purpose and direction which she, as a strong leader, was able to inspire and deliver.

Strangely enough, the pre-EU European Economic Community of which, in 1979, we had been full members for seven years, while it intruded into many aspects of domestic affairs, was not at the outset of the first Thatcher administration anything like the central political preoccupation it is today. The pioneers and leaders of the economic liberalism revival, the think-tanks such as the IEA[52] and the CPS,[53] who had inspired the Thatcher cause and more or less taken control of the Conservative party, curiously had very little to say on the EEC issue. It was certainly an irritant, as I discovered my first day as Secretary of State for Energy,[54] but not a central concern in the early Thatcher years. That was to come later – nine years later.

It was Margaret Thatcher's Bruges speech, in September 1988, followed up four weeks later at the Conservative Party conference, which marked the public turning point for the Conservatives from quite strong commitment to the EEC to the ascending hostility which culminates in Brexit today, and in unending divisions within the Conservative Party. This is what has been called 'the long shadow of Brexit'. It was to prove a bumpy road, bringing down Mrs Thatcher herself along the way. However, the deeper direction was already firmly set, made flesh by the speech Commission President Jacques Delors gave at the 1987 Labour Party conference promising corporatist socialism as the future European spirit, as much as by the Thatcher reaction to it.[55]

That Cambridge taxi driver echoed a widely shared view: A discontented and divided British nation is again seeking, yet fearing, radical change.

* * * * *

A Visionless Future

As time moves on, the insistent questions of history present themselves: Whatever account of the Thatcher period one wants to believe, has there been progress or regress (material or otherwise) over the four decades since the formation of the first 1979 government? Are we still on that 'irreversible' path to liberal democracy, both economic and political, promised by the likes of Francis Fukuyama?[56] Or have events and technology combined to block that path and make the questions it poses unanswerable, and have the very words 'liberal' and 'democracy' been unpicked and argued over to the point of meaninglessness?

Has history's trajectory, which seemed so clear and uplifting forty years ago, been reversed, leaving the modern world bereft of any direction or commanding set of beliefs? In his latest work, Yuval Noah Harari ruminates that with fascism and communism defeated, and faith lost in the liberal story, a visionless future without a single global story, a sort of nihilist era, may be our fate: a future without God, without humanism and without trust in robotics and artificial intelligence, or an understanding of where the awesome logic of science and technology may be taking us.[57]

Despite this pessimism from such learned and fascinating sources, the central message of our story is simpler and not so gloomy. Over the past fifty years or so, colossal forces have been sweeping through our lives, bypassing governments, altering relations between nations, changing behaviour and influencing the most humdrum aspects of everyday life. To stay afloat on these crashing waves of change, let alone to prosper, nation states – and they are still the boats on this heaving ocean – require not nostalgia, but new kinds of governance and leadership genius, with a new political language to communicate it.

Good leaders know they cannot command the waves; bad leaders pretend they can. Good leaders strive to explain, to reassure and help their followers in preparation for what is to come. Good leaders calm unrealistic expectations, while keeping hope and ambition alive. Bad leaders fail to explain, claim more control than they possess, raise expectations which cannot be fulfilled and offer clear-cut solutions which cannot be delivered in a political world of unfathomable complexity.

Forty years on from that 1979 Cabinet photograph and the Thatcher world, we are now the other side of the fall of the Berlin Wall, , the Brighton bomb ,the 9/11 horror, and the 2007 invention of the iPhone. We have seen the Lehman collapse and the 2008-onwards global financial crisis, more Middle East chaos, the rise of social media, successive waves of digitally driven globalisation, and the rise of new centres of power and influence, which were not even dreamed about in the 1970s and '80s.

Richard Baldwin, in *The Great Convergence*,[58] identifies these waves, or phases, as first, the early twentieth-century expansion of global trade of all kinds, with falling shipping and transport costs; secondly, the big late twentieth-century shift of technology and production to low-wage economies; and, thirdly, in the twenty-first century, the splitting in actual stages and processes, of production between different countries – the ultimate internationalisation of supply chains.

Old power has been fragmented (in the Middle East with catastrophic results). Old certainties have vanished. Old theories and doctrines have faded. New fears and hobgoblins hover, icons are torn down, truth debased, values derided, civilities forgotten, hatreds inflamed. Almost everywhere indignation and a sense of injustice seem to have taken over, disrupting and dispiriting young and old. The blessings are counted feverishly, but they no longer seem to add up.

The power of technology and communications together with information transmission of unprecedented intensity, have created a new world of ambition, envy and dispute. The world population generates 2.5-quintillion bytes of data by the day.[59] Peoples in their billions are better off economically, richer in circumstance, yet poorer and more restless and troubled in spirit, more connected by far than ever before, yet paradoxically lonelier and more introspective.

Left behind are communities living in deprivation and fear, without hope for themselves or their children, who are now able to see more clearly than ever before how others live and how life is better elsewhere. There is an irresistible call to get up and go. Call them migrants in search of a better life, or call them refugees escaping from terror and frightfulness, whatever the precise impulse, they now see how a better life could be reached. The world is on the move in numbers never before equalled.

Forty years ago, as well as a Cold War capitalism-versus-communism view of the world, another simplified worldview prevailed: the one which neatly divided humankind between the developed and the developing countries, the north/south divide. There was a perfect 'they' and 'us' syndrome, colouring our thinking.

Yet, today, this simple two-group categorisation, too, is now totally misleading. According to Hans Rosling,[60] only thirteen countries, representing 6 per cent of the world population, still live in what might now be called impoverishment, while 85 per cent live in conditions which only a few years ago were confined to the developed world. The gap between the world's rich and poor, he argues with detailed statistical support, is now, in reality, filled with middle-income consumers creating vast new markets and billions of new savers, reversing capital flows and upending old attitudes about who should be helping whom and how societies develop.[61]

Even more undermining of old assumptions are the challenges to all official statistics on which so much political debate and media commentary relies, and the questioning of the worth of old friends like GDP, or the very concept of economic growth and how it should be measured.[62] As Diane Coyle observes, a measure of national strength which includes prostitution and drugs activities but excludes unpaid work in the home and the family (often the hardest) hardly inspires confidence.[63]

With most of the world in a state of constant connection, the imperative now is to organise and conduct government on completely new terms. The good lessons of the past must be distilled, the bad lessons confronted and discarded. If this story assists in this filtration process, if it casts even a wavering light along the journey of the last half-century – its distractions, its barriers, its dangers and its hopes – and maybe along the treacherous path ahead as well, then it will have achieved, in however small degree, its purpose.

* * * * *

This account of the changes is not objective – it cannot be because it comes from one person's experience of, and involvement with, the key figures on the stage, and all the unfolding theories, debates, realisations and events over the decades, both here in Britain and across the world. Inevitably my description and analysis of the events and dramas of half a century are strung along with the thread of personal narrative, a thread with numerous knots and twists. Just how knotted and twisted can be confirmed by the job lottery of my career, as shown in the mish-mash list of sixty-two roles in Appendix One.

However, the story does try to inject into the picture of the world with which we are presented, the dynamics — fluidity and evolving change — which are the central feature of the age in which we live, making extreme views so dominant and moderation in all thing so necessary.

As we shall see, Hans Rosling and his co-authors — his son and daughter-in-law — are right. Nothing is anymore as it seems.

Chapter Six

Origins and Fears

ALL books have ancestors and one of the inspirations of the present one, although it may seem long out of time, is *The March of Folly*, by the American historian Barbara Tuchman, published in 1984.[64] She describes some of those fascinating moments in history when overwhelming opinion favours some course which seems right and obvious to most people at the time, but which turns out to be a disaster, leading to the very opposite results to those intended or hoped for. As so often through history, the ever-hovering law of unintended consequences swoops down and takes over. Barbara Tuchman starts with the classic example of the Trojan decision, agreed all around as a good idea, to take the wooden horse within the walls of Troy.

She describes the futile policies of the medieval popes to crush the rise of Protestantism which, instead, reinforced it, and the British hard line against the American colonists which had the opposite result. She finishes with America's well-intentioned 1970s interventions in Vietnam to uphold freedom and prevent nations falling to communism one by one, like dominoes. In the end, there were no more dominoes, only nations forcing mighty America into humiliating retreat – with 58,000 dead Americans to bury, and with Vietnam, ironically, now a fast-growing mixed-economy state.

However, follies of this special kind, with the full weight of authority and established opinion behind them, have marched on since then. The 2003 invasion of Iraq is a classic example of good intentions paving the road to hell. The explosion of the world financial debacle of 2007/8 was a rather different kind of disaster, but again spectacularly wrong-footing conventional wisdom. The common feature of these calamities is that very few see them coming (as pointed out by Her Majesty The Queen about the 2008 Lehman crisis). The minority who do find their voices are drowned out by the suffocating certainty of those in charge that they are on the right course.

Contexts change. What seemed like a good idea at the time turns out not to be. Events which no-one foresaw come spiralling out of nowhere and turn hopes and visions to ashes.

By the late 1970s, mainstream opinion agreed that labour unions had become over-mighty subjects and had to be curbed, that the state was too large, that markets would produce better results than central planning and state ownership, that inflation was a killer and had to be defeated by curbing the supply of money. There were sharp disagreements about the pace of reforms and the methods, which led to the famous labelling between Wets and Dries in the Thatcher administration and quite a lot of Cabinet reshuffles. However, on the broad objectives there was agreement.

On the whole, over the period of the Thatcher premiership these issues were successfully addressed and goals, at least in part, achieved. So how does that square with talk of follies and failures? After all it was Tony Blair who saw the benefits of privatisation and markets, harnessing New Labour to the market reform trend, and promised 'Thatcherism without the prickles'. At my last meal with Margaret Thatcher, then ailing, she kept repeating this very point to me and Charles Powell, our host that evening: 'Watch out. He (Tony Blair) has stolen my policies.'[65] If imitation is the sincerest form of flattery, then surely that makes the Thatcher era a success, not a failure or an age of folly?

Yet folly there was, even if it lay beneath the surface. It lay first in the exaggerated media imagery which was allowed and encouraged to develop. In appearance, though not in fact, the swerve away from state socialism and corporatism towards market doctrine went too far, too fast, skimming across a surface beneath which lay deeply flawed theories and concepts.

The problems lay especially in the narrowness of the economics profession and its loudest voices. We were using tools that worked for only half the picture. The almost unquestioned prevailing wisdom was that economic analysis explained how economies worked, and that policies bedded on this analysis would produce economic progress. If socialism had failed and was wrong, this alternative analysis must be right. If state control had produced miserable results, then liberated efficiency of markets must be right. That was all we needed to believe and know. That was Adam Smith. That was the dogma.[66]

You can usually sniff it in the voice and the tone. The test question is, 'Are you sure you are right?' If this is answered with a pitying half-laugh or a look as though it is a really silly question, then you are in over-the-top country, where conviction, doctrine and broad principles have mutated into dogma. This is the land in which a set of beliefs takes over which it is deemed stupid or downright impertinent to query. The voice of reason and moderation becomes still, small and hesitant, quite easy to distinguish from the loud and confident voice of dogma. Cross the border between the two and we are in the dangerous country about which Karl Popper warned.[67] The propositions cease to be refutable. It is time to sound the alarm. And we are usually, too, marching headlong to a Barbara Tuchman folly.

The obsessive and dogmatic atmosphere developing around 'scientific' monetarism has already been mentioned. Another sure danger sign, not recognised at the time, was a tendency to see remedies solely in terms of restoring *consumer* sovereignty as the foundation of free markets. Missing from the minds of too many around Margaret Thatcher (although certainly not from her own mind) was an understanding of the nature of and need for *political s*overeignty. This was the foundation of a free nation and a balanced democracy, where people are citizens first and consumers as a consequence.

Because British failures in post-war years had been so notably economic, this was an understandable narrowness of focus at the time. We were all dismayed at Britain's economic underperformance, trades-union paralysis, high inflation, the weak pound, poor exports and general humiliation. Comparisons with almost all our European neighbours had indeed become odious. Italy had proudly arrived at

Il Sorpasso, with a GDP larger than the UK's.[68] What on earth was wrong? Cure all that, bring back market-driven economic growth and a golden road of social harmony opened out ahead just what Margaret Thatcher seemed to be saying as she quoted St Francis of Assisi on the steps of No.10.[69]

The proper antidote to ideology is a mixture of balance, common sense and pragmatism. The more the replacement to collectivism and the Keynesian consensus of previous decades veered away after 1979 and became a counter-ideology, the more certain it would overreach, stumble and crash. All ideologies, Left and Right or any other kind, suffer from internal flaws and carry the seeds of their eventual failures. In this case the replacement was only half-formed. The ideologues of consumer sovereignty and free markets thought they had the whole story. The missing half was the social structure which supports economic activity; the source which determines the health, welfare, dynamic vigour, balance and contentment of a society or nation.

This is a universe which begins with the family in the home and in the humblest daily routines but which spreads right up to the unity and direction of a nation. It lies in the human impulses to share and co-operate, in the world of social relations and attitudes, in the surrounding environment and in the routine dealings and requirements of daily life, on which everything else depends. These are precisely the 'core' qualities that determine a country's strength or weakness. They are what decides whether the economic process pulls together or stagnates then falls apart.

Many of these activities in a society may be unpaid, but that is not the point; a not-the-point for which the more conventional economists fail to find a value. Intense efforts may be focused on improving market efficiency, raising skills and standards, building new roads, railways, schools, hospitals and distributing benefits across the board. In short, making the visible, money-measured, market economy work.

But if this focus on growth as presented by the statistics is in reality only half the story, giving only half a picture of the nation's real activity, vigour and welfare, it is bound to leave a sense of unfulfillment and discontent. The figures might insist that people were 'better off'. It just did not feel that way.

Could we but see it at the end of the 1970s, we were already living in a pattern of networks which placed large areas of national life above and outside our control, yet which were beginning to give new strength to localism and local identity. Changes in the international order of things, in the behaviour of others, in the influences of distant and remote actions on the most intimate of home affairs, were already at work in ways of which we had no inkling. What the imminent communications revolution was about to communicate, were resentments and senses of affront to human dignity on a scale we could not then imagine.

Besides Barbara Tuchman's grimly realistic tapestry of human folly there is a second inspirational book, with a somewhat less dispiriting message, from which to draw better understanding. This is Anne-Marie Slaughter's *The Chessboard and the Web*,[70] which explains how the international world of competing powers and interests now has to live alongside, and will in due course be replaced by, a series of networks so dispersed and yet so densely connected as to change the whole nature of international relations and the diplomatic strategies required to navigate them.

Another wellspring for the views in these pages is Parag Khanna's *Connectography: Mapping the Future of Global Civilization*[71] which reminds us that supply chains and connectivity, not sovereignty and borders, are becoming the organising principles of humanity in the twenty-first century — decades beyond the horizons of the '79 team as we began our reforming work. Another guiding light has been Richard Baldwin's already mentioned *The Great Convergence*, which describes how the new second wave of globalisation, beginning in the 1990s and well beyond our 1979 horizon, appeared to bring an era of unprecedented income growth and came to change not merely the pattern of trade but the very organisation of world production.[72] To this picture, Oliver Stuenkel's *Post-Western World*[73] adds the detail of the new non-Western networks of trade, security and interests of the twenty-first century which have largely replaced the world institutions of the twentieth century.

These new vistas were entirely hidden to us forty years ago. Yet our actions and decisions were the progenitors to all of them. Markets and competition unleashed innovation in every economic sphere and every corner of the earth, bringing a Cambrian explosion of technology, generating an unparalleled growth of finance capitalism and making an impact on even the poorest regions and societies – said by some, with an only shade of exaggeration, to be greater than the arrival of gunpowder, colonialism or Christianity.

Technological advances of unstoppable force, and consequent international shifts of power and behavioural changes barely suspected forty years ago, have reshaped our lives, altered social structures and trends and so, also, altered the course of politics. As G.M. Trevelyan long ago reminded us in his *English Social History*, politics is the *outcome*, not the *cause*, of social change.[74]

Chapter Seven

Unspinning the Past

'There is no such thing as fixed policy, because policy,
like all organic entities, is always in the making.'

—attributed to Lord Salisbury

'Even when I am giving ministers a hard time on
camera, I try never to forget that they are attempting
to do something very difficult.'

—the late Sir Robin Day, who knew how to interview[75]

'If old truths are to retain their hold on men's minds,
they must be restated in the language and concepts
of successive generations.'

—Friedrich von Hayek[76]

TODAY'S political debate has lost its bearings and almost its vocabulary. As technology races forward, leaving old arguments and ideologies hanging in the air, a polarisation of theories fills the scene. At one pole is the set of claims that capitalism is finished and that a new kind of state collectivism should prevail, despite the glaring evidence of past and current failures.

At the other pole is the claim that free markets are the only way forward, despite glaring evidence that they invariably lead to mega-cartels and monopolies, and so act against the interests of citizens and societies, just as Adam Smith warned – only far more intensely in the age of digital revolution and globalisation, of which we are now experiencing the second wave (as explained in Chapter Five).

Both sides twist and distort history to prove their case and perpetuate their theories. Both sides try to impose their versions of the past on an unfamiliar present. Neither side connects with what is really happening or likely to happen, in totally new conditions, whether globally or domestically (the two being inextricably interwoven). Neither side fully understands the Asian mindset which will do so much to shape the century. Both sides rely on economic concepts and models which were always flawed and have become many times more so.

* * * * *

Nevertheless, to see the situation more clearly and maybe to check the vortex of political extremism towards unbridgeable division, break-up and anarchy, it is essential to understand better what really happened in these past decades, how practice and theory were far apart, how governments were not what they seemed, and how the roots of present dilemmas can be disentangled from a misinterpreted past. Maybe to lay some ghosts to rest, too.

Forecasts, especially economic forecasts, tend to ignore human passions in favour of logic and have suffered many embarrassing failures as a result. Too often they are made by people who overlook, or are oblivious of, the consequences. Like bankers who collect the profits but leave others to bear the losses, or makers of fine policies who never suffer the experience of living under them, or designers who never use the things they design, those with 'no skin in the game', as Nassim Nicholas Taleb, author of *The Black Swan*[77] puts it, are on an easy, no-risk, ride.

All too often analysts and futurologists forget how real outcomes turn out again and again to be completely different from what they predicted. Certainly, we are now miles away from many of the hopes and predictions of 1979 and, it is absolutely safe to say, in ten years' time all sorts of completely unforeseen issues and problems will be swirling around us, and present problems and obsessions omnipresent in the current Brexit debate in the UK will fade into insignificance.

Even now, a revolution around us is making it harder to keep up, or to find a quiet pool amid the swirling waters by which to pause and reflect on life and progress and beauty and purpose.

Is there now an open slide to anarchy, at least of opinion, but maybe, soon, of behaviour, as the contract between government and governed finally collapses, as political fragmentation takes over (as has already occurred in parts of the Middle East) and as mass audiences, empowered by information, reject authority in all forms?

Or are there new binding forces at work, maybe the very forces which pulled apart the old-world order, which now give grounds for optimism and for the belief that there is a new era of stability and progress in reach? Are the pictures painted of a world without rules – with unrest, discontent, global threats and horrors, allegedly widening gaps of inequality and reams of statistics in support of utter gloom – misleading us? I argue that, yes, in many respects they are.

The proposition in these pages is that, today, power has come to lie not in the Cabinet (to anything like the past degree), nor in the will of one 'strong leader', nor in the jeers and cheers of elected parliaments, nor in the shrill media, nor in the banks, nor in Washington or some of the rising empires in Asia, but increasingly in the global networks which create their own pathways and impose their own agendas.

Some, such as Niall Ferguson, contend that the hyper-connected billions have finally defeated the hierarchies of the past, heralding a new openness and fluidity, but also a dangerous new volatility, in world affairs.[78] Others suggest that power has passed to the new giant global monopolies, born out of the information revolution and now far larger and more influential than even the largest nations.

These are the present-day dilemmas and dangers to which the political team of '79 could not possibly see their actions might lead. Yet the legacy and its confused interpretation, is there. And of course, the story is not over. The follies will continue. However, so also may the restraining moments of practicality and common sense which, along with basic civility and respect for one another, are the real ingredients of genuine democracy in all its aspects, and the real antidote to incipient anarchy, social breakdown and to the ideological excesses of the past.

PART TWO
ROOTS AND FALSE DAWNS

Chapter Eight
Roots of the Revolution

L ONG before the full impact of the microprocessor burst on the world, the signs of coming upheaval were there to be seen if one searched for them. This was the period – in the 1960s and '70s, a decade before the Thatcher era – when words and concepts from the military management sphere (which is, after all, where the internet originated) began to penetrate political language. References to the 'delivery' of goals, to objectives, to the rolling out of programmes, mission targets, benchmarks, operational readiness, resource planning, new configurations, and a host of other expressions, began to pepper the speeches of politicians who wished to show they had 'got it' or were 'with it'.

This alone was enough to trigger, about two-thirds of the way through the twentieth century, an avalanche of questions about the functions of government and the state: what they were supposed to achieve; whether they were best configured to do so; and which governmental functions needed to be in the public sector at all, or might be better handled by the market. A period of intense questioning about the role of the swollen state began, starting at its very heart.

The privatisation genie, although not at first recognised, was well and truly out of the bottle; the high watermark in the twentieth century of 'big state' beliefs and doctrines had been reached. A new revolution seemed to be under way, dubbed the New Style of

Government, and whether it was or not, this was the language in which the story was packaged and presented.

At the beginning of the '60s there had been a real anger and frustration, coming from many quarters – think-tanks, commentators (although less so from academia) – that public policy was on the wrong track, that the British had been almost uniquely let down by intellectual failure in the higher echelons of governance, both on Left and Right, and that a wholly new direction was required. Furthermore, many believed others in Europe were visibly doing better.

The election of Ted Heath (seen as a reforming figure) as Conservative Party leader, raised all kinds of hopes: This was the man who, as a Cabinet minister, had abolished Resale Price Maintenance in 1964.[79] Furthermore there was his brisk, not to say brusque, performance as Conservative Chief Whip – all in all, surely a new generation kind of classless Conservative leader.

In Opposition during the Harold Wilson administration Heath had been quite an easy person to advise. He was very open to new ideas, responsive, clear in his speech needs, amusing, friendly, accessible – all the things his detractors said he was not. Chatty handwritten letters flowed to and fro – I particularly liked the note to me in which he wrote at the bottom, 'Lord Annan praised you at length last night but I am prepared to overlook this.'

He was also very hospitable. The door of his Albany flat – large and nice rooms but a bit austerely furnished (too much black leather) – was always open, and he liked parties. Working with him was enjoyable as well as hard work.

For us advisers, itching for more free-market measures, whether in our undergraduate arguments or in organisations like the rising Bow Group, the journey had really begun ten years before Heath, back in the late '50s, with our dismay and sometime fury that by the end of the that decade Britain was still the sick man of Europe. It seemed incredible that our continental neighbours were powering ahead while we were still gripped by I'm-alright-Jack industrial relations, low growth, weak currency and a general feeling of impoverishment – except for the aristos who seemed to be carrying on with the Season, Ascot, etc., in a remarkably disconnected way from the general national plight.

One debutante dance at Claridge's, given by Árpád Plesch for his stepdaughters, was considered so spectacularly extravagant that questions were asked about it in Parliament.[80] However, on the whole, it amazed me how little egalitarian outrage was directed against the wealthy and well-connected, whose untroubled lifestyles could be viewed through the pages of *Tatler* – and in due course of *Harpers & Queen*, which Jocelyn Stevens pioneered into the glossy magazine front line.

Instead, the class warriors of the Left seemed determined to vent their anger not on the truly, quietly, landed rich who were, as ever, with us in post-war Britain, but on the salaries (by today's standards very modest) of one or two captains of industry or nationalised industry bosses, and of course on enterprise and the private sector. The staggeringly high high-income tax rates, maintained by successive Labour governments right up to 1979, were the flag of anti-enterprise in the shadow of which no above-board wealth creation via high income could flourish. Perhaps Labour thought that death duties had finished off the landed gentry (in practice, only partly) hence their preoccupation with attacking visible incomes rather than stately homes.

During my days as a *Daily Telegraph* leader and feature writer I penned a few articles for *Harpers & Queen*, although one was not strictly supposed to write outside the newspaper. Their offices were around the corner from the *Telegraph*'s Fleet Street building. The aim was to widen political coverage with some daring feature articles among the pages of fashion and society photographs, and thus lift readership beyond the Chelsea Set. I used to slip around there after finishing at the *Telegraph* and discuss new ideas for features with Jocelyn Stevens himself and his brilliant editor, Beatrix Miller, whose silver fingernails fascinated me.

I had served Stevens in a different capacity years earlier: At school he was the golden head boy, gazed up to by us juniors, the prospective heir to the Hulton publishing empire, and superb at the right sports – rowing and the field game, the perfect qualities for a public-school hero poised to move on easily to glittering prizes. He had specially chosen me as his fag (this was then the system) because of my skill – long since lost – in making fluffy omelettes.

As Conservative Government difficulties mounted in the early
'60s, so did the familiar attack on privilege and wealth, with fresh and
telling vigour. The super-sharp Harold Wilson – said by his Labour
colleagues to have the quickest mind of all – picked up the scent and
gleefully began to pin on the Tories the image of the 'grouse moor',
with the landed, old Etonian gentry in charge. This was an image
beautifully validated (for Harold Wilson and Labour) by photographs
of Harold Macmillan, indeed, right there on the grouse moor, with
the red telephone resting on the heather nearby, and of course with the
emergence of the fourteenth Earl of Home as Prime Minister – when
Wilson had a field day.

Those at the younger and impatient end of the Conservative Party
were as wrong as the Left about Alec Douglas-Home. He turned out
to be tough and shrewd and nearly won an election again, despite the
Government's failures and problems. Aristocrat he certainly was but,
far from being out of touch, he was probably the most matter-of-fact,
down-to-earth and accessible national leader of his age, much closer
to everyday life and feelings than some of the socialist grandees or
trades-union barons.

I knew perfectly well what a charming, straightforward and
sensible man he was. Some years before he 'emerged', first as Foreign
Secretary then Prime Minister, I had been invited by his daughter to
stay at Dorneywood (then allocated to him as, I think, Commonwealth
Minister) to attend a nearby dance.

The morning after, the earl seemed worried. I found him in the
big drawing room in an armchair surrounded by papers. It was the
weekend of the overthrow – and murder – of King Faisal of Iraq.
'What shall we do?' asked Alec – a very flattering question to ask of
a wet-behind-the-ears opinionated *Daily Telegraph* leader-writer. Of
course, I had no idea, but the whole thing was typical of his relaxed
style and ultra-accessibility.

Later on, when he was Prime Minister (by then, Sir Alec), I met
him in St James's Park, walking across from Downing Street to his club
for lunch, and fell in with him for a chat. One rain-coated Inspector
Knacker trailed about twenty yards behind. Nowadays such things
would only happen in a Mary Poppins storybook – but this was, of

course, long before the days of swarming security men and forbidding iron gates at the mouth of Downing Street.

Much later still, after Alec had ceased to be Prime Minister, I saw him and Lady Douglas-Home sitting in the front upstairs seats of a Number 9 bus and enjoying the experience – a return to ordinary life which some of his successors do not seem to have followed. So much for the stereotyping nonsense about grouse moors and old Etonians, it was as silly then as it is silly now – not least because toffdom and Eton are not the same thing and never were, despite the famous image of top-hatted youths.[81]

Even after the grouse moor story had died away and Ted Heath had been elevated to Tory leader – not least because he was considered to be a break from the old ruling class, being a scholarship boy and the son of a Broadstairs carpenter – I was still being told, in 1965, that my own attendance at Eton was an impassable barrier to being chosen as candidate for a 'safe' Conservative seat or any seat at all. This, I was warned, together with my role as director of the Conservative Political Centre – where, in the view of some Tories, far too much thinking went on – and with my then still unmarried state (this was just after the Vassall affair,[82] with its negative connotations at the time about single men), would make me the least attractive candidate and pretty well unelectable if ever chosen.

Luckily, the Guildford Conservative Association selection committee thought otherwise. 'Never mind,' said the commanding, do-not-interrupt-me chairwoman of the committee, when my bachelordom was raised, 'Never mind. There are plenty of nice girls here.' I did marry a year later (1967), although not a girl from Guildford despite the undoubtedly impressive local selection, and we have lived happily ever after.

It may also have helped that I had spent three years – a hard grind – earlier, fighting a massive Labour stronghold, the Dudley and Stourbridge constituency in Staffordshire (and also Worcestershire). For some historic reason connected to the Duke of Northumberland's Percy family interests, Stourbridge, although entirely surrounded by Worcestershire, was in Staffordshire. A mild snag for a vote-seeking parliamentary candidate was that the Dudley Tory colours were red, the traditional colours of the Percy interest, while those of Stourbridge, the seat of Lord Cobham, were blue. A change of tie had to be hurriedly conducted in a lay-by between the two towns.

The friendly Dudley people were a brave little enclave of Tories in a fiercely Labour area. When I was adopted as candidate, I was much struck, as I shook hands with the Tory elders of Dudley, that so many of them seemed to have lost their thumbs – in the war, I presumed. Afterwards it was explained to me that this was the masonic handshake and they were just checking – in my case, in vain.

The constituency had a massive majority and was held by George Wigg, the much-feared Wilson condottieri and look-out man. To me, he was friendly and even seemed to be confiding – but I was advised to be always on my guard. After losing the 1964 election my Dudley friends were totally understanding in letting me go to seek more promising pastures. Dudley and Stourbridge, they said, would obviously always be Labour. Three years later, when George Wigg died and there was a by-election, it went Tory with a large majority.

However, for the restless younger generation of Conservatives, and especially the critics of Britain's continued poor economic performance, the worry was not about too much wealth but too little. Our eyes were focused on the German recovery miracle (*Wirtschaftwunder*) and the *Ordoliberalismus* of Ludwig Erhard, which was pushing the Germany economy well ahead. I had seen the growing achievement of rebuilt German cities and main streets at the end of my time as a national serviceman in Germany. The picture of plumper German ladies tucking into *erdbeertorte mit sahne* – a luxury unknown in austere post-war Britain – was wedged in my mind. The war-time losers in Europe were clearly doing better than the winners. It was plain as a pikestaff that Britain was on the wrong track and that radical change, of philosophy, of policy, of organisation and of mindset – in short, a whole new style of government – was needed to catch up with the rest of western Europe.

In the early '60s I visited Ludwig Erhard to interview him when he was Economics Minister, at the height of his powers and success (this was before his subsequent less happy period as German Chancellor). Erhard had already become a hero to some of us and his book,

Prosperity Through Competition[83] had served as a kind of economic (and political) bible to us at Cambridge as we searched for an alternative to the consensus which seemed to paralyse the post-war British economy. I see I wrote in my new copy 'the only hope'.

The German Economics Ministry was housed in an old Luftwaffe barracks in the suburbs of Bonn. I was distracted by the minister's tight lace-up black boots. Apparently, he nearly always wore them. My German was not good enough to grasp every word of our talk (there were no interpreters) but I picked up enough to get the picture.

His guiding philosophy was liberalisation and competition – liberalisation of the currency, of trade, of regulations. Germany was back in business and the business was going to be an army of family-owned and mid-sized enterprises (with one or two giants from the pre-war period still going strong as well, once awkward de-nazification questions had been navigated) and with no paralysing encumbrance of mastodon state-owned and slothful monopolies, as in slumbering Britain. Wealth would be shared and used to underpin sensibly designed social benefits on the Bismarckian pattern. In its new form this was the famous *Sozialmarkt* concept – a wonderfully practical German expression of an idea that eluded the polarised British debate then, and now.

This idea is that, far from capitalism and socialism being opposites, they combine powerfully to deliver social benefit, raising living standards, dignity and equality of status. It is the very opposite of the fashionable claims made today, for example by the French sociologist Thomas Piketty, that capitalism, as it expands, increases inequality. This, of course, depends on what you mean by capitalism, as well as how you measure inequality.

So, even in the early 1960s, this more generous and wider type of market-driven growth seemed the right model for Britain. It was why we wanted the new style of government: freer, less state dominated and, if possible, with large sections of the state either contracted out or pushed back into the private sector – the very approach that laid-back Reggie Maudling thought was 'all balls' (see below), as did many others.

We were trying (in vain at that time, as it turned out) to advance the notion in the British context that regulated and modulated capitalist free enterprise could deliver the biggest, fairest and most sustainable outcomes of all – and the fastest rate of economic growth, not that there was some mythical choice of economic models between socialism and capitalism, nor even that there was some halfway house between the two (the famous Butskellism).

Earlier in the '60s some of us had formed a small cross-party, or maybe non-party, dining club we called the Economic Growth Group. The members included William Rees-Mogg, Nigel Lawson, Samuel Brittan, Andrew Shonfield, and me.[84]

We aimed high. Faded papers in the Churchill Archives show that during 1962 and 1963 our dinner guests included Harold Wilson, Hugh Gaitskell, Reggie Maudling, Rab Butler (the prince of ambiguity) and Sir Maurice Parsons, George Brown and Iain Macleod. Dinners took place at Andrew's house in Paulton Square, at William's house, then 13 Cowley Street, or at my bachelor flat in Abingdon Gardens. An invitation to the Prime Minister (Sir Alec) resulted in a kind counter-invitation to drinks at No.10 instead.

After the Gaitskell dinner in Paulton Square, where Gaitskell and Nigel Lawson clashed sharply, William Rees-Mogg suggested we should aim even higher and ask General de Gaulle to dine. Somehow this did not get off the ground.

This was certainly one forum – there were undoubtedly others – in which thinking began to turn strongly to free markets, large-scale privatisation, deregulation and monetary policy prudence, and away from more consensual concerns about trades-union power. However, these were very early days. All that can be said is that the seeds of a very different approach were being planted, which would take well over a decade to come to any kind of fruition.

'What's All This Balls?'

While Ted Heath was always open to new ideas, the same openness was not shared too strongly by some of his shadow cabinet colleagues. Here's a conversation, overheard by Douglas Hurd, which took place just before the shadow cabinet went to a dinner at the Carlton Club in February 1970, at which some of us concerned with a very detailed programme of preparations for a radical government had been

The Cabinet of 1979. At a crossroads. No-one possessed, or had ever heard of, a mobile phone.
(Author's collection)

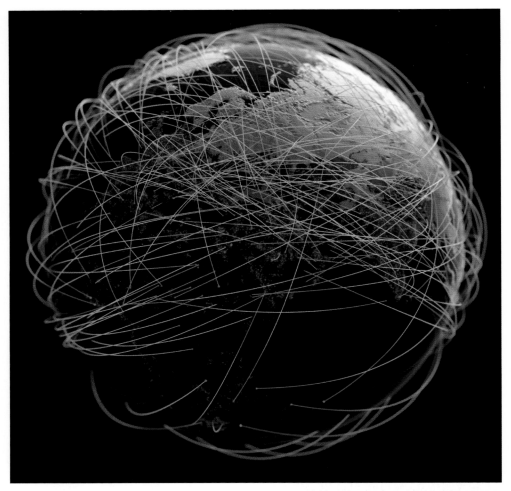

The explosion in connectivity. Nothing like it in history (iStock)

Burke spoke of democracy's 'Dangerous and angry passions', and reminded us about 'unpopular minorities' – a caution lost on today's demagogues who persist in confusing democracy with majoritarianism and the myth of 'the will of the people'. (Duyckinick, Evert A./University of Texas Libraries) (WikiCommons)

Keith Joseph and Jim Prior – at opposite poles in yesterday's debate (Author's Collection)

The new Prime Minister visits the Department of Energy –and does not like what she sees.
(Author's Collection)

Really quite close. (Author's Collection)

The Go-between. Heath kept dropping off. Not much policy discussed. (Author's Collection)

Ernest Marples. Contempt for politicians. Heath 'not the boss'. Began the questioning of all government functions and operations. (Alamy)

Mark Schreiber, now Lord Marlesford. Insisted from the start on ceaseless and systematic questioning of all government functions – which began the unravelling. (Author's Collection)

PRIVATE EYE

No. 99
Friday
1 Oct. 65

1/6

With the new Conservative leader in the South of France — Private Eye version. He regretted the visit. (Public Domain)

Beginning the peace process leading to Sunningdale One. Sunningdale Two (the Good Friday Agreement) took another twenty-five years. (Author's Collection)

commissioned to explain our ideas for 'a new style of government' (less of it) and how to get there.

Reggie Maudling: 'What's all this balls we're having a dinner about at the Carlton tonight?'

Peter Carrington: 'Well, Reggie, I'm sorry you feel like that. I regard it as very important.'

Maudling: 'Well I can't say I understand what it's all about. Still, hope it's a good dinner.'

There was something wonderfully encapsulating and defining about this exchange. Some months before this Carlton dinner, Angus Maude had written a fiery piece in the *Spectator*, with the same disparaging tone as the Maudling remarks, of the Heath approach to policy reform, as well as a highly critical letter in the *Daily Telegraph*. For him, the Heath line was far too managerial – all objectives, systems, missions and jargon. Ted Heath, he opined, was 'a dry technocrat'.

Maude was sacked from the shadow cabinet for his pains. In one sense he was right – we probably did sound much too technocratic and so did Heath. To please the Tory intellectuals and cheer up the demoralised backbenches we needed to couch our ideas in more high-flown and philosophical terms; less jargon and more of the beautiful English language.

Angus was a master of this style. He spoke and wrote with refreshing clarity and was the darling of Tory conferences. However, on this occasion he was missing the point, or perhaps we were failing to get it over. The basis of our 'New Style of Government' thinking was that the centralised corporatist state, as bequeathed by the Attlee administration, had failed: the private sector could, on the whole, do better; the swollen state sector had to be unravelled, however much opposition there would be from entrenched trades unions, academic 'experts' and the political Left wing; private enterprise could be harnessed to public purposes.

In our naivety we thought this position was clear to everyone. We thought it was understood that the liberalised market economy had to find new ways of working with a less dominant state, as in Germany – and to some extent, France. (I was taken by Jean Monnet's indicative planning model in France – framework guidance without control – and had visited the French planners at their attic offices in the Rue Martin.)

What we were really concerned about with our New Style of Government 'playbook'[85] was the mechanics of translating a heavily socialised economy into a free-market and enterprise economy. In our eyes, it was not just a question of making speeches about liberty and freedom and the market economy, however finely phrased. Even the wonderfully persistent proselytising of the Institute of Economic Affairs (IEA) was not enough. We had to figure out how these ideas and ideals might be turned into policy in hard, practical, step-by-step detail. How, in short, the transformation away from the state socialised era might be accomplished, and not lost in the consensual quagmire of ineffective state intervention.

Not content with mere speeches, we compiled a 'black book' of forty or so immediate administrative actions to be taken by an incoming Heath-led government to make a reality of the 'New Style of Government'. This list had a wide circulation in Whitehall and caused general alarm.

The administrative approach to greater issues of reform and principle was the aspect Angus Maude and many Tories, and for that matter Reggie Maudling, had not cottoned onto – but I think that Ted Heath had, at least for a while, until he was later overwhelmed by events during his premiership. Maybe our ideas and proposals sounded too Keynesian, or maybe they did not fit clearly into the polarised British ideological debate?

Either way, they antagonised both the Left, inevitably, for attacking the sacred cows of state socialism and nationalisation, and the Right who felt they were not truly conservative enough and began to question whether they had made the right choice for leader with Ted Heath. Much later, when Heath, having defied predictions and become Prime Minister, was driven on the defensive, these were the cracks in the new edifice for which there was going to be a heavy price to pay.

The other worry among the Conservative faithful and grass-roots membership was that their leader was not married. The word was that Heath had had an early but unhappy love affair with a senior mistress at a private school. It had all gone wrong and, went the story, and he had vowed never to commit himself again, or succumb to vulnerable passion.

The message now went around that the Conservative Party leader must be introduced to suitable partners. With a youthful sense of duty, I felt I should take some action and brought round to dinner at his Albany flat a truly dazzling girlfriend – ready to make any sacrifice in the interests of the party.

It was a hopeless mission. She sat down very close to Ted on his black leather sofa but he immediately rose, patted the cushion and went to stand behind the sofa, well out of her aura. There was no interest and there was to be no sacrifice.

Contrary to some assertions, Ted liked accomplished women and had several close female friends. However, none close enough for partnership or marriage to be in the frame. So, the Tory faithful would just have to lump it.

* * * * *

The *Daily Telegraph* was a good perch from which to observe and contribute, as much as commentators can, to the unfolding Conservative story and the new thinking as the 1960s opened up. It was a very different paper from today. Wise and quite elderly editors gave the paper an authoritative tone of calm and reassurance. Today, although it is difficult to pin down, the *Telegraph* radiates a more crusading tone which seems at odds with its conservative tradition.

Back in the '60s, editorials (called leaders) were not the best way of propagating ideas, first because they had to be a maximum of 350 words and often only 250, but much more because the editor, Sir Colin Coote, had the alarming habit of deleting the last two lines of a carefully argued piece and substituting the opposite conclusion. Thus a balanced view of, say decimalisation of the currency (over which Trollope's Duke of Omnium agonised a century earlier), which had taken me two or three hours of thought and research and which concluded magisterially with the view that it should now at last happen, would simply be turned on its head, with the end crossed out and Sir Colin's view that it should be resisted inserted.

Perhaps it did not matter since it was the view of the tough old news editor, who occasionally attended our 3 p.m. editorial conferences where we decided what to write in the leader columns, that the percentage of readers (then about 1.4-million) who took in our editorial views was miniscule. More readers, he opined, checked the price of lard in the commodities section of the *Telegraph* than read our weighty leaders – a humbling thought.

Feature articles (nowadays called op-eds) were a different matter. Here one was permitted to spread one's wings and try to shape the future. I was allowed to dilate at length on the need for new economic policies and for fundamental changes in the machinery of government to push them through, as well as on the apparently better and more successful practices going on across the Channel, not just in Germany, but in France, Belgium, the Netherlands and even Italy, whose GNP – a shaky concept at the best of times – had overtaken Britain's. As Italy sags into recession again today, this picture of an Italian miracle taking Italy way ahead of Britain seems incredible. Yet it was the fear at the time, and it is a reminder of the vastly different context in which decisions were then – almost half a century ago – made.

Some of my advice and ideas were complicated and difficult to get across. Journalist Colin Welch expressed the view that I had been reading too many books. Welch had been the originator of the Peter Simple *galère* of characters – mostly parodies of preposterous and self-centred lefties, which Michael Wharton brilliantly brought to life – with some of whom we continue to be saddled. With a not-unkindly sigh, Colin explained that my Middle Way-ish feature articles were for display, not reading. They were useful (i.e. sold more copies and filled up space) only in that they could be seen when the *Telegraph* was tucked under the arm, thus proving that the buyer or reader was concerned with deep and complex issues rather than just polarised clichés or the sports page or the latest juicy crime report.

Colin Welch and Peregrine Worsthorne, his associate, were seen in the distorting mirror of those times as *les enfants terrible* of the Right at the *Daily Telegraph*. Their remarks, often tongue well in cheek, were usually greeted with cries of outrage from the centre-left and were doubtless intended to do so. If they went too far, it was because the suffocating consensus of a Britain in decline had gone much too far the other way.

We were left remarkably alone by the *Telegraph* proprietor, Michael Berry, a man of great charm and gentleness who occasionally asked us to lunch in his panelled offices on the fifth floor. The only ruling to emanate from that level was that we should write carefully about anything to do with gypsies. It was asserted that this was because the proprietor's wife, Pamela Berry, who gave glittering soirées in Cowley Street, had some connecting thread back through her father, F.E. Smith, the great Lord Birkenhead, to gypsy origins.

For the rest, we could say what we liked, and what Sir Colin would accept. He himself retired after a while and was replaced by the equally mild and wise Maurice Green, who had been deputy editor of *The Times* (and who ironically had turned me down, in the kindest possible way, when I applied for a job at *The Times* two years before, on the grounds that I was 'too political').

This was also the time (February 1961) when the decision was made to launch a Sunday edition. The terse, but kind, Donald McLachlan, was appointed the first editor and asked me to introduce some of my Bow Group friends to him as possible contributors, such as Geoffrey Howe, Tom Hooson, Tim Raison, and others. A dinner was arranged at the Davidson mansion in Chiswick Mall and I drove him down in my newly acquired Mini, which I was anxious to demonstrate as the cutting edge of British automotive technology. This was the earliest model, with an asthmatic gear change and, incredibly, an unprotected carburettor just behind the front grille. In wet weather, when overtaking a goods vehicle, the spray would drown the carburettor and cut out the engine in mid-manoeuvre. Later a yellow plastic guard was supplied to avoid this hair-raising experience.

McLachlan was not impressed, but several of us were invited to contribute feature articles to the new paper. One reason for launching it, he confided, was to offset *Daily Telegraph* tax bills with the inevitable initial losses the new paper was bound to occur.

* * * * *

Daily Telegraph travel also took me to Washington several times. The legendary figure, Peregrine Worsthorne, by now deputy editor of the *Telegraph*, seemed to know everyone there and gave me a sheaf of introductions to the Camelot court of President Kennedy. Presidential advisers were the crème-de-la-crème in Washington circles, hovering on the edge between the luxury of opinion and the responsibility of power.

Arthur Schlesinger, a central figure in the Kennedy cosmos, took me out to lunch and drew a picture on a napkin to explain how communism and fascism ended up as the same thing. I had read – avidly – his book, *The Vital Centre*[86] – more 'Middle Way' stuff but of great sophistication and with a very American context. (I 'borrowed' it from Capesthorne[87] and to my embarrassment found that I had kept it decades later. It happens.) Ted Sorensen, star Kennedy speechwriter, was also very friendly and Carl Kaysen, the head of the Bureau of the Budget (subsequently Office of Management and the Budget) invited me to stay at his house in Georgetown, where most of the Camelot group lived and dined.

Jo and Polly Kraft also became good friends – Jo being the number one columnist and Kennedy admirer in the Washington press. Peter Jay was at that stage *Times* correspondent in Washington and he kindly took me home for lunch. (Later, of course, he came back in glory as British Ambassador, but that is another story and a rather less comfortable one.)

Arriving back at his home, his then wife, Margaret (née Callaghan), greeted me bravely but probably with the inner lack of enthusiasm which any struggling mother with young children must feel towards an unplanned lunch guest wafting in – a feeling with which I totally sympathised.

Henry Brandon, William Clark[88] and Henry Fairlie were the big British names in the Washington whirlpool. Fairlie was the inventor of the phrase 'the Establishment', which had real resonance and impact in the still class-ridden Britain of the 1960s and '70s. To be anti-establishment rapidly became the 'in' thing and Nicholas Luard's London Soho club, 'The Establishment', attracted all who fancied themselves as critics of the current order and hierarchy.

But terms such as this one have never been very helpful; they confuse and distort the realities of power. There is nowadays no such thing as an Establishment in a permanent sense: Newcomers arrive in short order at the top and new networks replace established ones all the time. Political analysts in this field have never understood social mobility, merit-driven but, in the past, often assisted by marriage upwards and downwards, the fluidity and constantly shifting nature of classes or even good old social climbing. Furthermore, setting up some inner clique as 'they', 'the Establishment', then endowing it with elitist and conspiratorial qualities and attacking it, is always a good political football and widely used to denounce opponents.

Whether it has any relevance in today's world, where celebrities are the new 'upper' class and where social mobility and changed lifestyles have drained most of the class structure of meaning, is more questionable. Journalists cling to it, because they must have a punchbag and politicos of the far Left, along with the ambitious climbers on the Right, still try to position themselves as being on the side of the masses against a malevolent controlling class which they depict as 'out of touch with the people' (the favourite denunciation).

Of course, these are fantasy images, made the more so when the arch-attackers are themselves from classic establishment backgrounds. However, it is an old trick. William Gladstone got a long way as 'The People's William', proclaiming that he was 'one the side of the masses against the classes'. The claim was as absurd and transparent then as it is now.

The message for me from Kennedy's Washington, romantically compared to King Arthur's court at Camelot, was two-edged: On the one hand, it was a lesson in how to create a new sense of direction for a nation – the USA – which was beginning to feel that it was not winning the Cold War after all; on the other hand, it was a naked appeal to the worst kinds of celebrity and youth culture – all of which were to leave a legacy of cynicism which the subsequent information revolution has amplified much further.

Later in the '60s, after the Kennedy assassination and with Lyndon B. Johnson in office, I would return to Washington with Mark Schreiber[89] to penetrate the mysteries of American budgetary techniques from which we derived our ideas for budgetary and administrative reform in the British machinery of government. Mark had a wonderfully innovative mind, to which people greatly warmed. He also had an ability to pinpoint the absurdities and inefficiencies of current practices – in this case, in the inner workings of British government – which made the case all the more vividly for implementing new methods and radical change. If any single person can be credited with levering open Whitehall and Westminster minds about the possibilities of questioning government functions, and maybe moving them outside government altogether – the seed and genesis of privatisation – it is he.

Charlie Schultz in the Washington Bureau of the Budget (BoB, later rechristened the Office of Management and the Budget) was the driving force in curbing official spending and questioning the purpose of public spending programmes, persistently and with real inquisitional power. Later on, we brought him to London to tell the Conservative shadow cabinet how to go about the task and to start shaving down central government and public sector functions. We believed the BoB approach could be replicated in Whitehall.

Very few seemed to understand this message and those who did, did not like it, especially in the senior reaches of the Civil Service. The impact was minimal. The idea that swathes of the state 'empire' in so-called 'public' ownership could be transferred, systematically, to the private sector and might perform better there, had simply not moved into the 'thinkable' category in mainstream British political debate.

As we were to learn later in government, the time had not yet come for this kind of radicalism.

Chapter Nine

Heath and Hopes

WHEN Harold Macmillan fell ill in the autumn of 1963 and the time came to find a successor, the *Telegraph* leader writers took a somewhat hostile line to the Earl of Home (about to downsize himself as Sir Alec in order to enter the Commons), with my support, for which I subsequently felt slightly ashamed. At first glance he was even more 'grouse-moor' than Harold Macmillan and very much in 'the magic circle', about which Iain Macleod wrote so bitterly in the *Spectator*, to which he had moved as editor. To Macleod, and to the younger Conservative echelons, it seemed that the democratisation of the Tories and the break-up of the old upper-class network had not happened.

The critics of the new leader (and Prime Minister) were to prove as muddled-headed, trapped by stereotyping and fazed by Harold Wilson's attacks as much of the media. Douglas-Home's integrity shone through, and his party and public appeal were far wider than the Young Turks of the party feared and the editorials predicted.

His emergence was not quite the surprise for me that it was for some, including much of Fleet Street. I had been staying at Capesthorne Hall, the massive mid-Victorian Bromley-Davenport mansion[90] in Cheshire and commuting each day to the Tory Party conference in Blackpool. The leadership issue was being fought out in full daylight, with active campaigning for the various contenders along the sea front and in the foyer of the Imperial Hotel.

By far the most popular contender among party workers was Viscount Hailsham (Quintin Hogg), famous as the bell-ringer at an earlier Tory conference and a formidable orator and audience-rouser. At the packed fringe meeting organised by the Conservative Political Centre, of which I was shortly to become director, Hailsham ended his speech by saying he had decided to throw his hat into the ring. The audience rose as one with a mighty cheer. Unfortunately, it was the wrong audience and the high priests of the party did not like what they saw and heard. Nor did Macmillan from his sick bed. Other candidates were in the wings.

Bill Deedes (later Lord Deedes), who had been appointed Minister of Information by Macmillan, kindly asked me to lunch at the conference, where I was part of the *Telegraph* team covering the event and dictating the leaders back to the copy tasters in Fleet Street. He spoke in coded messages, some of which I was not sharp enough to grasp.

Speculation was swirling through the media around other names. Months later he told me that he had been giving me a scoop about the Earl of Home being Macmillan's first preference. However, if he was, I was not quick enough to pick it up.

Nevertheless, having heard the earl's name mentioned more than once at lunch I had some clue that he might be part of the new picture. Another vital clue was about to be put into my hands. Also staying at Capesthorne was the chairman of the 1922 Committee, the legendary John Morrison (later Lord Margadale), as well as several other mighty 'knights of the shires', Walter Bromley-Davenport, of course, being the presiding host. (It was his marvellous and very rich, American wife, Lenette, who organised everything. She brought the place to life and gathered around a her a brilliant circle, of which Walter was happy to be part.)

Coming down late to breakfast I found the knights[91] discussing who would be 'the winner'. I listened electrified but discovered they were talking about the flat season's champion jockey. Would it be Scobie Breasley? Nonetheless, the other winner – of the Tory leadership – was clearly on their minds and there were quiet meetings that morning behind closed doors.

Later that day Walter, gave me a letter to catch the afternoon post. It was addressed to the Earl of Home. My half-formed journalistic instinct told me that was odd. Walter had a buffoon-like image at Westminster – which he played up to – but a shrewd political brain. Nevertheless, he would have had no contact whatever with Alec Douglas-Home and had never before, to my knowledge, ever mentioned the name. His only instinct as an archetypal loyal backbencher was to back to the hilt whoever was going to win. Amid the media speculation and questioning as to Macmillan's likely successor I realised I had the answer in my hands.

For all the criticism, Sir Alec Douglas-Home nearly led the Conservatives to another victory in the subsequent 1964 general election. However, 'there is a tide', as Jim Callaghan observed about a later pattern of events, and the country wanted change. This was most emphatically on offer, at least verbally, with Harold Wilson's promise of a revolution spurred by 'the white heat of technology'. This gave him a tiny majority and clearly another election lay not far ahead. The Conservatives in unfamiliar Opposition also wanted change and Heath was clearly the coming man – or, in practice, not quite so clearly since there was the genial, clever Reggie Maudling waiting on the side lines.

Now in Opposition, Douglas-Home gave Ted Heath responsibility for policy development. He rang (while I was in the bath) and asked me to go with him to the Hirsel[92] for an overnight visit to receive various papers from Douglas-Home and discuss strategy and policy for the imminent next election. The expedition was much publicised, with photographers both at Euston as we climbed into our sleepers, and at Edinburgh Waverley as we decanted, slightly dishevelled, early the next morning. Sir Alec came to meet us and drive us home.

I have written elsewhere about this rather odd occasion at which, to my certain knowledge, nothing in the way of strategy or policy was discussed.[93] Instead, there were several icy walks along the banks of the River Tweed. When it came to hand over papers, Ted Heath dozed off (as was his habit) while Sir Alec was trying to hand him documents. I had to reach over and take them (see plate section). Ted then asked me to write up the conclusions from this non-conclusive meeting, which I did with gusto. Such opportunities are gold for advisers, who can, of course, put down anything they like in pursuance of their favourite causes, of which I had plenty.

All this, as the media sensed, was the prologue to Alec Douglas-Home's announced retirement and the leadership election, which Heath won easily. Maudling lacked the edge needed and, while a few still hankered after Rab Butler who had been passed over in favour of Douglas-Home two years before, the outcome was decisive.

Almost immediately, with congratulations pouring in, Ted Heath decided to go to France to stay with his oldest friends, the Seligmans[94] and he asked me (again) to accompany him. In his memoirs and with hindsight, Ted thought this visit was a mistake. The media were all over him, his *bête noire*, Edward du Cann, was staying at a nearby hotel in Villefranche. The feelings of distrust and dislike were mutual. The lampooning *Private Eye* pictured with me raising a warning hand just behind him – one of its most famous covers, subsequently on the front of the annual *Private Eye* calendar (see plate section) – was one outcome of the visit with which he could have done without.

After some confusion over my arrival at Nice airport, where I was mistakenly swept up with a team of top Treasury officials who had been summoned by George Brown[95] to a nearby villa where he was holidaying, Ted Heath arrived to pick me up. There was no room for me at the Seligmans' quite modest villa, so he drove me up to a glittering establishment nearby, owned by the Necchi family (whose fortune came from sewing machines). Ronnie Grierson, who knew everybody, appeared on the scene and swept off the Conservative leader, with me in tow, to meet the great, the good and the not so good on various yachts and in mansion-like villas along the Riviera. Gianni Agnelli, Drue Heinz and others were on his list.

To visit Agnelli we boarded his motor yacht in the harbour at Antibes. At the time it seemed awesome: state of the art, complete with 4000 HP Fiat engines and a main lounge filled with Impressionist paintings. However, it was nothing compared with what was to come, such as in the way of five-storey floating palaces: rooms stuffed with priceless artworks; lifts between the floors; and, one case, a complete trading floor occupying the forward bow area of the craft, keeping the owner in instant touch with global trading across world markets.

The Heinz mansion, where we lunched and played tennis, was set on the shore line and to reach it one had to cross, rather strangely, a main railway line. (Drue Heinz remained a friendly acquaintance after the visit that day with Ted Heath and always recalled it when we occasionally met.)

The Conservatives lost the 1966 election by a large margin and Labour turned a small majority from the 1964 contest into a big one – a clever move by Wilson although, in the wrong circumstances, it can easily backfire (as Theresa May was to discover fifty years later in 2016). Advice poured in to Ted Heath, not all of it helpful, on how the Conservatives should rethink their policies and overall attitudes.

Advice comes in many forms. For the adviser, as for the master chef, new and more appetising ways of preparing ingredients are always needed. In my days as adviser to successive party leaders it was usually via policy papers, speech drafts, and the like. Iain Macleod, who was highly receptive, sent me a card within minutes of being appointed shadow chancellor in 1965 saying: 'Will you come around and see me soon. I have much to learn but then I learn quickly.' With Ted Heath, it was a matter of long conversations in his Albany flat (and on our travels) mulling over ideas before I went away and wrote speech drafts.

Ted asked me both to put together a grand statement pamphlet on where we were heading under our new, dynamic, non-grouse-moor, non-old-Etonian leader – called clumsily 'Putting Britain Right Ahead' – and to work up a first draft of the Tory Manifesto for his 1966 election, which I named, a bit naively, 'Action not Words'. This I drafted over three days, shutting myself in a room at the top of Boz and Hilary Ferranti's house in Chelsea Park Gardens, which they kindly made available.[96]

Both draft documents were torn to pieces by the shadow cabinet. Sir Reginald Manningham-Buller was particularly scathing. He had read it, he explained, coming up in the train. I listened from a chair at the back of the room, dismayed as my efforts went up, almost literally, in a cloud of smoke.

The pamphlet title had started from the then current Esso slogan 'Put a Tiger in the Tank' which was on posters everywhere and had caught my fancy. The resulting mutilated title was what emerged after everyone who thought they should be in on the project had had a go at it. Not much tiger left by then. It was an early and abject lesson in what happens when committees get hold of ideas. My thoroughbred – or perhaps my tiger – became a camel.

The manifesto title was meant to purvey the view that Harold Wilson, the agile Labour Prime Minister (whom I always respected and who was quite friendly to me) was all talk – 'the white heat of the technological revolution', etc. – and not much action. Heath, by contrast, was going to be depicted as Action Man. It didn't work, of course, and Wilson, who had been living with a minority government since 1964, was re-elected with a vastly increased majority.

Meanwhile Ted himself – unlike 'the colleagues', as he always scathingly referred to his shadow cabinet and backbench MPs – was hearteningly receptive to new ideas and new phrases, sending me a stream of handwritten letters of encouragement.

Critics of Ted Heath, who are many, have always taken offence at his evident contempt for much of the Conservative Party. However, when were things different? Stanley Baldwin said he would as soon consult his valet about any policy matter as the Conservative Party. Willie Whitelaw, master tactician, of whom more later, proclaimed the golden rule was never to listen to the backbench 1922 Committee – the grumble forum for backbench Conservative MPs ever since, in a moment of glory in 1922 at the Carlton Club, they had finally revolted against the coalition with the Lloyd George Liberals and chosen Stanley Baldwin as leader instead. (J.C.C. Davidson, the great fixer of Conservative affairs in the inter-war period, once showed me the voting cards for that meeting. They were almost unanimously in favour of Baldwin. They hated the coalition.)

The emerging line of advice from Mark Schreiber and myself to Heath was that the time had come for a new style of government: transformed and curbed trade unions; privatisation all around; much lower taxes; and a powerful new Prime Minister's office.

Reflecting on the widespread view that the incumbent Prime Minister, Harold Wilson, was a man of many words and fewer deeds, and that Ted Heath was seen, at least by Conservatives as a man of action rather than clever remarks, the 'Action not Words' slogan seemed just right. In practice it was a resounding flop, and probably helped Harold Wilson to his enlarged majority.

Becoming an MP (for Guildford) I moved away from almost daily closeness with Ted Heath although we still kept contact. Maybe as a marker that, with my membership of the House of Commons, a phase of our relationship had closed, he sent me a book – Kenneth Young's *Arthur James Balfour*[97] – inscribed with his thanks for my part in our unsuccessful 1966 election.

This was the time when a breakaway research group, from the official Conservative Research Department, was formed. It was named the Public Sector Research Unit under the auspices of Ernest Marples and staffed by Mark Schreiber, David Alexander, Laurance Reed and me. We did our own fund-raising, to the annoyance of Conservative Party officials but with Ted Heath's blessing. As mentioned in Chapter Nine, Mark Schreiber and I toured America and Canada and began importing radical ideas for change in the machinery and policies for a future Conservative government in Britain.

We spent time visiting not only the Washington gurus but also the various think-tanks around the country, including the Rand Corporation in Santa Monica and Tempo in Santa Barbara. The big new thing was systems analysis which, it was believed, could be applied to government and policy-making with highly beneficial results. In Washington, we talked with Robert McNamara at the Pentagon, who explained how his new tools of management were going to be applied in future conflicts. This was a year before the unfolding Vietnam War was to prove their very limited success. Sometime after that I again visited the US with some parliamentary colleagues and this time we were invited by Lyndon B. Johnson to sit around the Cabinet table in the West Wing while he explained how American airpower was going to 'solve' the deepening Vietnam chaos and crush the Vietcong (see plate section). Once again things did not quite turn out this way.

Nevertheless, Mark Schreiber and I were deeply impressed by the systematic approach being used in containing and increasing the efficiency of public spending, as well as the potential for harnessing the private sector far more to deliver public objectives. This was the machinery of systematic questioning and pressure that we believed would lead to better government and also to the possible privatisation of a wide range of government activities, not just state-owned industries but many other functions – agencies and government services – as well, some of them lost inside departments or conducted without regard to clear objectives or the regular measurement of outputs. Way-out thoughts began to enter our minds, such as that prisons and detention centres could be run by the private sector, branches of military organisation could be privatised, numerous smaller agencies, like the Ordnance Survey or the Forestry Commission, could be reconfigured as private sector companies. Most of these ideas were, of course, unthinkable. Within a couple decades most of them came to be realised.

Among our innovations, which Ted Heath later adopted when Prime Minister, albeit in somewhat diluted form (although oddly without any acknowledgement in his memoirs), were the Policy and Programme Budgeting System (PPBS), Programme Analysis and Review (PAR), and a new central government capability for giving strategic shape to all government programmes and expenditure – the so-called Central Policy Review Staff. We intended this to be located right there in No.10, but the mandarins had other ideas and it ended up under the wing of the Cabinet Office and – surprise, surprise – under the control of the Cabinet Secretary, Sir Burke Trend, and the head of the Civil Service, Sir William Armstrong.

In a pamphlet the Conservative Political Centre published just a few weeks before the 1970 Election, duly called 'A New Style of Government' (CPC, May 1970), we brought to together our proposals for central government reform for privatisation, for the departmental structure of Whitehall and for new policy machinery. These backed up previously circulated 'Black Book' projects (see plate section) and also linked them with the need for similar parliamentary reform and a stronger committee structure to hold a new type of decentralised government more effectively to account. This was, in fact, the genesis of the modern select committee structure which emerged ten years later.

The pamphlet argued that, 'somehow the formidable preliminary task of establishing what everyone is doing now (in Whitehall departments) has to be tackled. In other words, before reorganisation and redirection there has to come diagnosis – to find out and set out in terms which are bound to be unfamiliar to departmental civil servants and their ministers the aims or "outputs" of the whole range of a department's activities.'

The pamphlet went on to propose new central machinery and accounting methods to drive the questioning process through Whitehall and to get real dispersal and decentralisation programmes under way. We argued both for a kind of 'bureau of the budget', as a separate entity from the Treasury and its economic policy functions, and, somewhat contradictorily, a powerful new capability right inside No.10 to increase strategic prime ministerial power. Questioning procedures had to be highly informed and related to objectives. It was the old Gladstonian syndrome revived: not whether the money allocated for paper clips had indeed been spent on paper clips, but for what end-purpose paper clips were needed in the first place.

A brand-new parliamentary committee system was proposed, to keep better track of departmental expenditures and to match a re-orientated Whitehall system that would have clearer objectives and the appropriate spending programmes to achieve required outputs.

These proposals may sound obvious now but they were revolutionary then. The dovecotes fluttered both in Whitehall and Westminster. An older generation of MPs was confused – as evidenced at the Carlton Club dinner described earlier. Surely, argued the old school, MPs should not move from just questioning estimates (did you spend what you should?) to actual matters of policy (e.g. why is this expenditure taking place at all, and for what purpose?). This, we were warned, was dangerous ground and might implicate Parliament in the Executive!

The pamphlet acquired a niche in political history. It was the first time a political document of this kind contained the word 'privatisation' (in a footnote), borrowed from Peter Drucker, the American management consultant super-guru.

All these devices and plans, which Reggie Maudling, Angus Maude and others found so arcane and technocratic (or, as Maudling had put it at the Carlton dinner, 'balls'), were designed to put the whole range of central government functions through the mincer and squeeze out the ones that were unnecessary, inefficient or could be performed as well, or better, by the private sector. In other words, we were really talking about the genesis of the process which could lead to large-scale privatisation and the total reconfiguration of Britain's lumpen and paralysing nationalised sector.

Part of the new brew adopted by Heath was a heavily changed pattern of Whitehall departments. Ministries of Works, Local Government and Housing were merged into a new giant department with a new name not previously used in Whitehall – Environment. The Board of Trade and the Ministry of Industry were joined into a new Industry and Technology Department. Social Security and Health were all to fall under one centre of social policy.

The theory (our theory) behind these changes was not to create giant entities but, on the contrary, to establish high-powered policy-integrating and convening hubs from which much of the implementation and management would then be outsourced or even (a daring thought in 1970) privatised. Heath carried through the first part – the mergers – but not the second. The result was to accentuate the disadvantages of size, while losing the benefits of streamlined government.

Another departmental novelty was to create a separate, smarter department of procurement for the Ministry of Defence. This was the brainchild of Sir Derek Rayner, MD of Marks & Spencer and part of our small businessmen's team. He had been seconded to us by Marcus Sieff who promised us, at a meeting in his flat, to provide his very best man, and did so.

Ian Gilmour was appointed as first Minister of Procurement, but complained that it sounded as though he was being put in charge of a brothel. Derek Rayner lasted eighteen months in the Heath government but left in some despair, arguing that not much was happening in the 'new style of government' programme. (He returned eight years later to work under Margaret Thatcher with much better results.)

Our other innovation was to propose a central capability unit to be firmly located under the Prime Minister's control in No.10. This would be staffed by people with business acumen who would ask the tough questions about objectives and outputs around Whitehall; it would give the Prime Minister adequate firepower to control the great new Whitehall departments and to knock heads together.

Sir Burke and Sir William thought otherwise and insisted that the new body should be behind the 'green baize door', tucked into the bowels of the Cabinet Office. Otherwise, reasoned Sir Burke, it would give the Prime Minister an undue advantage over his Cabinet colleagues. That might have been permissible in times of war but not in times of peace. Instead of being a powerful policy unit giving the Prime Minister more power over the great departments of Whitehall, it was reduced, in the words of the White Paper announcing Heath's reorganisation plans, to 'a small multi-disciplinary staff in the Cabinet Office' – far from what we had intended, what was needed, or what, years later, came into being – namely being fully ensconced in the No.10 system. Instead it was to be safely installed on the fourth floor of the Cabinet Office, well away from ministers. There would be no 'undue' advantage for the Prime Minister in challenging the great Departments of State as they went about their separate ways.

We tried to point out that this 'undue' advantage was precisely the intention, doing no more than putting the Prime Minister on equal strategic terms with his administration. But it was too late. The Central Policy Review Staff (CPRS), as it was christened, was thus born inside the official machine and never really fulfilled our hopes as the Prime Minister's new instrument of coordination and power.

Chapter Ten

Wrong from the Start

S O it was that our plans for a new 'central capability' unit went wrong from the start. We wanted a ruthless and tough individual to head it and use the scalpel to begin the dismantling task throughout central government. However, somehow it was offered to Victor Rothschild, whose brilliance was unquestioned but who was not at all what we had in mind. He assembled a team of young stars, both from inside and outside the Civil Service, such as Robin Butler (future Cabinet Secretary), William Plowden (future Treasury mandarin par excellence), William Waldegrave (future Cabinet minister), Tessa Blackstone (from the London School of Economics), Robert Wade-Gery from the Foreign Office, Adam Ridley, also working at the Treasury, Peter Bocock from the World Bank and Tony Fish from Shell.

In intellectual terms this was an impressive team but not what we had intended. Their studies and reports spread out to cover the whole of government strategy, or what this strategy was deemed to be by the CPRS, along with detailed one-off studies of such things as Britain's motor industry or the effectiveness of the Foreign Office, rather than the guts of existing departmental programmes and purposes.

This turned them into just another think-tank – albeit at the heart of government – rather than the sharply focused and challenging capability, based in No.10, we had planned.[98]

A particularly pointless exercise launched by the CPRS was to ask each department what they felt their most important future challenges were likely to be. Hours of time and reams of paper were wasted on pointless rumination from the departments, much of it amounting to plans for larger budgets for favourite causes. In due course, the project was abandoned.

Even less did Sir Burke favour the idea of having a minister (a politician, if you please) sitting beside the Prime Minister in Downing Street. This was an idea we had drawn from the German example, where the wily Herr Horst Ehmke filled the role of Minister of State under the German Chancellor we thought to great effect.

However, apparently this model was not acceptable in London, as outlined in the previous chapter. Behind the green baize door, the new central unit to track and oversee departments, available to all Cabinet ministers via the Cabinet Office, began to be mysteriously vague, defined as 'helping to formulate overall government strategy' – eons away from the sharp expenditure-challenging operation we had designed for it.

By June 1970 I was a humble Parliamentary Secretary in the brand-new Civil Service Department (CSD)[99] and my only hope of influence was to get our new thinking circulating, and at least seriously discussed, in Whitehall, especially in the Treasury.

It was going to be uphill work, as an early visit from Sir William Armstrong (head of the Civil Service and also Permanent Secretary in my new department) confirmed. Sir William had a particular way of slipping into a room almost unseen. Now he was there, in my ridiculously capacious office overlooking St James's Park, and he apparently had some advice to offer. I rose from my desk out of respect and we sat down in armchairs opposite one another.

He had come to talk about 'our' ideas, that was to say the programmes and proposals some of us – Mark Schreiber and I in particular – had outlined for the reform of central government itself, while we had been in Opposition. We had lifted the actual expression 'A New Style of Government', in part from the Fulton Report on the Civil Service , which had been published a few months before the Conservatives took office, and which Sir William was specifically assigned to implement.

Sir William told me that he often bore in mind Hymn 266 in matters of administrative reorganisation and reform. This was Cardinal Newman's masterpiece 'Lead, kindly light, amid th' encircling gloom'. However, that was not the line Sir William was alluding to. His guidance was in the next line: 'I do not ask to see the distant scene. One step enough for me.' For young green ministers stepping into the Civil Service and Whitehall jungle, bursting with plans, strategies and reform programmes, this, he felt was the wisest advice. It probably was.

Meanwhile, support from No.10 and Mr Heath began to fade away as the huge issues of trades-union militancy, oil shocks, inflation and Northern Ireland began to closed in on the Prime Minister. My friends and I, with our radical ideas, had lost our patron. Advisers without a patron are simply snails without shells; the birds will always get them.

With Victor Rothschild things were different. As explained earlier, he was not the sort of figure we had envisaged for the powerful and probing 'central capability' we wanted to build up around the Prime Minister. But we still had common ground with him and greatly enjoyed the way he saw the knights and mandarins though the green baize door from the Cabinet Room as schemers and opponents. Once a week I breakfasted at his flat in St James where he went over his latest plans for outwitting them ('Burke 'n William'), as he referred to them) – or at least for preventing them from outwitting him.

Over at the Treasury, which in Opposition we had talked of dividing into a new Bureau of the Budget, on American lines, and a Finance Ministry, the slide into apathy about any of our radical ideas became evident from the tragic moment Iain Macleod died (after an appendicitis operation) – about three weeks after Heath entered Downing Street.

Tony Barber took over as Chancellor and Maurice Macmillan, the gentlest of men, moved in as Chief Secretary. I had a few desultory meetings with him. Everything I wanted to do seemed to raise an objection, not from Maurice but from the Permanent Secretary, Sir Sam Goldman, and the Treasury figures sitting around him, for whom all was impossible. We were even barred from the modest idea of raising the toll on the new Severn Bridge as a preparation for privatising it.

The Prime Minister had said during the election campaign, daring, drawing on a brief from Brian Reading, that we would 'cut prices at a stroke', so anything that raised them was ruled out.

Needless to say, my ideas for changing the shape of the Treasury itself, which had interested Iain Macleod, were not even discussed.

The questioning and 'blue skies' documents from the CPRS leaked out, as was bound to happen. In 1984 it was abolished by Margaret Thatcher, sensing it to be a fifth wheel on the coach and a source of potential political embarrassment with its way-out thinking. By then, Sir Burke's reservations had long been swept away and a strong new political unit created right inside No.10. The unthinkable of one era had become the necessity of the next.

Chapter Eleven

A Diversion: What If?

MUCH of the reform of government and the dismantling of the ramshackle apparatus of collectivist administration should have happened under Heath. It was undoubtedly the fertilising and propagating phase of the intellectual revolution to come under Margaret Thatcher a decade later. The radical new ideas were there to be incubated.

What derailed it all? There were chance outside events and distractions (outlined below) but a prime reason was the sheer mass of resistance from the Civil Service itself. In too many areas of the central administration, streams of awkward questions about why things were being done and whether they should be done better, or at all, was seen as both disruptive and a waste of good administrative time. In some quarters it was considered outright dangerous.

One of the advisers (or consultants) brought in to Whitehall from America at this time was Hugh Heclo, who had been a professor at MIT and was fully versed in the Charlie Schultz methods. (Later, together with Aaron Wildavsky, he wrote the definitive book on this period of attempted budgetary revolution, *The Private Government of Public Money*.)[100]

Heclo plunged into the Whitehall jungle with enthusiasm, but came out a little bruised, explaining that there was a limit to how much longer he could continue to batter against the brick wall with his questioning around central government. 'Socrates,' he gloomily observed, 'went on and on asking questions and looked what happened to him.'

The 'what if' thought is that, if Ted Heath had won the 1974 general election instead of losing it by two seats, or if he had made friends rather than enemies of a handful of Ulster Unionists (see below), the processes of decentralisation of government functions, leading to full-blown privatisation, would have gone forward even earlier than they did and with, perhaps, less confrontation and frenzied argumentation. Alternatively, if he could have persuaded Jeremy Thorpe to join him with fourteen Liberal Party seats, that would have kept in him in office. However, Thorpe wanted to stay well clear of the Tories and had his own agenda.

There can be no doubt that it was the Sunningdale Agreement (the culmination of the so-called First Northern Ireland Peace Process) that turned the Unionists decisively against both Heath and Whitelaw.

Had it been otherwise and had the Unionists agreed to some sort of conditional support arrangement in the Commons (not dissimilar from the Democratic Unionist Party support for the May administration today, at the time of writing), Ted Heath could have stayed at No.10. That was the heart of the Heath tragedy. He made no secret at Sunningdale of his view that the former Unionist ascendancy 'had abused its responsibilities'. He believed, in a quite straightforward and honest way, that this was a wrong to be righted and, to save Northern Ireland, he was prepared to take an open stand. Almost without sleep for seventy-two hours, he chaired the discussion at Sunningdale which slowly forced the Unionists into concessions. They came to hate him.

It was therefore for honest and upright reasons that Heath lost power and destroyed his own career. This is why it is impossible to forgive the sneering ignorance of those who, in many cases with hindsight, paint him as a dishonourable failure and a deceiver. His failure was honourable, and the alleged deception – mostly in the mind of those who came after him – was no such thing. Almost the entire political establishment except a fringe believed that Common Market membership was right for Britain at that time. Jean Monnet's passion for a federalist Europe was widely known but there were a dozen other ways in which the European Community might evolve.

Had Heath survived with Unionist support there would have been no talk of revolution, but there would have been steady and calm transformation and reform. Heath was, without question, a reformer. And since revolutions do indeed devour their own children, as the Thatcher one certainly did, would that have been a better experience for the British nation, reaching the same point with less revolutionary fervour and frenzy?

Commentators and biographers write as though the Thatcher 'revolution' arrived out of thin air. It didn't. It took years of preparation, argument and debate. The Thatcher reform years could not have happened without the Heath years. That is when 'thinking the unthinkable' in British political circles began.[101]

Something happened to Ted Heath once he became Prime Minister. The old sparkle vanished and No.10 sank into a quagmire of crises, with officials closing around the Prime Minister and suffocating all real radicalism. Our reforms were just 'not on' – that familiar phrase resounding down the years, and now being used to frustrate any serious and fundamental reform of the European Union.

The last time I was close to Heath and felt any real warmth between us was when he called me to Chequers one wintry afternoon in January 1971. He was kind, interested, friendly, wanted to know how I was getting on. However, I could feel things sliding away. He said 'they' were pushing him towards a prices and incomes policy. Who were 'they'? The answer in part had come out of his study door just before I went in – three mandarins, Sir Burke Trend, Sir Denis Greenhill and Donald Maitland (later 'Sir', and also Press Secretary at No.10 in more civilised days and, after that – almost a decade on – my Permanent Secretary at the Department of Energy).

Two years later, in October 1973, it would be Sir Burke plus Sir William Armstrong (not to be confused with Robert Armstrong, later Lord Armstrong of Ilminster and a future Cabinet Secretary, who was there that day as Ted Heath's principal private secretary) who sat either side of him as he announced his conversion to a new incomes policy – an occasion which took place – fatally – not in Parliament but at Lancaster House. William Armstrong told me years later that he always regretted being there. It was his nadir as well as Ted Heath's.

The ostensible purpose of that Chequers afternoon in 1971 was to give me a pay increase. Why? Because there was apparently no legal backing for a salary for a Parliamentary Secretary at the new Civil Service Department and I was instead listed as a Lord Commissioner of the Treasury, salary £3,000 per annum. Heath now told me that I was also to become Parliamentary Secretary at the Department of Employment. It would involve a pay increase of £750 but would not involve me in the department's work. He had obviously taken some trouble.

We chatted on. He came to the door to wave me goodbye, asked after my family, told me to take care of myself and watched as I drove away. It was the end of something.

When I got back to London the Permanent Secretary of the Employment Department, Sir Denis Barnes, rang to tell me that I would be answering questions in the Commons on employment affairs and would I please attend meetings in his department. So much for Heath's well-intentioned assurance. As Ernest Marples was fond of saying, Heath was 'not really the boss'.

The irony of the Heath tragedy is that, but for a couple of colossal misjudgements (and which governments have not made a few of those?), one tragedy – the very early death of Iain Macleod, the new Chancellor, in 1970 – the loss of Unionist trust for the noblest of reasons, and a chance error of precise timing in calling the 1974 election, he could certainly have won and survived.

The miners' strike of 1974, for all its subsequent romanticisation and surrounding legends, was widely disliked. And the three-day week, which some of us helped organise from the newly set-up Department of Energy under Peter Carrington's direction, was a firm piece of government in face of a direct political challenge by over-mighty union leaders to the state. The Tory backbenchers who muttered against their leader – as they nearly always have against most leaders (except, perhaps, Margaret Thatcher, and even her end) – would have been mostly silenced by a Heath victory. Election success would have been the conclusive argument and answer to serious challenges, complaints and grumbles – just as electoral failure is almost never forgiven.

Had Heath won, Europe would certainly have been a bone of contention but the younger wing of the party was solidly in favour at the time. So indeed, were the leading figures on the Conservative side, including Thatcher. It seemed, in the contemporary context, so utterly the sensible thing to do, joining Britain with a largely market-driven Europe (as it then was) and escaping the stifling atmosphere of socialised corporatised Britain.

In due course, the negative aspects of the European Community (as it then was) would have become increasingly visible. But one has to remember, as many people conveniently fail to do, that for at least ten years after Heath's defeat, UK membership of the EU was still widely considered to be 'a good thing', with only a tiny, marginalised minority against it. The persistent hope was that some of its dynamism would rub off on us (just as a decade later some of the hardest line Eurosceptics still believed that joining the European Monetary System would, by some kind of osmosis, lead to better British budgetary discipline, tighter public sending and tougher, less accommodating monetary policy).

The referendum of 1975, although in its genesis a device to deal with internal Labour Party divisions, produced a large national majority in favour or staying in the EU. It was only after Jacques Delors that the rot set in, the corporatist character of the EU began to show through and the first steps were taken towards the shaky architecture of the euro – a true cornice without pillars if ever there was one, as events came to demonstrate all too clearly.

* * * * *

My very last truly friendly and warm encounter with Heath was when he called me over to the Cabinet Room eighteen months later and asked me to go to Northern Ireland with Willie Whitelaw. The conversation was almost fatherly. This would be my big opportunity. I should make a go of it. It was a huge challenge, etc.

He was right. It was not only a challenge but a strangely enjoyable one, despite the hideous, continuing and murderous violence. This was because William Whitelaw, the Secretary of State for the new post, had in abundance the very talent which Ted did not – that of winning his subordinates and assistants' total devotion and loyalty. His wasn't just charm for the day but a real and sincere bond, expressed by Whitelaw later in his memoirs where he has many kind things to say about the jobs we did and the support we gave. (More of this in Chapter Twelve.)

After that morning being sent to Northern Ireland as the security and political situation there crumbled, I scarcely met Heath again and after his defeat there was coldness, even hostility. For about twenty years after his fall we did not speak, until at a dinner at the Guinness's Hampshire house he, after a rather silent meal, began dilating on the good work I had initiated in changing the structure of government decades earlier. However, then he closed down again, and he had nothing to say about our days and hours of work together in the early '60s.

Later, it turned out, there had been papers from this period but they had been lost in a basement flood and, with the publishers clamouring for a draft of his autobiography, *The Course of My Life*,[102] it was decided simply to leave the whole phase out. This may be one explanation as to why our core ideas for bringing a new and more systematic approach to the evaluation of government functions appeared in the Heath memoir without a word said about their source.

Iain Macleod saw all this even if he did not fully understand where we had to start – which was right at the heart of the central government administration. When appointed by Heath as shadow chancellor, he had rejoined the Tory mainstream; the despised magic circle had melted away. 'Come and see me soon,' he scribbled on a card I kept and to which I have referred previously, 'I have much to learn quickly but then I learn quickly.' His oratory and wit, in that penetrating, almost grating voice, would have been the ideal counterpoint to Heath's undeniably dull chant-speech style.

Deprived of Macleod's vision, Heath fell back rapidly, too rapidly, on official advice. With clever and clear-minded civil servants he felt at home – far more so than with 'the colleagues'. One could go back to those three high advisers and officials leaving Ted Heath's Chequers' study that winter afternoon – and to their confrères hovering behind the arras.

All were wise, dedicated, experienced servants of the state. However, their skill lay in managing situations, not changing them. Everything started from the 'given': things, it was constantly repeated, had to be taken 'as they are' and were to be managed from there; realities had to be faced and handled. Challenging the realities was for blue-sky thinkers, for ivory tower academics or unreliable politicos. 'Sound' official views and judgments ran along a single valley, with no inclination to move laterally and see or connect with what might lie over the mountain ridge. That kind of thinking and advice had to wait another decade for its moment to come.

Nor did they always get everything right by their own standards. A small incident: We set out one day to attend the official opening of the new Civil Service training centre at Basingstoke under its new director Sir John Hunt (later Secretary to the Cabinet). 'We' in this case were the head of the Civil Service, Sir William Armstrong, his two immediate deputies in the Civil Service Department, the Lord Privy Seal George Jellicoe, a couple of private secretaries, and me (Parliamentary Secretary CSD). It could be said that little group was the brain box of civil service administration and reform. The future of the Civil Service was safely in our hands.

Or was it? The plan was to go by train from Waterloo to Basingstoke where an official party would greet us. Unfortunately, we got on the wrong train which took us to Alton; we were on the wrong track. At Alton there were no taxis, only a helpful youth in a battered Mini. He offered to drive Earl Jellicoe, Sir William and myself to Basingstoke. We were quite heavy for such a small vehicle and each time we went over a bump the bottom of the car scraped the road. We arrived in not very dignified fashion an hour and half late.

Had these great advisers and masters of administration put the reform-inclined Heath on the wrong train? I believe so. What they had to offer was essentially more of the same medicine that had brought Britain to its knees in the '60s. Yet what is really needed from effective advisers is not to be too narrow and accepting of the 'givens' but not too be too impractical either. A modern cliché has emerged since those days about 'thinking outside the box'. However, the lesson is the same. Like an innovator in science or industry, the good adviser must draw

126

on other disciplines, do other things and pursue other occupations and interests.

We could see that the century was coming to the end of a phase of big-state socialism and corporatism. We were carrying in our pouches the seeds of great new ideas to come, which were to grow into the privatisation and decentralisation movement with Margaret Thatcher a decade later, and which were to sweep around the world.

By 1970 we had a sense that immense developments of this kind lay ahead and we believed that, with Ted Heath in office and the 'New Style of Government' as our credo, we could set out on this radical new path into a new era. Yet we failed and in doing so, left Heath entrapped, as did the officials that had closed around him.

Maybe the hostility which Heath showed afterwards to friend and foe alike was because of that. Maybe it was because, along with others, some of us carried on working with his successor – because that is what you do in a political vocation, if asked, and that is where the ideas he had espoused to strongly in and before 1970 were bound to take us years later. Maybe in Ted Heath's eyes those of us who went on and served in Thatcher administrations were some kind of traitors. It is a word he used about one my colleagues who took the same path.

Perhaps he regretted giving so much attention to our radical plans, many of which were either naive or premature. Or perhaps he regretted not doing so. Anyway, there was something missing in the man and seemingly, at least for me, no middle ground between being very close and being shut out completely.

His future would have been much happier if he had accepted the job of British Ambassador to Washington, which the new Prime Minister proposed. Who knows where it might have led? He forgot the Whitelaw adage that you should always dutifully take what is offered in politics. And he was, without doubt, a bad loser.

Whatever happened, all sense of affinity was gone.

Chapter Twelve

A Tale of Two Roles

'Avoid taking advice from someone who gives advice for a
living, unless there is a penalty for their advice.'

—Nassim Nicholas Taleb, Skin in the Game[103]

T HE Thatcher era can be understood more as a sequel than a
reaction to the preceding Heath administration. The belief,
almost universally accepted, was that Heath had failed
electorally because of the miners' strike and the nation giving the
'wrong' answer (for him) to the question, 'Who governs Britain?'

The originating trigger for this sequence of events was far away in
an office in Vienna, where the headquarters of OPEC were housed.
There, it had dawned on the leaders of the oil-producing countries,
mostly of the Middle East and dominated by the mega-producer Saudi
Arabia, that they still had control of world oil supplies and the power
to exploit it. Perhaps their opportunity would pass, with new oil fields
such as the North Sea and Alaska coming online, but meanwhile the
oil producers seized it. A British government disoriented by the oil
shock blow made an ideal target for militant miners, seeing their
own monopoly opportunity and the perfectly timed chance to use it,
before coal became less dominant and before governments succeeded
in passing laws curbing their power.

Half a decade after the frustrations of the Heath government,
as one political orthodoxy evolved from another and as Margaret

Thatcher replaced Ted Heath as Conservative Party leader, I found myself in a role similar to the one I had played back in the 1960s with Ted Heath. However, in practice it was very different. Acting as what was laughingly called the 'head or coordinator' of Margaret Thatcher's speech-writing 'team', my job was to pull together drafts for all the major speeches the new Conservative leader was going to make during the expected 1978 general election.

At first it was something I did not much want to do. At the time I was the number two shadow spokesman on home affairs under Willie Whitelaw and, while the portfolio held limited pleasures (it required me to spend my time going around prisons), I was enjoying working for Willie again after our stormy years in Northern Ireland. One day Willie said that Thatcher had asked for me (apparently impressed by something I had written). I dutifully agreed. (See my account of Willie's good advice in Chapter Four: If one wants to climb the political ladder, one should do what one is asked. Once it is climbed, then the time comes not to be pushed around.)

I felt that there was a chance here to be a sort of carrier between the old and the new governments, to resurrect some of the incipient and lost ideas of the Heath period, as previously discussed, and make sure they were carried forward.

I describe the title of my new role 'laughingly' because if ever there was a collection of people who were not going to be a 'team' and would not be 'coordinated', this was it. The task involved working for Margaret, night after night in Flood Street, through bowlfuls of coronation chicken and mountains of smoked salmon. Margaret Thatcher was extremely hospitable. It was almost overpowering. At one stage she said I reminded her of some film star of her youth of whom I had never heard. For all that, very few of my fancier phrases or literary allusions, let alone my attempted jokes, survived her pen.

Furthermore, half the 'team', which included such stars and polymaths as Paul Johnson (a genius), Peter Utley (blind and brilliant) and Ronnie Miller (who gave birth to some truly famous phrases including 'the lady's not for turning'), felt that their pearls of wisdom must go to the lady direct, unsullied by any kind of composite editing or redrafting by a lowly MP. Adam Ridley and Douglas Hague were the economic heavyweights in the so-called team. However, their views, too, got short shrift as, by then, Margaret was thoroughly in thrall to the beguiling simplicities of monetarism and needed no further advice.

How we ever succeeded in producing in time six speech drafts for the six major speech occasions around the country during the general election campaign I cannot now imagine. Certainly, Jim Callaghan's fateful delay from the winter of 1978 to the spring of 1979 didn't help. It just meant further redrafts and more coronation chicken. Perhaps, in the end, we didn't quite succeed – I have vivid memories of drafting and redrafting until the dawn hours before each event, with the marvellous duo, Caroline Stephens (later Caroline Ryder) and Alison Ward (later Alison Wakeham), pounding away on ancient typewriters with a special large script. On some occasions we were rewriting these speeches minutes before Margaret walked onto the platform. So much for months of preparation.

Caroline and Alison were the great unflappables. Leaders could rage, press and PR advisers panic, strategists shout and quarrel; they just went on in quiet amusement, turning out the drafts through the night, calming the over-agitated staff and steadying the otherwise fraught mood that always runs through a leader's office at campaign time. Both went on to become the partners of, supporters of and, I am sure, strongest and best of advisers to, leading Cabinet ministers.

The first volume of Charles Moore's Thatcher book[104] does not quite catch this drama – but drama it was, particularly when, towards the end of the campaign, there was a suggestion the Tories might lose after all, at which point the central office publicity gurus became quite critical of Margaret's performance. However, they were wrong and the rest is history. My job was to be at her side on each of these occasions to make last minute adjustments, a sort of verbal version of a dressmaker/couturier frantically adjusting the diva's gown seconds before the curtain rises.

Being in attendance on the leader meant I hardly had time to visit my own constituency of Guildford, leaving meetings and events to my wife, Davina. Without my presence, my majority was the highest ever of my nine elections there. Maybe Davina was the better politician.

The most visible high spot of my Thatcher advisory role, prior to her premiership, came when I co-authored a pre-election economic document with Geoffrey Howe, Keith Joseph and Jim Prior, 'The Right Approach to the Economy'. It was edited by Angus Maude and published in October 1977. I wrote in Chapter Eight of how Angus (father of Francis Maude and husband of before-her-time green campaigner Barbara Maude) had been sacked by Ted Heath ten years before for criticising our reform efforts as 'far too managerial'.

In essence, 'The Right Approach to the Economy' was a truce-seeking document in the age-old war between traditionalists and free-market radicals in the Conservative Party (subsequently depicted as between the Wets and the Dries and the latest incarnation of the much longer running civil war between the conserving and liberal reforming streams in the party). It was an attempted bridge between those who believed a deal would have to be done with the all-powerful trades union leaders, through some kind of wages and prices trade-off, and those who believed that, with tough monetary policy and lots of supply-side reforms, the wage-price spiral could be broken. The pamphlet hummed and hawed between the two approaches and Margaret Thatcher disliked it.

The civil war continues to this day and will only be ended by a Conservative leader who can somehow hold the two sides together. This is difficult but not impossible, as some latter-day Conservatives lament. It can be done, but not by lamenting the lost consensus of the past, or mouthing generalities about aspiration, staying in touch and appealing to the young, etc. A much deeper understanding of the past, and of the roots of discontent, are needed.

For ten years after leaving the Cabinet, I chaired the Conservative One Nation Group – traditionally a hotbed of Wets, deeply suspicious of privatisation, monetarism and the like, strongly pro the welfare state and uneasy about the Thatcher departure from the old consensus tone of Conservative government. Indeed, One Nation had originally been formed in the late 1940s to nudge the post-war Conservatives into committing to strong social and welfare programmes.

To shift these Tories from Heath managerial harmony (sort of) to the rhetoric of free-market Thatcherism, without party splits, there had to be a new, reconciliatory theme. This theme, we argued, was that wealth – assets and capital (savings) – could, and would, be widely spread. Personal ownership could deliver welfare, security and dignity on a scale that the old welfare state could no longer match.

The One Nation Group even succeeded in publishing a fully-agreed pamphlet under my chairmanship in May 1996 – 'One Nation: At the Heart of the Future'. Still worth a read, as Ed Miliband seemed years later to have found out.[105]

This link between patrician conservatism and free-market liberalism had proved elusive in the past and was to do so again in the future. The next chapter will discuss the practical aspects of wider ownership in detail. It remains the key to reconciling (and curbing) populist sentiment with a social market under a Conservative mantle in a new age. During the Thatcher era it helped unite extraordinarily diverse parts of the Conservative Party and kept it in shape as a winning force. The civil war between Wets and Dries was cancelled for the duration – at least around the One Nation dinner table on a Wednesday night.

* * * * *

Enoch Powell once pronounced, in his ex-cathedra manner, that all political careers end in failure. Not so. The Thatcher revolution and the years leading up to it, which lifted Britain from being the sick man to be the pace-setter of Europe, at least for a while, were driven by advice which, after many tribulations and setbacks, was at last taken. This advice, ultimately, succeeded.

I never felt the need to share the Powell pessimism. The time from the 1970s to the mid-1990s was a phase of enormous policy success for Britain, shrewdly built on, rather than rejected, by Tony Blair as the successor to the Tory years. Despite numerous tactical blunders, the entire period was based on the overriding success of the one enormous, central idea and one picture of the possible future, to which all our advice had built up, drawing on events, analysis and observation from far outside politics and outside even the realms of governance.

This idea was that a hundred years of growing belief in state centralism was over, and that a new era of markets, not unbridled

– the critics' mistake – but operating in an entirely new e-enabled context, was dawning. Technological change, on a scale and with a ubiquity and intensity unmatched in the past, even by the Industrial Revolution, was just beginning to do its work, not merely in Britain but across the planet. The new paradigm, overworked though the expression may be, had arrived.

Among many errors, this was one successful call and the one that mattered more than all the rest put together. Excesses there may have been later. As we shall see, the seeds of troubles to come , both different and destructive, were being planted, some to lie dormant for a decade or more . However, in its time the Thatcher experiment, as some called it ,was no failure; it was an unqualified success. For once in politics it was becoming possible, for those who wanted insight into the near future's shape and its implications, to see where we were going.

Chapter Thirteen

Ireland, Europe and the Eternal Question

THE unity of the United Kingdom was not high on the 1979 Thatcher team agenda. However, Northern Ireland certainly was, both during the Heath and Thatcher administration periods, as it is today, and as it has dominated the premierships of Major, Blair, Brown and Cameron in between. The Irish Question may have kept changing but it is nearly true to say that no government since the time of Elizabeth I has been free from the Irish issues in some form or other. No government since 1844 – the year that the horrors of the great famine began to make their full impact on English politics and parliament – has been able to escape endless debates about Irish governance.

For most of the last 200 years we may have avoided a Cornish Question, a Welsh Question and, until recently, a Scottish Question,[106] but the Irish Question has always been there: at the heart of nineteenth-century politics, cascading over into the twentieth century, slicing into party politics before, during and after World War I, and again in post-war Britain. In 1979 it was there once more, even as we assembled for our Cabinet photocall. The Irish Question has become the Irish legacy, always being handed on.

Now it has returned, but the guise is different again. This time it is a central and intertwined part of the Brexit negotiation. It never was, and never will be, part of the Left–Right political debate. Instead, it is part of a new debate about the integrity of the UK, compounded by the Scottish independence movement (so far non-violent) and the complexities of devolved government. What follows therefore belongs to both halves of the fifty-year period that this book surveys. It also belongs to the on-going conflict and tension between localism and identity on the one hand, and the pull of international and supranational collaboration which stretches far into the future, on the other. There will always be an Irish question, just as there will always be a debate between national sovereign control and European unity. There will always be a contradiction tugging at the human soul.

Some have predicted a new era of Anglo-Irish bitterness, resulting from the Brexit issues, and even a new period of violence, similar to the one which is recounted in the pages which follow. But it will be argued that this sort of thinking depends on stereotypical Irish and British views, which a new age is washing away. The forces now pulling the two islands together, Great Britain and Ireland, are now greater than the forces which have for so long pulled them apart.

* * * * *

One of the greatest pleasures of my life and certainly of my political career, was to enjoy the company and, so I believe, the confidence of William Whitelaw. A truly big personality, his large frame and his outward bonhomie concealed qualities of leadership of the most subtle and agile kind. The image of him in some quarters as bumbling and indecisive (Willie Whitewash) were light years from the reality and reflects only on the small minds of those who held it. Contrary to many opinionated judgments, he would have made an excellent prime minister and leader in the stormy days to come. Micro-details of economic policy may not have interested him any more than they interested Churchill, but his grasp of the major issues of government and politics of his time was complete.

His period in Northern Ireland (1972–74) was, of course, only part of his career. However, it laid the foundations, as I shall explain below, of the Good Friday Agreement eighteen years later, as well as being the origin of today's challenges.

Willie Whitelaw liked a good lunch. He particularly liked one before he made a statement in the House of Commons, often at Buck's Club, to which he frequently took me. I would watch with some alarm as a giant martini, almost entirely gin, went down, followed by several glasses of club claret, and wonder whether and how the statement would ever get made. It always was – quite safely and with the full use of Whitelaw's ingenuity in pleasing the House.

One of his best and often repeated adages about political life was that 'nothing is ever as bad as it seems and nothing is ever as good as it seems' – a sobering judgment amid the hyperbole and excitement of the media and newcomers to the parliamentary scene, which would have had a useful influence on today's Brexit dramas.

Many accounts have been written of the first Northern Ireland peace process, as it came to be labelled. This is not the place to go into the labyrinthine negotiating detail between the disputing parties. The issues are probably best covered in Ken Bloomfield's book *Stormont in Crisis*,[107] or in Thomas Hennessey's book[108] on the process, which goes into the full filigree detail of negotiations, exchanges and contacts between the various parties, including the UK Government and the Provisional IRA. A more immediate account, written in the direct aftermath of the period and just after the collapse of the Sunningdale Agreement, is my 3,000-word article which *The Times* carried on 10 February 1975. It is reprinted in full in Appendix II.

The central feature of the process was the endless, tortuous stream of events and arguments attempting to square the circle between Dublin's immovable claim over the jurisdiction of Northern Ireland, embedded in Article Two of the Republic's Constitution, and the bottom-line refusal of the Unionists to countenance any dilution of the Province's status as part of the United Kingdom.

Northern Ireland was not only a challenge but a strangely enjoyable one, despite the violence. This was because Whitelaw had in abundance the very talent which Ted did not – that of winning the total devotion and loyalty of those who worked for him.

I took detailed notes during my two years as a Northern Ireland Minister, a time that covered Bloody Friday, Bloody Sunday and

Operation Motorman, and in which we were treated like an occupying power. It took us weeks to repair relations and establish speaking terms with the Unionists. The last picture in the plate section one shows us at the first coming together (at least of democratic parties) at Stormont Castle, taking the first step towards some sort of agreement that discussions should begin on a power-sharing settlement. Even this was a step which faltered, since – when the time came in the autumn of 1973 – Paisley, who was smiling in this picture, was no longer smiling around any table and would, in due course, bring the whole enterprise crashing down.

Repeated attempts followed to bridge the two irreconcilable standpoints, buttressed by decades of the deepest mistrust. The eventual 'device' used to reach and ratify a power-sharing agreement at the three-day conference at Sunningdale in December 1973, was simply for each side to accept differing interpretations of the role of a new Council of Ireland. For the Social Democratic and Labour Party (SDLP), the Alliance party and, behind them, the Catholic community and Dublin itself, the fear was that the council was being reduced to a mere talking shop. For Unionists and, behind them, the whole Loyalist movement, it was the opposite – the absolutely unacceptable, unthinkable beginning of the slide to a united Ireland.

These efforts lay a long way ahead in the late summer of 1972, as violence kept escalating. The culmination would be the decision to mount an all-out, large-scale military operation to reclaim sovereignty over the no-go areas of Derry, codenamed Operation Motorman.

This intervention took place in the early hours of 31 July 1972. My diary for ten days before – July 21 and 22 – gives a good flavour of the mounting tension and violence.

Arrived with Frank Steele[109] in warm mist and fog at Aldergrove and went straight to Chichester House to do Commerce business [I was, inter alia, the acting 'direct rule' Minister of Commerce]. *From there to lunch at the EBNI* [the electricity authority].

Suddenly, just at the end of lunch, there was a not so distant boom, then another. Outside, the police told me that bombs were going off everywhere in the city. I give orders to return straight to Stormont

Castle. There I am told that 14 bombs have already gone off and there are many killed and wounded. Every minute the telephone rings out with more and more news of bombs — in all 22: 10 killed, including two Welsh guardsmen; 130 in hospital.

I ring WW and he says, with my encouragement, that he will return at once to Belfast with Peter Carrington from London.

Many more calls and press releases etc. The world wants to know what is happening. A deputation of senior civil servants comes in to urge me to take new measures.

At last the GOC and military men arrive. General sense of crisis with only hours before the Protestants finally boil over with anger and frustration.

WW and Peter Carrington arrive and we begin. Meeting puts aside longer-term issues — for which WW and Carrington keep saying they have no authority. We discuss a variety of short-term measures offered by General Ford. At last we decide on some. News comes in that the army are already involved on the edge of Andersonstown. So, we change the plan a bit. Ford very clear, although somehow sounding a bit boy-scoutish.

Peter Carrington amazingly relaxed, perhaps not quite grasping the intensity of the situation. Willie saying repeatedly 'but what can we do?' General pressure from civilian advisers to get a statement out quickly. It is agreed to, 'make the most' of the military operations by the maximum sabre rattling. A statement is drafted by WW. PC suggests changes. Willy Whitelaw loses his cool and begins shouting. PC suggest he goes to bed.

After that we all have a drink. WW tells us that he has already threatened to resign once that day, earlier in the day — before the bombing — over the fact that the Cabinet had refused to let him go ahead with the plebiscite legislation — which he had firmly promised to the Unionists. Eventually all to bed.

Tuesday July 22, we meet at 10 and decide what line to take with the Army. GOC tells us that operations have been 'reasonable' and fifty-eight have been picked up. We then have a long rambling discussion on Regulations 10 and 11 and whether people picked up by the Army can be interrogated. Then we adjourn to WW's room for what PC calls 'the crucial discussion'. He seems to be getting rather impatient.

He (PC) suggests three options, ranging from military saturation down to selective attacks. All would involve going right into Bogside and the Creggan estate. We agree that these are the options although they will need to be accompanied by new attitudes and policies vis-à-vis Dublin.

PC flies off to see the PM at Chequers. I see the Ulster Unionists – who are insultingly rude – then lunch with Ossie King at Radcannon. Back to Stormont where WW is just off back to Westminster to make a statement. We read it and suggest redrafts. It sounds very weak.

The night of Operation Motorman Willie Whitelaw was agitated. Bill Nield, the Northern Ireland Department Permanent Secretary, who had a short fuse at the best of times, kept on exploding in angry bursts and Peter Carrington, who had flown over for the evening to be with us, kept telling everyone to calm down. The troops were going into Provo heartland and there was a real prospect of casualties.

In the event it was a non-event, largely thanks to Whitelaw's wise decision to issue warnings before the operation began (which the military, believing in surprise, only reluctantly agreed to). The Provos melted away, the area was fully reoccupied and the stigma of a no-go area removed.

From the start, our arrival and work at Stormont had been facilitated by the Northern Ireland Civil Service. My own Permanent Secretary at the Ministry of Commerce, Ewart Bell, was the perfect support. I do not believe there could be a better civil servant anywhere at any time. In a situation of obvious delicacy, when we could have been made to feel like an occupying force (which we were), he mixed wisdom, friendship and diplomacy in equal measure as we struggled through the thickets of division, tribalism and animosity.

The other tower of strength and endless source of good humour was Ken Bloomfield, who had been Brian Faulkner's closest adviser but whose talent Whitelaw had swiftly recognised and employed. His inspired insight into the very heart of the problem, the need for what he christened 'the Irish dimension', opened a gateway between the seemingly irreconcilable stances of the Republic, the North and the British Government.

Later on, when Nield retired, we were fortunate to get Frank Cooper as his successor. Frank was a no-nonsense operator of the highest skill (and later Permanent Secretary at the Ministry of Defence, where he was an even greater success).

Bloody Sunday had, of course, put an end to all talk of truces. At the time of the earlier truce, in June 1972, the evangelist Billy Graham had been visiting the province and had attracted large crowds despite the high security and tension. We were giving a him a splendid dinner at the Culloden Hotel when the news came through that the Provos had declared a highly conditional ceasefire. Billy Graham rose in his seat, radiating optimism.

Of course, it was a shallow and meaningless manoeuvre (all troops out of Northern Ireland), mostly designed for propaganda purposes and intended to allow the Provisional Irish Republican Army (PIRA) to regroup and rearm. But Graham was convinced that a great moment in Irish history had arrived, almost certainly by the power of prayer. I hadn't the heart to tell him what it was really about and he continued the evening in an elated mood.

The truce lasted three days and was followed, as recounted above, by renewed bombing and killing of unparalleled ferocity. The morning after Motorman, nine innocent civilians, including a schoolboy, were killed by a bomb in the village of Claudy. I visited grieving relatives later that day. What was the point? What was the point?

I have a note in my files of a 'normal day' Royal Ulster Constabulary (RUC) report of what was described as 'low level, routine violence'.

Minister

Situation Report 11.40 p.m. 21/5/73

1. *There was some stoning in the Mt Pottinger area this evening.*
2. *A bomb thrown into a butcher's shop in Lisburn at 10 p.m. this evening exploded damaging the shop – no casualties. The owner, Mr Carr, was recently a witness in a case in which a UDA man was sentenced to two years' imprisonment. Probably retribution.*

3. A bomb exploded in Londonderry at 17.43. Considerable damage but no casualties.

4. A blast bomb damaged a police Land Rover in Londonderry this evening. No casualties.

5. A crowd hijacked a furniture lorry in Armagh. It was then set on fire and used as a barricade by the crowd. The crowd was dispersed by the army, using rubber bullets.

In other words, a very quiet evening: low level routine violence.

So much for 'normal' days. There were many horrifically less normal days ahead.

The signing of the Sunningdale Agreement was the summit of the Whitelaw era in Ulster. Whitelaw himself had moved back by then to take change of the deteriorating industrial relations scene in Britain, leaving Francis Pym to take over as Secretary of State.

Sunningdale seemed like a real step forward, involving long nights of negotiation at the Civil Service College (which had been opened by Ted Heath three years earlier) and not much sleep. Waiting around through the early hours for some working group to reach agreement, I fell into long conversations with the Irish Taoiseach, Liam Cosgrave. He was a gentle leader, immersed from childhood in Ireland's stormy and bloody years of civil war, his father having been Taoiseach in the early 1920s.

Within months though, the agreement painstakingly worked out between the moderate parties had been overturned by Ian Paisley's Democratic Unionist hardliners. It came to be seen as a failure. In fact, it can more fairly be regarded as representing the essential early steps on the long road leading to eventual agreement between the warring parties twenty-five years later, when Tony Blair brokered the Good Friday Agreement. Many people called this occasion Sunningdale Mark Two in view of its strong resemblance to the original agreement twenty-five years earlier.

These days and nights at Sunningdale were my last in the quagmire of Northern Ireland. We had done our level best. It was to be more than twenty years before I spoke again on Northern Ireland and its travails (after the Omagh bomb and mass killings). In January 1974,

Heath brought me back to start yet another new department – this time the brand-new Department of Energy under Peter Carrington: the department and policy area that contained within it Heath's eventual nemesis.

Of the four ministers who ran the Stormont government, I am the only one still alive. As we all know, the Irish Question is with us again, but in one important sense the Whitelaw mission was the end of a chapter in UK-Ireland relations: It was the last phase before the onset of the digital age, bringing with it the mobile telephone, the internet and the World Wide Web, the empowerment of public opinion and of course the empowerment of new and more deadly methods of terrorism.

Perhaps it could be more optimistically argued that it was the last phase before the people of Ireland, in the North and the Republic, discovered their own voice. They ceased to be dominated by myth-makers and religious authority and dogma and gained the power and information to influence events directly, rather than leaving their views to be shaped and interpreted by demagogues, media-spinners, bend-it-any-way opinion polls, historicists, determinists and generalists, to suit particular interests.

Irish issues remain at the centre of British politics today, having been brought back into the limelight by the Brexit issue and the super-sensitive conundrum of how to keep the island as one, yet keep it divided between the Republic in the European Union and the North inside the United Kingdom but outside the EU.

A huge debate has built up about the need for a new frontier between the two, based on a totally erroneous view. The mistaken assumption is that, as long as both sides were in the EU, there were no differences – and therefore no border checks or border of any kind were needed or existed. In fact, there have been considerable differences between North and South, existing long before either Ireland or the UK joined the EU and continuing over the years of common membership. Currency and VAT rates are obvious examples from recent years.

From the trade point of view, the border has all along been lightly policed (military control for security reasons was another matter), but it existed – just as borders of a kind exist between every member state within the single market). This can and will continue. There is no reason whatever for change, bar some more online form filling for the bigger and more regular road freight businesses.

However, behind the debate is a much deeper factor at work – again unappreciated in much of the political or media-fuelled debate. What too few seem to appreciate, or want to build on, is that the entire atmosphere of Irish politics and opinion has changed, thanks in part to economic and social advance in the Republic and the weakening influence of the Catholic Church, as exemplified by the Republic's liberalised abortion laws. The romanticised but bloody battles of the past no longer have the same appeal to a younger generation who want sleeping dogs to be left undisturbed.

In the current debate about the Northern Ireland border issue we return to the either-or mindset – which distorts so many situations – and to the common failure to see that almost every set of assumptions behind this mindset is changing all the time. Just as protagonists in the Europe debate fail to see that Europe is changing, both within and between every member state and in relation to the wider world, so the older generation of Irish affairs experts remains locked in the assumptions and arguments of thirty years ago.

Ireland, the Commonwealth and Brexit

We now turn to a completely different UK–Ireland story, one which had begun to look possible before Brexit and may yet bear fruit long after Brexit and border issues have been settled.

The Republic's recent interest in engagement with the Commonwealth is a case in point. There are states where serious voices are talking about Commonwealth membership, or at least association, but nothing is said by ministers or at government level. One of the most interesting countries in this category is the Republic of Ireland. The historical baggage here is almost crushing. Ireland declined to join the Commonwealth at the time of the 1949 London Declaration. This was the moment when a new Commonwealth was conceived, admitting republics as members (notably Nehru's India). While history has it that Éamon de Valera, who could hardly be described as pro-

British, wanted to stay in, there would have been an instinctive dislike of any British-tainted institutions and the 1949 Commonwealth must have looked to many very much like the old British Commonwealth in new packaging.

Today the picture is very different. First, the Commonwealth is no longer such an Anglo-centric entity, whatever its origins and history. Secondly, Ireland has been wounded by its European association. Commonwealth membership would not be some sort of ricochet impulse, but it might be a steadying reinforcement for a nation temporarily knocked off balance by the crisis in the euro system of 2008–2011, which rocked the EU as well as the global financial structure – a situation in which Britain was ready with prompt and substantial help. Thirdly, the Queen's visit of May 2011 proved outstandingly successful in healing old wounds and promoting reconciliation. Fourthly, there is a question of mindset: Bringing Ireland and the UK alongside each other, as fellow members of the Commonwealth, ought to be an opportunity not just for widening Ireland's economic and business ties far outside the EU, but for reinforcing the many longstanding links with its neighbour of which the Common Travel Area (from 1922) is a strong example.

The Council of the Isles has long existed, although hardly in a state of public prominence. The new thought, yet to mature fully, both in Dublin and London, is that Britain and Ireland need each other as never before. The combined voice of the British Isles would carry new weight both in a European and a wider international context. The Northern Ireland issue would fade away into inconsequence. The mutual economic benefits would multiply. New areas of co-operation in everything from cultural creativity to offshore energy possibilities would open up. Inter-island transportation might lend itself to revolutionary technical possibilities.

These are the areas to which the first step, association of some kind with the Commonwealth network, might lead.

It will take time, but there is a growing campaign for this to happen, interrupted though it undoubtedly has been by the Brexit/border issue. No allegiance to the Crown is involved and the Commonwealth of today is a very different institution to the one from which Ireland walked away in 1949.

Lingering Fenian suspicions, of course, remain of anything that appears to involve British intrusion. However, this would be partnership without dominance in a changed world. And fellow membership in the worldwide Commonwealth network would open links and access opportunities to many other regions. What a partnership it could be. Value would be added for both countries. In a way that has never occurred within the EU context, joint Commonwealth connection would enable the so-called Irish dimension, seen from the London side, to begin to fuse with the English dimension, as seen from the Dublin side. There would be the question of the impact on the North, but the supporters of the idea in Dublin see such a move as a strong gesture of reconciliation.

In reality, far away from the headline politics, the overlap of interests between Ireland and the Commonwealth already exists and is growing. Some forty-million Irish people live in Commonwealth countries. A changing world landscape may have turned the idea of Ireland's return from a possibility into a probability.

Unity of purpose with Ireland would give Britain new meaning and status in the global network. It would be the crowning reversal of the 'break-up' of the United Kingdom again which has dragged on through public discussion for years past, reaching a culmination in the 'near escape from death' outcome of the Scottish independence referendum in 2014.

Far from it being time to wring hands over the break-up of the United Kingdom, a new 'Irish dimension' (Ken Bloomfield's phrase in a totally new context) would signal the opposite – a new era of British Isles unity and cooperation.

Is that impossible with the Republic in the EU and the UK out? Only if you believe that the EU power structure is immutable and a United States of Europe inevitable. I do not.

All along some of us have queried the great diagnostic alliance which unites both extreme Brexiteers and extreme Europhiles: that the EU is heading inexorably for a powerful federal state, bound together by a single foreign policy and in due course a single defence and security strategy. The Brexiteers say that is just the reason for not being trapped and crushed in this ever-advancing machine. The Europhiles assert that this is precisely the reason for being part of it instead of standing aside while the leviathan marches on.

As events will prove, both are wrong, locked into a dangerous misunderstanding of the forces dominating the international landscape in the digital age. There will be no great EU federation with a single policy, single budgets or even a single broad direction. The centrifugal powers of the digital age have long since unravelled the old centralist EU model. Good Europeans should long ago have understood this and devised new and looser forms of cooperation in Europe, striking a new balance between national identity and international connection.

Britain could have played a major part in this pattern of fundamental alignment had it not been both rushed and sidelined into a shopping list of self-serving 'demands', most of which were rejected. The advice to go early with the referendum and not on any account to challenge the 'fundamentals' – for example the four EU 'indivisible' freedoms, the alleged sacred tablets of EU unity – was to prove completely fatal to David Cameron and his strategy. It created the most favourable possible conditions for the leavers to prevail.

The setback to a new era of Irish–British relations is undeniable. However, it is not permanent. The repeated theme of this volume is that the forces at work bringing countries and societies together are now much stronger than those tearing them apart – even the seemingly unending quarrels between Britain and Ireland.

PART THREE
THE INHERITANCE

Chapter Fourteen

Technology Unravels
the Global Order

THE post-Thatcher era and the dawn of a new political age began for me on the Charles Bridge in Prague on 17 November 1989.

On that day a gigantic protest rally (estimated at 100,000), mainly students, assembled on and around the bridge with demands to bring the Communist government to an end. Later there was to be an even bigger rally in the New Town Square (750,000 people) as the final days of the Husak Communist regime unfolded.

The Charles Bridge event and the massive protests following the fall of the Berlin Wall a few days earlier (9 November 1989), in Prague and elsewhere in the former Soviet satellites, were evidence of something completely revolutionary – perhaps even more defining than the collapse of the Soviet empire itself. They were gigantic gatherings mobilised electronically by email and the internet, with an impact never before seen on such a colossal and instantaneous scale, realising Václav Havel's famous identification of 'the power of the powerless'. People power had arrived, this time not just in street rallies and banner waving but in a form turbo-boosted by the microchip and the information revolution.[110]

This phenomenon occurred decades before social media would arrive to play such a big part in the next century. The iPhone had not been invented. Blogs had barely begun. By today's digital standards, it was quite primitive. However, it was the first call of a new age of empowerment. By using emails and personal computers, the organisers were showing what power could be used to summon enormous numbers of people to demonstrations at very short notice. The old world of painstaking preparation – months of contacting people and making arrangements, of furtive telephone calls on tapped lines – had given way to something completely new.

Of course, the Prague rallies were forbidden and police tried to break up some, such as also the earlier ones in Bratislava. However, the authorities had been by-passed by the microchip and they knew it. The will of the Communist regime to break up the crowds, once they had coalesced in such enormous numbers, was fading. Power was passing to the street and to the network in increasing strength as mass-connectivity took over from elite control. Although they were yet to become aware of it, governments everywhere were being dragged into a new era in which the techniques of governing, of maintaining legitimacy and of leading popular opinion, had changed.

Power was seeping away from traditional styles of 'strong' leadership and heavy centralism, not just in the crumbling Soviet Union and its satellites, but in Britain, too. Although it was not seen that way, the immense and dominant personal strength of Margaret Thatcher was giving way to poorly understood power centres and to increasingly e-enabled discord and rival groupings. Perhaps the power and reach of the strong leader had always been exaggerated, as Archie Brown suggests in his book on that very theme.[111] However, the information upheaval across the planet was about to transfer the instruments of power and persuasion out of the hands of elites and authorities. The so-called Velvet Revolution[112] in Prague was the harbinger, warning governments, staring leaders in the face.

Later I was to pay many visits to what was then Czechoslovakia – first in the final months leading up to the Velvet Revolution, then after the Revolution itself and the actual liberation from the Communist regime, although before the velvet divorce (Slovakia's breakaway).

In the period just before the final Communist collapse, an odd atmosphere prevailed in Prague. Visiting with members of the

Commons Foreign Affairs Select Committee, I attended a dinner arranged by the very switched-on British Ambassador. He had invited all the 'dissident' leaders who were clearly lining up to be the next government, including Václav Havel himself, Jirí Dienstbier and others.

They still had their pre-revolution 'hard labour' jobs as permitted under the old regime – Václav Havel as a window-cleaner, Jirí Dienstbier as some sort of engineer on the Metro system, another as a taxi-driver.

By this time the police cadres, who were supposed to be corralling Havel and his colleagues, had turned into sort-of security guards. On this occasion they followed Havel and his colleagues to the embassy then sat outside while we dined within, not sure what to do and only cheering up when someone brought them cups of coffee.

All this was about to change dramatically. Only two months later we were again with them at dinner in a Prague brasserie, but this time they were mostly all cabinet ministers in a new government. Peter Shore and I, as the two senior members of the Commons Foreign Affairs Committee (FAC), were travelling together at the invitation of Havel to a historic evening. There were things to be said about the past and about Britain and Czechoslovakia, that perhaps were easier for parliamentarians rather than governments to express – things for which to say sorry, such as Munich – and things for which to give profound thanks, such as the role of brilliant Czech airmen in the Battle of Britain.

We were met at the airport, still in a 1930s-time warp, by Karel Schwarzenberg, then a sort of PA and adviser to Havel and a major supporter of the growing Civic Forum movement, but later a distinguished Foreign Minister of the Czech Republic. He had an ageing car and his driving was atrocious, but luckily Czech liberation had not yet reached the transport sector and there were hardly any cars on the roads.

Prince Schwarzenberg was a perfect example of the dangers and idiotic wrong-headedness of classifying people by provenance and background – the Douglas-Home syndrome again. On paper he was a classic *ancien régime* character, a dynastic prince complete with great estates in different parts of the Hapsburg Empire. He even looked a bit Hapsburgy. In practice he was an absolutely determined liberator, his eyes fixed on the future of the Czechs and the way they were going to re-enter Europe and prosper after the long darkness of the fascist/ communist years.

The evening at the Prague brasserie was both emotional and humorous. Jirí Dienstbier, now Foreign Minister, had just discovered his phone was still being tapped. When he asked the former secret police authorities why this was so, he was told by the commandant that, despite the dramatic change of government, no-one had told them to stop.

Two years on, in 1991, I visited Havel yet again – this time in his presidential role, in Hradcany Castle. I passed through vast halls, saloons and double doors. Eventually there was the great Havel – a diminutive figure in a light-blue jumper looking oddly out of place amid the gilded furniture and mirrors. Here was the ultimate word-master of the late twentieth century. His phrases ran like gold threads through my mind. 'I really do now inhabit,' he had written, 'a system in which words are capable of shaking the entire structure of government, where words can prove mightier than ten military divisions.'[113]

I don't remember much of what we said that day. The Czechs were free but facing agonising economic and political problems. The velvet divorce of Slovakia lay just ahead. The inevitable disappointments, after the elixir of freedom was attained, were setting in.

I myself was part of a Coopers & Lybrand consultancy team trying to reform and privatise the Czech power industry. However, the old apparatchiks and their attitudes, were still ensconced. The prospect of privatisation, let alone connecting up with neighbouring countries' power systems, was anathema. We were getting nowhere.

Beyond that day lay the botched attempts at privatisation under Havel's very different successor, Václav Klaus, whose purist free-market economic theory clashed with political reality but whose logical views about European integration remain full of potency – and a grimly accurate prophecy about the problems ahead for the whole European integrationist project as it ran up against nationalist realities and the centrifugal tendencies of the digital era.

On the way out, the cloakroom attendant in the castle hall spoke to me as she gave me my coat. Was I not, she asked, an expert on returning state industries to the rightful owners, and on restitution? Her brother had owned a restaurant which the communists had seized. It was time to get it back. Would I help? I explained feebly that I couldn't.

Already by then, the early '90s, we were an age away from the mood of Western triumph which rose as the Berlin Wall fell – and from unipolar American hegemony, buttressed by unswerving, Thatcher-led, British support.

Now the ground was shifting and power with it. Bonn was heading back to Berlin; Prague was becoming the centre of a greater and different Europe; China and India – in fact, almost the whole of Asia – were awakening. Asian cities were outstripping the old Western world, with Western political elites only dimly understanding that things were changing fundamentally, and not liking what they saw. It was to take decades for the penny to drop.

Even Moscow was shedding its communist shabbiness, although very slowly. The Foreign Affairs Committee team had visited Moscow in 1987, where we were put up at the old National Hotel, now long since dismantled and replaced. As chairman, I was assigned the very room overlooking Red Square in which Lenin had slept the night he came to Moscow in February 1918, after his triumphant return to the Finland Station in St Petersburg. Or so the management said.

It was a modest enough single bedroom, with a picture of Lenin over the side table. I felt the surge of history running through my veins. Afterwards I learnt that the management designated whichever room happened to be free on the street side of the hotel as the 'Lenin' room, presumably moving the picture around as required. A colleague, visiting a month before had been given quite a different Lenin room. So much for the surge of history.

Meanwhile, what was so special about Prague, aside of course from the incredible beauty of the city areas out of which it has grown – with the Old Town, the Lesser Town, the New Town (not so new – fourteenth century) and the nineteenth century, layer upon city layer, like some fabulous cake of history?

In part it was that, in the twentieth century, Prague had lived through the very darkest eras of both nazi-ism and communism, trying desperately to escape from each – and failing until this moment. The hairpin bend where partisans assassinated the monster gauleiter, Reinhard Heydrich, and the spot in Wenceslas Square where Jan Palach immolated himself in the brief Prague Spring – all at the time hopelessly in vain – cried out from the past each time one drove by them.

However, in even larger part, it was Prague's return to freedom, something that most of my generation had never expected to see. We had been assured by the great gurus such as Zbigniew Brzezinski, that the Soviet empire was here to stay and that the Cold War would continue indefinitely. There had to be engagement and containment, but there would be no room for freedom and cooperation.

Yet the edifice that would always be there had crumbled. Now open and free, Prague was totally accessible – an hour or so's flight away from London, closer than Marseilles, closer than Barcelona – unbelievable, unthinkable. Yet it happened and the midwife at its rebirth was none other than the amazing internet, with its connectivity, its mobilising powers, its shattering impact on centralised control and official myths.

In Europe the internet age had arrived and the politics of Europe would never be the same. All the twentieth-century models, not least the model of the European Community itself, would have to be adapted and refashioned. This imperative will continue to unfold as the outdated structure struggles to escape stagnation, instability and global irrelevance, and as Germany – once seen as the motor which would drive European recovery – drags itself into self-inflicted energy and environmental chaos.

Two decades on from the end of Soviet Europe lay the Arab 'awakening', likened, quite wrongly, to the liberation of Central European. Incredibly the experts, followed by Foreign Office officials and ministers, came to confuse process with outcome, assuming that what the information revolution and the internet had done for Prague, Budapest and Warsaw – the restoration of democracy and the rule of law – it would do for the totally different social conditions of the

Middle East. Officials and ministers alike plunged into a symphony of false comparisons between the two eras and the two events. While dictatorially inclined leaders toppled, they talked of liberty, dignity and the Arab 'Spring' as though it was the European experience all over again.

It was not. The restorative powers of the internet in bringing Eastern and Central Europe back to democracy became the fragmenting powers of Middle East history and rivalries, returning the region to bloody chaos. Same technology – disastrously different outcomes.

* * * * *

Meanwhile, my time throughout the 1990s advising the Swiss Bank Corporation – largely on Asian projects – made for an exciting ride. The SBC had been a pillar of the Swiss banking establishment for at least two centuries. Fleeing French aristocrats had deposited their gold with it at the time of the Revolution, saying that they would be back to collect later. Needless to say, a lot of them failed to return.

The SBC had pots of money and now wanted to spread its wings in London and international markets. Its investment arm expanded rapidly, driven by big hitters like Hans de Gier and Andrew Large. Brilliant operators like Brian Keelan, audacious inventor of many of the new financial techniques and instruments in wide use today (but who sadly died young), gave the bank added momentum.

Soon we gobbled up the great house of Warburg, full of talent but temporarily off balance, and I found myself an 'advisory director' there, whatever that meant. At first, I shared an office with Sir David Scholey, the master networker of all time who was never off the telephone, although some said that, as his voice was so mighty, he hardly needed a telephone (the same used to be said about Willie Whitelaw).

By this time, we – SBC Warburg – were advisers on privatising the world. The Warburg stars included people like James Sassoon and David Freud, both later becoming stalwarts of the 2010 coalition government. Not all our advice worked. One overseas government, which I visited several times with Brian Keelan, listened attentively as we explained how to privatise their state energy company. When we returned, they said they were grateful and had followed our recommendations. The chairmanship of the state oil and gas industry had now been taken away from the Finance Minister – and given to his brother.

Working at the same time with the then Coopers & Lybrand (and often bringing the two – Coopers and SBC – together), we also advised the huge Czech state energy company, CEZ, on how to modernise and privatise – with little effect, as in our previous experience, described above.

Coopers was also asked by British Rail to work on impending privatisation. The view was that the break up should be by liveries and the old company brands revived – London North Eastern Railway (LNER), Great Western Railway (GWR), Midland, Southern, etc. On no account should track and stations be separated from operators. This was the same view as that put forward by Simon Jenkins, the highly influential journalist, former *Times* editor and former British Rail director.[114] It was all ignored and the separation of track and franchisees went ahead, with distinctly mixed results.

Later, when I worked as adviser to Japan Central Railway, their boss Yoshiyuki Kasai, a true railway genius, made no secret of his view that the British railway model was flawed. He wrote a book to say so. He wondered how on earth one could establish a good career structure. Station administration, platform organisation and track management are inseparable from train operation, and staff need to develop their skills and careers through all aspects of the operation. He had a point.

My own journalist activity received a surprise boost when the formidable John Junor, *Sunday Express* editor, took me up as a feature writer. There was a slight problem in that his views of the messages his readers required and how they should be presented were diametrically opposed to mine. However, it did not seem to matter. He remained very supportive, even running a piece in his own rancorous and scourging Crossbencher column that I should be recalled to government – for which, of course, there was a fat chance.

We lunched regularly in Kensington and although it sounds a bit ridiculous in the case of this Fleet Street Beaverbrook dragon, I had a soft spot for him. Of course, we compromised and my centre-page features appeared regularly for a while. Anyway, the money was nice even if the articles had zero impact – on *Sunday Express* readers or anyone else.

* * * * *

By the millennium American global dominance, on which the Reagan-Thatcher bond had rested a decade before, was waning fast. Network power was growing. America was about to be hit by the most vicious, inflaming, unprovoked and unexpected assault from outside forces in the history of the republic – the 9/11 New York massacres, in which 3,000 people died in a single morning.

Huge consequences were set to flow, of which the Iraq invasion was one of the biggest. My place for the next ten years was going to be at the despatch box in the Lords, first as Opposition spokesman, then as deputy Opposition leader and finally as Foreign and Commonwealth Office Minister. Hours and days of debate on the 9/11 aftermath and the Iraq invasion lay ahead, with the talented Liz Symons (Baroness Symons of Vernham Dean) opening and closing for the Labour Government while I did the same for the Opposition.

Neither of us really knew why Iraq was the chosen first target in George W. Bush's war on terror. The evidence of weapons of mass destruction was shaky and based on a few sepia-tinted photos of desert sheds and caravans. And the links between Saddam Hussein and the real terrorist movements were slender, almost non-existent. However, led by Bush, with Tony Blair at his side, and misled by shockingly weak intelligence from both sides of the Atlantic, we went ahead.

Chapter Fifteen

Asian Reset

IN a way this chapter you are about to read is the most important in the book, because it demands a fundamental shift in attitude in British minds – and in Western thinking generally – about status, position and behaviour in the new world. We have to say goodbye to moral superiority, lecturing others on values, asserting the virtues of the Westminster model and other psychological relics of a vanished age. It will be difficult.

The '80s and '90s were a time when far more could have been learnt by the old Western powers from the rising stars of Asia – not just from their economic brilliance but also from their culture and evolving social and governmental systems. There should have been a much clearer idea of where the e-enabled world was bound to be heading. Visiting Japan frequently, I learnt one obvious lesson – constant innovation combined with a unifying sense of purpose, first-class education and a high moral sense of parental commitment to children's literacy and numeracy, could do more for any society than a thousand lectures about economic theory and good governance.

Although Japan was about to run into a period of apparent stagnation – the so-called lost decade (much exaggerated and better called consolidation) – I was struck by the central concept of obligation on the part of each citizen towards each other as a central part of Japanese philosophy – and of daily behaviour and business relations. This has not changed.

Nor in China, despite the revolutionary upheavals of massive economic growth and the bourgeoisification of 600-million people, have the underlying binding characteristics – although somewhat different from those of Japan – been weakened. They are the Confucian precepts – quite simply, that the family, its ancestors, its children, its learning and its saving, come first.

In both cases – the world's second and third largest economies – there can be no doubt at all that the overwhelming emphasis on family cohesion and mutual obligation, and respect for the role and status of the elderly, is the underlying bonding agent which drives and strengthens, in bad times as well as good. It is certainly the quality which helped Japan through its decade in the '90s of lower growth and lost momentum.

Martin Jacques[115] reminds us that it is filial piety, combined with profound respect for history and the collective memory, and towards those who teach the story of the past, which gives China the binding sense of continuity and stability in face of breakneck economic change.

The point so often missed by global analysts is not so much that the Asian and now African economies seem to have found the secret of fast growth – albeit from very low levels. It is that they are philosophically free of the 'isms' which have bedevilled Europe in the twentieth and to some extent in the twenty-first century. What Disraeli long ago called 'all the baleful European ideologies' have been left behind – in practice even in China. Elsewhere they scarcely ever surfaced.

As chair of the UK-Japan 2000 Group (renamed the 21st Century Group when we got to 2000), I had to deal with a bewildering series of Japanese Prime Ministers – they were 'dispensable' a Japanese elder told me, hence the rapid turnover. Maybe, since the Japanese are well ahead of us – as they are in living standards, technology, transportation, social organisation and much else – it will become the pattern here in the West, too.

Maybe, too, the Japanese have at last escaped from the rapid prime ministerial turnover pattern just as Western leaders are finding their tenure getting shorter and shorter. Junichiro Koizumi was the first of the long stayers in recent times and Shinzō Abe is proving to be the next.

Another area where we have been left far behind in Europe, although at last catching up, is in railway development. I have for some years been a paid adviser to the Japan Central Railway Company, the main operators of the amazing Shinkansen system, and have therefore been admitted to some of the secrets of the world's must successful, advanced – and safest – passenger railway network in the world.

However, there is no secret, just a constant incremental application of innovations and the most scrupulous and detailed administration of the whole system. Very high speed and very high frequency require controls of intense accuracy and precision. The frequency is the key, meaning that every train has to be precisely on time, in exact place in every station and performing to exact speeds. When one period showed that punctuality had slipped by four seconds, a special board meeting was called to consider this terrible lapse and how it could be swiftly corrected.

The electronic controls to prevent these trains, travelling at 370 kph, from running into each other, have been honed and improved with fifty years of technical ingenuity and training. A state of mind has to be built up and inculcated. One cannot just construct and operate from scratch a high-speed train network as if it were a Hornby train set.

The Chinese have sought to do just that on a huge and super-fast scale. Wiser heads predicted that without a full and deep understanding both of the intricate technology and the underlying mindset, acquired over decades, there would be crashes in the Chinese system. There were – terrible ones.

Transport and Infrastructure are not of course the only manifestations of Asian advance. Physical triumphs spring from deeper cultural, social and educational progress at a pace which Western thinking has been slow to embrace. They have now created a new era (or the historian might say, recreated an old one) of Asian predominance in both economic and, *parri passu*, political and global affairs. To the colossal, pervasive and growing implications of this advance for the Western world, and our British world within it, we now turn.

My contention back in the '90s was that Asia was overtaking the West not just economically and technically, but in terms of moral conduct and societal behaviour as well. This assertion was met with cries of dismay and disagreement by the commentariat — *The Times*'s columnist grandees in particular. How could Western superiority be outclassed? I outlined my position in a Demos pamphlet in 1995 in which I argued that Western societies had to adapt to the higher standards of Asia – especially in education and in family commitment – or knuckle under. The time had come, in short, for Easternisation as the reverse of the Westernisation of the past two centuries or so. It was not a popular message and has still not reached large parts of Western leadership circles, even as we face the new crisis of violence and disintegration in the Middle East and the juddering impact of populism throughout Europe.

One could argue that none of these trends, and the values behind them, are new. In fact, they are very old. However, there is a massive new dimension to the picture. It is the marriage of new information technology and its planet-wide connectivity, with old Asian thought and behaviour patterns which transform, uplift and accelerate the shifting Asian phenomenon. The union of peoples and technologies alters everything, and it was the reason why the book that was beginning to form in my mind after 1995, *The Edge of Now*,[116] began by talking about 'a new epoch in human affairs and in human institutions, especially, but not only, the institution of government'.

I am not sure even now that the public, or the British media and the British body politic, have grasped the significance of Asian economic power, or of the rising middle-class momentum of most of Africa. People still gasp at the appearance of dozens of Manhattans across China, the spread of a 12,000-mile network of both railways and high-speed ultra-modern rail services, at the endless spaghetti junctions of railways and motorways, and the factory complexes as big as large towns. What they do not see is the wave of new technology racing ahead, overtaking all but the most advanced forms in the West. What they do not see in Africa is the enormous revolution in agriculture as a new middle class demands home-grown products and as the old pattern of commodity groups and semi-processed foodstuffs for export melts away.

As Hans Rosling reminds us in *Factfulness: Ten Reasons We're Wrong about the World*[117] – the book Bills Gates said was the most influential he had ever read – this polarised picture of developing versus developed countries, and of a world divided by a widening gap between rich and poor, bears no relation to what is happening. The 'gap' is now where most people in the once stagnating but now transforming regions of the world reside. They are creating the largest and fastest expansion in history of middle-income consumer markets. They are mobile-enabled, Web-connected, e-empowered – today, now.

The statistics lag way behind. As Rosling remarks, most of our global statistics, purporting to inform on economic growth, per capita income, national output and other aggregates, were designed for an age of wheat and steel, now gone. They tell us little about the data-based patterns of economic activity and commerce which have emerged in the last decade and even less about the social transformations these strong and rapid trends have brought about.

Yet these are the societies and the markets and the cultural conditions with which a country like Britain must struggle to come to terms and in which it must succeed, or die.

This is the new reality slowly beginning to dawn on British policy-makers. As Brexit Britain prepares to re-enter the international scene in more of a solo capacity – although, of course, still tied to numerous links of interdependence (perhaps more than ever) – the sheer size to which the Asian factor in world affairs has grown is challenging old assumptions.

Four and a half decades ago, when Britain first joined the EU bloc, of course there were signs that the Chinese giant was stirring, although it still kept to itself on the world stage. The USA was the unquestioned superpower.

However, since then it has been 'all change'. The growth, first in the Chinese economy and now in China's world footprint, has been earth-shaking and has defied every prediction.

In the past five years alone 30 per cent of total world growth has come from China, vaulting it into second place in industrial size (and likely to overtake the USA before long), becoming the world's biggest energy player and extending China's reach and influence in every corner of the globe. In the words of the Chinese all-powerful leader, Xi Jinping, now elected for life, we are witnessing 'a rise in China's international influence, ability to inspire and power to shape'. China, he added, is becoming 'a nation of innovators'.[118]

In the next five years, Chinese production could grow at least 50 per cent more, see China take the lead in many new technologies, bring middle-class standards to another 100-million or more Chinese people (on top of the 600-million who have already arrived), expand China's trade and investment around the world exponentially, and greatly increase China's weight in almost all aspects of geopolitics. One does not have to believe all the forecasts and claims to see that China is becoming the indispensable economic power, incidentally leaving Russia far behind.

This new reality demands a major and difficult shift of mindset in many countries, nowhere more so than in Britain as it looks for new allies and new markets. This is because, for Britain, the USA was always the bedrock – the founding partner in the post-war liberal order, far the biggest investor in Britain and the biggest single country for British exports of goods and services.

So, for British strategists, an adjustment to the prospect of another power of equal or even greater global importance was always going to be a wrench. Yet it has become an urgent task to decide how to react and relate to the growing Chinese presence in every continent – throughout Africa, in Latin America, the island states of the Caribbean and the South Seas, the Middle East, Pakistan and Sri Lanka, and across Central Asia. And now the Belt and Road strategy stretches out and right into the heart of the European continent – and, indeed, deep into the British economy itself.

The depth of this penetration is illustrated by recent Chinese interest in Macclesfield. Macclesfield? A strongly pro-Chinese London business figure explained to me that since Macclesfield was the great nineteenth-century silk industry centre, that is where the new Silk Road should end in the UK.

The plan was to open a new silk museum in the town which would bring in streams of Chinese tourists. Early local investigations suggested that the plan was not all that welcome locally. Could I help? Well, yes, by advising the Chinese to go a bit easier with local sensibilities.

But Britain's China-inclined business community, as well as its diplomats and national planners, have a further challenge, when handling relations with China, which complicates and compounds the difficulties – Britain has another relationship with a major Asian power to cherish and safeguard against Chinese involvement, namely its ties with Japan.

These are not minor issues. On the contrary Japan has long been seen as Britain's 'best friend' in Asia, just as Britain has been regarded as Japan's best friend in Europe. And with good reason. Massive Japanese investment in Britain over fifty years helped transform the British economy. Nor has the connection been solely economic. Japanese-British cooperation on security and military affairs has been moving onto a new level of detail, with officials from both sides in increasingly close contact.

Honda may have decided to move back to Japan, from which it can now sell its cars into Europe without tariff, thanks to its completed free-trade agreement with the EU. But other auto producers remain here and plan expansion. If and when the British grow and reshape their own automotive industry, after years on relying on foreign ownership, close partnership with Japan will be needed more than ever.

So, Britain confronts a tricky double dilemma and balancing act. It's interests and future are becoming more than ever bound up with Asia and with the second and third largest, and most dynamic, economies in the world. Yet it's traditional instinct and reflex has been to look westwards, to the American giant. As the former British Minister, Tony Blair, wrote unambiguously to George Bush Jnr back in 2003, 'We will be with you, whatever.'

That was over Iraq, where the 'whatever' turned out to be disastrously different from the outcome the two leaders hoped for and which, indeed, remains elusive to this day. Despite the American setbacks, and the extreme unpredictability of the Trump regime, over trade protection, over Iran, over the 'fire and fury' handling of North Korea, and even over Russia, the bulk of British official opinion clings doggedly to what used to be called the 'special relationship', long after its nature has in reality changed radically.

Now along comes this even bigger new reality of China. How is Britain to measure up to that? Napoleon long ago warned that when China awoke it would shake the world. And the British Prime Minister, Benjamin Disraeli, once proclaimed that Britain should become 'an Asian power'. Disraeli was, of course, referring to Britain's Indian empire. However, what will happen when modern China and modern India start talking about a partnership instead of pursuing endless disputes, as Xi Jinping plainly seeks to do in his persistent courting of Prime Minister Narendra Modi?

This is Asian power on a new scale and, for Britain, the testing moment has arrived. Brexit may be a headache but there is an entirely new agenda calling. The power, wealth and ubiquitous influence of China leaves Britain no choice but to adjust its stance, for reasons of both prosperity and hard global strategy. From relying on its membership of so many twentieth-century international and multilateral institutions, from the permanent membership of the UN Security Council downwards, it is now confronted by a string of twenty-first century international networks and bodies in which, or alongside which, Britain needs to be active.[119] If British diplomats and policy-makers still believe these regions are of lesser importance then they have another think coming. In the next five years the regions connected by Belt and Road linkages will account for 46 per cent of total world growth. That will be about twice that of North America and four times that of Europe.

The section of the world we loosely call Asia now contains far the largest part of the world's population (five-billion out of seven) and which, between now and the mid-century, is set to generate the overwhelming proportion of world economic growth. Parag Khanna puts it at $30-trillion for Asia against $1-trillion for 'the West'. These figures, rough though they may be, remind us that, while sheer numbers of people seemed to mean little (the phrase 'teeming Asia' rings from the past), today, as 'people' turn into swelling consumer markets, numbers means economic weight and, coming hard on its heels, political power, on a scale and at a speed never before comprehended.

What they also show is how Asian societies want quality government first and foremost. By this they mean excellent education, reliable social and home security, well-regulated market freedom, combined with environmental improvement. Corrupt regimes and self-serving elites cannot deliver these things – or not for long. Sensitive technocracies can and do. Where a genuine rule of law prevails, applying to both governors and governed, so much the better. But authoritarian regimes can do as well – increasingly so if advanced data technology allows them to pick up and respond swiftly to public desires and ambitions – possibly more efficiently than unstable and constantly shifting multiparty coalitions.

The kernel of the issue, the hardest part of all for British policy-makers in particular to crack – is that the Asian issue is the flip side of the American issue. The two aspects are inextricably woven together. Many of Britain's leaders remain immersed in the habitual idea that the USA is the fountainhead of security and technology, with the deepest capital markets and the largest military power (in conventional terms of sheer spend). In the words of a very recent official Foreign and Commonwealth statement of British foreign policy priorities in the digital age: 'The UK has a special and enduring relationship with the US based on our long history and commitment to shared values. We are natural, resilient and strong allies and we do more together than any other two countries in the world. The US–UK security and defence relationship is central to our interests.'[120]

It would be hard to put it more bluntly than that, nor find more definitive proof of the lag in understanding of how Britain's position in a new world of networks and Asianisation has to change.

But there is one more area where British – and indeed all Western – thinking has yet to connect fully with the size and power of Asia. In the central issue of climate change, Asia (Pacific and Central) is now by far the biggest factor. Asian energy consumption, which was 18 per cent of the global total in 1980, is now (2019) just under 50 per cent. And this is the half which is growing fast, while Western levels shrink.

Carbon emissions at world level are still rising far too fast. The biggest rise for seven years was recorded in 2018, reducing the Paris Climate Change Accord of 2016 (signed up to by 191 countries) to mere gesture diplomacy. The battle to curb carbon emissions will be won or lost entirely in China, India, Indonesia and South-East Asia generally.

Even in the USA, which still has far the highest energy consumption per person, total carbon emissions have been falling fast until recently, thanks to the huge switch from coal to cheap gas, although now they, too, are starting to rise again.

Most Asian countries will continue to rely on coal for the bulk of their swelling energy needs, while also being, as in China's case, the biggest importers of oil (China buys in nine-million-plus barrels a day). The best that Europe can offer to halt climate change is example. Britain has come quite near its targets (although at the cost of heavy energy cost burdens) with Germany the worst big performer in Europe (thanks to banning nuclear expansion and burning more coal), and France the best (still with largely nuclear electricity).

Overall, the European contribution to curbing emissions is statistically negligible. The real impact in fending off climate upheaval can only come from major advances in renewable energy in the Asian giants (including big further cost reductions), from breakthroughs in cleaner coal and in electricity storage methods and, above all, from carbon-free nuclear power – which again has to become much cheaper to build. Reaching into a utopian future, global agreements on carbon taxes will be essential.

While the last can be no more than a wish for now (requiring, as it does, virtual world government), Asian progress on the other fronts is quite encouraging. Solar and wind costs are falling fast, coal-burning for electricity is being cleaned and curbed, and Asian technology is delivering nuclear power plants at increasingly competitive costs. Ultimately, cheap, super-safe nuclear power could prove the lowest carbon economic source of all for Asia's massive electricity requirements. End-use efficiency is also rising, but net consumption is rising much faster.

Already China, Korea (and also Russia) are becoming the suppliers of choice in nuclear power to the Middle East and to the Indian sub-continent. China's nuclear power reach also already extends deep into Britain, to an extent of which the British media and public seem largely unaware.[121]

Thanks to poor and inaccurate teaching, a similar unawareness about the real sources of the climate threat extends to parts of the younger generation, including climate 'activists' and school children. Protest and concern are understandable. But they should be aimed not at the UK's good performance, but at policies in regions where emissions continue to rise and which will heat the atmosphere everywhere regardless of good and bad performers and regardless of national boundaries. It is Asian technocracy, rather than Western democracy, to which the world will have to look to save itself from a frighteningly disruptive climate future.

In the front line of threatened communities are the many island and coastal states of both the Caribbean and the Indian and South Pacific Oceans, and of sub-Saharan Africa. This makes the fifty-three-nation Commonwealth 'club' especially important in providing focused and tailored help to island states and African Commonwealth countries, as explained in the next chapter.

It is going to mean new engagement with global networks and political pressures which barely register at present on Western agendas, and for which Western protest movements and costly interventionist green policy gestures are no substitute (and in some instances, such as with Germany's *energiewende*, ineffective and counterproductive).[122]

British adjustment to these realities, which are already upon us, requires a new governmental and parliamentary focus. Forty years of seeing the world through the EU prism have to be dismantled. Seventy-five years of looking almost exclusively to the USA for security have be unravelled. Closer to home, a cluster of EU-related committees of in the Westminster Parliament have to be redirected. Government departments have to switch long-standing priorities. Maybe a new and powerful Whitehall department is called for – an ultra-strong Ministry for Asian Affairs.

If that is where the future lies, that is where both Britain's hard resources and its considerable soft diplomatic power must now be deployed with the utmost concentration and effort.

A Note on a Sensitive Aspect of UK–China Relations, Namely Hong Kong

This period of accelerating Asian economic , and then political, power and influence coincided with my decade long chairmanship of the

House of Commons Foreign Affairs Committee. One of the trickiest times we faced was in June 1996 when the Committee transferred to Hong Kong and set up shop in the old Legco building (Legislative Council Building) to conduct an enquiry into rising tensions as the 1997 handover day approached. It was widely assumed in Hong Kong that we were an official government review committee and we probably fostered this impression by requiring all our witnesses to start by taking an oath about giving the whole truth, etc. Martin Lee refused to comply.

Most Hong Kong citizens at that time were getting nervous and wanted proper British passports in case they needed to escape to Britain – an influx which would have truly dynamised the British economy, though it was not quite clear where they would settle. Anyway, they weren't going to get this precious document and we had no power to help them. Tension was heightened by the head-on squabble which seemed to have arisen between the Beijing authorities and the governor, Chris Patten, with insults flying on all sides.

When I polled them, most of my committee felt Patten had erred and tripped into an unnecessary spat with the Chinese over a complicated but quite minor issue – to do with how local councillors were to be elected after the hand-over. However, I felt it necessary to have a report which did not overtly criticise the governor. My feelings were divided since, before he left for Hong Kong, Chris Pattern had courteously taken the trouble to visit me at my house in Pimlico and ask what I thought his priority should be. When he had said there might be room for 'scoring a few points on the blind side', I had nodded in acquiescence. In fact, there turned out to be no 'blind side', just a lot of apprehension-inducing Chinese fury. I was certainly not in a position to join the critics and we managed to produce a final report which offered reasonably balanced advice about Hong Kong's future and prospects, despite the very strong representations from old 'China hands', like Sir Percy Cradock, that Chris Patten and the British Government were mad to get up Beijing's nose so unnecessarily.

After Hong Kong, the committee moved on to Beijing and were entertained by the ambassador, Sir Donald Donaldson. He and his advisers assured us that the regime was rock solid, although there had been fragments of news filtering through about riots in distant Chinese cities. However, there would be no big upheaval here in the capital. All would remain quiet. We were free, we were told to wander up the road to Tiananmen Square and chat to some of the students squatting there, which we did. Six days later the tanks arrived and Tiananmen Square exploded, creating a global sensation.

Hong Kong will prosper and remain a 'super-connector' between Western and Chinese business. The technological facts of life will ensure that. Modern China needs the free-market 'valve' of the Hong Kong Special Administrative Region' as a component part of its complex and evolving state-and-market mix.

But the tensions over the interpretations of democratic governance will continue and are an inherent feature of the digital age, and of its paradoxes. Here, as everywhere, we see working the push-me-pull-you strain between local freedom and central strategic power, between identity and the necessary connection and collaboration, between we-us-ourselves – each with the colossal new power and reach in our handsets and on our screens – and the counter-magnet of belonging and being securely embedded in the bigger cradle of networks and algorithms, without which survival for any community is impossible.

The vast Hong Kong street protests in the summer of 2019 against Chinese extradition plans mark one more stage in this unending process. The conflict between Hong Kong civil liberties and the Chinese imperium can never be settled in conventional Western political terms or in the language of the pre-digital age.

For Britain the key will be how quickly, and with what agility, the strategic mindset can be adjusted away from twentieth-century Western thinking and towards operating in a world of numerous new and evolving networks which provide the entrée to the new power centres, the new pace-setters and the markets of the future.

That will require new kinds and techniques of engagement on many fronts. But there is one network above all to which Britain has ready access, more by luck than by planning, and which offers both a new role and an inspiring way into the new international world order.

Chapter Sixteen

The Mother of All Networks

*The Commonwealth: 'A soft power network which
represents the realities of a changing world,'*

—former Australian Prime Minister, Tony Abbott

W E are now moving fast into a world of networks and
supply chains of infinite complexity. To prosper, even
to survive, Britain has to lay hold of every available
instrument, asset and connection it can find. All along, some of
us have argued for, pleaded with, begged officialdom to recognise
that one of Britain's best, but most under-used access routes into
this new milieu is the vast system of Commonwealth links and
ties with which (more by good luck than good planning) we
happen to be embedded.

* * * * *

On 22 November 1995 the Foreign Affairs Committee of the House
of Commons at Westminster issued a report. The report contained a
revolutionary message. The message was that the Commonwealth, far
from being a redundant organisation, was transforming into a modern
network of enormous potential, both economic and political.

From the UK point of view, it argued that this network offered
new opportunities which should be recognised and seized and indeed
exploited with vigour and imagination.

171

The view that Commonwealth relations had become the Cinderella in the shaping of British foreign policy and the promotion of British interests, although refuted by ministers who appeared as witness to the inquiry, seemed all too clear to the committee. The report urged a stronger emphasis on the Commonwealth dimension right across the government as a whole.

The report concluded that 'the Commonwealth is acquiring a new significance in a rapidly emerging world'. Policymakers, it urged, should bring this major change to the forefront of their thinking.

The message went nowhere. A tepid response came from the Government some six months later, assuring the committee that ministers would 'discuss the priorities', that they were 'conscious' of the advantages which the Commonwealth links could bestow on British companies and institutions, and would examine how these links 'could be used to best effect'.

However, that was it. The rest was silence. Hardly any of the recommendations from the committee were put into effect. Within the Whitehall hierarchy the Commonwealth remained a fractional part of its concerns. The Commonwealth Office had long since vanished, as had the post of Commonwealth Secretary. Inside the Foreign and Commonwealth Office (FCO) a handful of officials were still struggling to keep the issue alive at all. Indeed, within a few years, trendy voices in the Foreign Office would be arguing that the name of the department should be changed and the word Commonwealth dropped forever from its title. Fortunately, they were frustrated.

A year or so after the report, the government changed and the preoccupations of the new administration turned elsewhere. Some speeches about the Commonwealth were made by the Labour Government's eloquent new Foreign Secretary, Robin Cook, but he was almost alone in doing so. Little or no action followed. Minds were elsewhere as New Labour discovered its new-found interest in the European Union and addressed European issues with the zeal of converts. In effect the Commonwealth sank from sight, or at least from the sight of policy-makers, opinion-formers and the Westminster world.

From one source, almost alone, came the reminder that the modern Commonwealth was a hidden asset. That source was Her Majesty The Queen and members of her family. While ministers in successive governments looked the other way, her insistence, in line with her very first vows as monarch, was that it would prove, in her words, 'to be in many ways the face of the future'[123] not the past.

In the preceding Thatcher years there had been little time for the Commonwealth as an entity. Like most people, Thatcher wanted to see the ugly apartheid situation ended, but – again like many people – she wanted to see it happen gradually and without violence. In an era of increasing intolerance and polarised debate, any kind of moderation was, of course, labelled reactionary.

Zimbabwe was the other Commonwealth-connected issue of the 1980s. Christopher Soames carefully manoeuvred the situation towards peaceful handover – not to the preferred leader, Joshua Nkomo, but, facing political reality, to ZANU-PF leader Robert Mugabe. Margaret Thatcher attended the Lusaka Commonwealth Heads of Government Meeting (CHOGM), danced with Kenneth Kaunda and was on best behaviour. Everyone was pleased and the final phase of Zimbabwe independence was navigated in April 1980.

However, that was it. The Commonwealth network played no further part in British foreign policy from then on.

Today the situation has changed beyond recognition. In place of a lonely single-numbers group within the Foreign and Commonwealth Office, a lively Cabinet Office unit was set up in 2017 focusing entirely on the issues and on the preparations for a major Commonwealth summit, held in London in April 2018. At one stage, between sixty and eighty officials were at work where six had struggled before. For the first time in history both Buckingham Palace and Windsor Castle opened doors for conference activities.

More recently the Cabinet Office unit has been moved back to the Foreign and Commonwealth Office, but on a much larger scale than before and with firm cross-government, interdepartmental links. Meetings of Commonwealth trade ministers had already been revived[124] and Commonwealth education ministers now meet regularly and generate new ideas. Cyber and intelligence co-operation is being expanded, especially with India, building on the already close ties with Australia and Canada.

After more than twenty years, the Commonwealth is beginning to be viewed anew from London and across the nation, as it was urged to be all that time ago. The contrast between the 1990s and today could hardly be greater.

How has this extraordinary, if very belated, change come about? For some, it is the culmination of years of persistent argument, advanced through many channels to a hitherto largely disinterested media, that a great opportunity was being missed. For others the trigger has been the British decision to leave the EU. Without a doubt this has led to a sharp revival of Whitehall interest in wider global networks of which the Commonwealth is undoubtedly one, possibly the biggest.

However, in truth, the build-up to the new mindset has been taking shape spasmodically over many years, driven by a number of forces bigger than any government. As it has slowly dawned that some of the Commonwealth economies offer the fastest growing middle-income consumer markets of all times, a different message has begun to sink in. Those who had previously viewed the Commonwealth as a left-over liability, marginal to Britain's future prospects, now found they were looking at something entirely new.

Between the world of the Seventy-Niners and the world today, a very different Commonwealth network has opened up. The failure to grasp this earlier had its roots not just in static political thinking but in a much deeper conceptual error. This was the tendency to assume that trade was purely about commercial dealings. In practice, trade is about trust – more so than ever today when at least half of international transactions are in the form of services rendered, data transmitted, information shared and knowledge-filled products delivered.

In the digital age this is the part of international trade and exchange that will grow fastest. It is already doing so. Trust is generated by familiarity and reassurance, which in turn spring from such things as common language, common standards, common attitudes to the law, common educational and cultural links, common values and maybe common origins. The modern Commonwealth fits this model like a glove.

Present levels of export from Britain to the rest of the Commonwealth are low – certainly compared with trade with European neighbours and with the United States. Therefore, in the minds of leading policy-makers (and alas, this includes a succession of senior UK Foreign Office officials), the priority for increased engagement is low. That is the static assessment.

The mistake is a specific example of the problem which gives economic theory generally such difficulties and which leads to so few successes in predicting the future and the best way of preparing for it – as was noted in Chapter Three. The downbeat assessment seals off the wider complexities and unexpected twists and turns in human behaviour. While some sophisticated models of economic and trade theory attempt to project their narrow data into broader patterns of behaviour, what most economists offer is a much too limited canvas. Even a degree of solid verification against other disciplines and other 'externalities', such as biology, psychology, the natural sciences and even the weather, would help. This is what the philosopher Edward Wilson, already referred to earlier, calls 'consilience' – the bringing to bear of all the disciplines to avoid at least some of the so-called 'exogenous shocks' (what Taleb calls 'black swans') that seem invariably to falsify economic and foreign policy forecasts, at such a dreadful cost, and leave diplomacy floundering. More still of this in the next chapter.

One thing that is clear is that this is not just an argument about the Commonwealth; behind it lies a much bigger story. Down the years, a case has grown for a fundamental change in Britain's foreign policy strategy and in the way Britain views itself in a rapidly changing world landscape. Long before Brexit it had become increasingly clear that it was no longer enough for Britain, in the new conditions of the twenty-first century, to see its main destiny as lying within Europe.

The staggering expansion of communications technology, the implications of the rise of Asia and the extraordinary changes in the past two decades brought about by this latest wave of globalisation all conspired, long before Brexit, to impel Britain to rethink its world position.

Seemingly by chance, the decision was made at the Commonwealth Heads of Government in Malta in November 2015 to locate the next conference in London early in 2018, at which point Britain would take over the chairmanship of the Commonwealth itself, previously held by Malta and before that by Sri Lanka.

The decision at Malta that Britain should be the next Commonwealth HGM host had nothing to do with Brexit and was made at a time before many people saw the Brexit decision as at all likely. How the decision was made is not clear, although there were certainly some articulate voices urging this course. Perhaps it should be put down to serendipity. Indeed, that the Commonwealth leaders were meeting at Malta in the first place, rather than Mauritius as earlier intended, was due to a chance conversation in an aeroplane between the Maltese Prime Minister, Joseph Muscat, and Mauritian leaders, with Muscat learning in casual conversation that Mauritius was backing out and agreeing to take its place. This tumble of events provides a classic example of the way chance factors coincide and, in doing so, alter the pattern of history.

The Commonwealth connection is by no means the only answer to Britain's post-Brexit role in the world. At the risk of repetition, in a world of expanding networks driven by algorithms of unimaginable power and influence, the Commonwealth is one network among them – large, admittedly not strong in every sinew, and very widely misunderstood.

Its potential derives not from any central authority or government strategy but from almost the opposite – namely that power now lies increasingly with the grass roots, and with the myriad impulses of markets, interests, professions, civil society groups of almost every kind, and individuals, as well as with cities, as much as it does with states.

This is an entirely different world, a web rather than a diplomatic chessboard and it happens, by nobody's plan, that the Commonwealth structure has evolved in a manner uniquely suited to it.

Every prejudice will find a little on which to feed in the Commonwealth story. Some still sneer at it as pure nostalgia, without seeing that everything has a changed. One misguided official even tried to label the new interest as Empire 02.

When all is said and done, the forces which are pulling the Commonwealth together are getting much stronger, than the forces pulling it apart. The failure lies in the inadequacy of statistics to reflect this, in the inability of forecasters to surmise what is coming and, perhaps greatest of all, in the blind disregard of the giant global networks and their algorithmic engines which pursue their own agendas at every level of human activity, regardless of national governments and their intentions.

Not Alternatives

The Commonwealth today is the newest and most dramatic example of a network in the modern sense, living and growing as all networks do. The successful expansion of free trade depends not just on World Trade Organization (WTO) rules but on trust and affinities between trading entities. That is the Commonwealth 'premium' – the estimate that the conduct of intra-Commonwealth trade and investment costs some 19 per cent less than the global average, thanks to common language and background legal, financial and general cultural affinities.

The Commonwealth summit and gathering of more than fifty heads of government in April 2018 was rated a big success. It presented a massive opportunity for Britain to set its new direction in the transformed international conditions unfolding before us in the twenty-first century. Britain's withdrawal from the European Union treaties is a part, but only a part, of this new scene. The Commonwealth network and a vibrant flourishing Europe are not alternatives.

However, one crucial and differentiating factor about the Commonwealth needs always to be borne in mind: Unlike the EU, it is more than an assembly of governments and officials within a strong central hierarchy; it is a network of peoples – far the largest and most extensive in the planet. And, like all large networks in the modern digital age, it behaves and develops in ways that conventional thinking and conventional diplomacy find hard to explain or keep track of.

Some call it the fourth industrial revolution. Some call it the second globalisation wave. Whatever the label, it is unquestionably the hour of the Commonwealth network, linking up no less than 2.4-billion peoples, a third of the world population, larger than any nation – larger still, by a head, than Facebook.

Trendy historians and journalists churn out books and columns nowadays about global networks and clusters and their predominance in the pattern of international events, as though they were new discoveries. However, these are developments which some have been pointing out ever since the digital age began some thirty to forty years ago. This is the reason we now see the world and the UK's position within it, in terms of 'old links and new ties'[125] or, to use the former Prime Minister Theresa May's language, in 'old alliances and new partners'.

The hub-and-spoke model of the past typically put Britain at the centre of a sort of wheel with lines extending out to all our Commonwealth partners, now fifty-three in number (with more lining up to join). The network-and-cluster concept is quite different. Instead of links from a central point to the various points on the rim, there emerges a fantastic network of linkages without any particular centre. In the case of the Commonwealth, this currently means not fifty-three connections but 1,326 individual connections – a very different story.

Is such a network possible or practical? Yes, in the digital age it is. Of course, some of the linkages will be stronger between bigger trading partners and associates and some will be thinner, but the modern network is a pattern without a dominant or dictating centre. Furthermore, because networks talk to other networks all the time, it is a continuously growing system so, unless one is deliberately exclusive, fantastic sets of linkages open up and, in effect, lead to networking the entire planet.

While national borders will remain in some form, time-consuming impediments to trade flows will be largely eradicated by split-second digital clearance. Decisions from official authorities will become instant. Customs officers and much of the paraphernalia of frontiers will become redundant.

All networks, of course, require a framework or what used to be called, in the language of the past, a hierarchy of control and governance. Today the old links about which we are talking provide the framework (in some cases, such as Hong Kong, quite regardless of national boundaries). Meanwhile, the new ties provide the explosion of connections and gravitational effects which now govern international trade, made vastly more powerful day-by-day with the emergence of new technologies such as block chains, which allow the ever-multiplying part of the microchip to handle and validate the commands, wishes and opinions of tens of millions of people instantaneously. There has been nothing like it in human history. Even the largest super-powers have to accept nowadays that they are part of this ever-evolving global network of networks.

However, in making sense of this new world two cardinal points need to be born in mind. The first is that the successful expansion of free trade depends not just on WTO rules[126] but on trust and affinities between trading entities. In more practical terms, successful trade depends upon intimate and closely linked patterns of finance, trade insurance, common approaches on tax, interpreting a range of regulations and, above all, on a degree of trust.

This is a pattern which has to be replicated in relation to every market. An American shipper exporting into the European Union has to conform with a vast variety of EU regulations and legal requirements as well, and — dare I say it — with the rulings of the European Court of Justice. The same goes for Chinese or Japanese exporters into the EU. And the same will go for the UK, too, whatever the final outcome of our negotiations with the EU. Every market has its rules.

When exporting into the EU, just as much as into the USA, or China, or India, or Commonwealth countries, trust is the key and trust comes in many forms. It is worth noting that the present badmouthing of the European Union by some of my countrymen, and the constant reference to UK negotiations with it as seeking a deal with a hostile body, when it should really be described as an agreement with friends and neighbours, hardly helps build up this trust we are going to need in that direction.

What those who yearned for 'a clean break' failed to appreciate is that successful and open trade in any region or any part of the global market, under WTO rules (under which more than half UK trade now operates anyway), far from automatically ensuring a nirvana of flowing trade volumes, requires a massive amount of conformity with the systems, habits and jurisdictions of other markets. As argued above and in the case of the Commonwealth, trade requires trade *relations* – a whole hinterland of connections, understandings and friendships. They extend into fields far away from narrow business dealings, such as education, medicine, security and defence, energy and climate change concerns.

The Commonwealth's network characteristics make it especially suitable for focusing in the most practical ways on the specific environmental problems and fears of the many small island and coastal states who are part of the 'club' or 'family'. While climate issues are certainly being addressed (if not all that successfully) at global level, via the UN, etc., the vastly varied and detailed needs of different small communities tend to get lost in the generalities and preoccupations with the big offender nations. This makes the Commonwealth the ideal forum in which to shape responses to the precise needs of the long string of small islands around the world and the coastal ocean states of Africa, who happen to be part of the network.

Another highly relevant point is that services are the new growth area in international trade. They now make up a quarter of all trade receipts. McKinsey suggests that more than half the wealth generated by international trade comes from services and various forms of data transmission.[127] All the trends point to much more expansion of trade in this form, especially with the growth of digital fabrication.

It is good that the British Government is aiming for a new global services trade framework because the services aspect of the European single market has yielded very slim pickings over the years. Trust is the key ingredient when it comes to trade in services, data and knowledge products. And remember that the UK is overwhelming a services economy (83 per cent of GDP is the latest – 2018 – figure.)[3].

Trust also means a high degree of mutual respect. It means treating the citizens of the particular country with whom one is dealing in a respectful and sympathetic way. It means making one's nation attractive in all respects, and exemplary. It is quite deplorable that, in British

---

3   although always be careful of these fixed categorisations in a fluid and
    evolving economic process.

attitudes to students from India, we have deliberately discriminated in a hostile way, halving the number of Indian students in Britain, seeing them diverted to America and to Germany, and making life as difficult as possible for many other newcomers and visitors from India. That is not the right basis for trust and no satisfactory expansion of trade will be built without it. Our actions harm ourselves, harm our brilliant universities and the Commonwealth.

So, while world free trade is a powerful force for good (and, indeed, the key means nowadays of upholding a rules-based order), as previously outlined, the key ingredient is trust and its supporting pillars of common language, common values, standards and above all, respect for the rule of law, underpinned by close affinities and feelings of fair dealings, friendship and cultural and educational exchange.

Nowadays it is called soft power. It is no surprise that China, like many other nations, is investing on a very large scale, dwarfing Western efforts, in soft power and persuasion of all kinds.[128]

The Commonwealth has emerged in the digital age in a way that is organic rather than governmental. It is increasingly woven together not so much by governmental linkages and directives but by professions, civil society and interest networks of incredible density and power, all *outside* the governmental range.

Examples are the networks of scientists, schools and universities, creative industries, parliamentarians, doctors, financiers, farming reformers, veterinary experts, engineers, architects, environmentalists, women's groups of all kinds and all ages, energy and climate specialists, judges, lawyers, small business promoters – the list goes on and on. These are the skills and binding forces which generate trust and attract capital investment, from which trade follows.

Networks connect with other networks all the time; they never rest. sleep. Networks allow the opening of links for the United Kingdom through the Commonwealth to the great trading groups in Southeast Asia, such as Mark Two ASEAN (the Association of Southeast Asian Nations), the emerging trading groups around the Indian Ocean, the entirely new networks and clusters forming in Central Asia, in Africa and in Latin America, the Pacific Alliance, the Comprehensive and

Progressive Agreement for Trans-Pacific Partnership,[129] and to the North American Free Trade Agreement (NAFTA).

Above all, we should expect to see massive connections grow between like-minded networks of democracies (the Commonwealth again, for example) and the great China networks, clusters and global supply chains now snaking across the world. These are bound to expand with the (BRI) Belt Road Initiative and the tying up of Chinese, Central Asian and European markets as never before in history. And, of course, all this has to move forward with the necessary infrastructure of finance, trade facilitation, insurance, and so on.

These connections are already producing new levels of relationships between China and the UK and between China and the network of Commonwealth countries.

This is the new world which leaves the old twentieth-century centralised European model of integration and protection far behind. Indeed, in this new age, the Commonwealth has been described as the 'the mother of all networks'. It may not yet be quite that but, through the energy of its peoples, the understanding of its leaders and the unstoppable powers of communications technology, that is what it is destined to become.

This is an odyssey unfinished, with one enduring and central fact standing out, just as clearly as it did to some of us twenty-three years ago, at the time of that first parliamentary report: In the age of digital revolution – disrupting, connecting, empowering, challenging – the Commonwealth network continues to acquire, momentum, potential and significance on a scale hitherto unimaginable. The transformation continues in a radically changed international landscape, driven by immense new forces. This is what makes it both a key feature of the future, both for Britain and for the global trade concourse. Today's Commonwealth, six times as large in membership as in 1949, and transformed by total connectivity, has entered a third age.

Above all, this massive and unstoppable exercise in connectivity means that the Commonwealth assumes, or reassumes, a central place in our nation's overseas priorities and policies; it becomes a vast transmission system in the exercise of soft power.

This may not be what national governments or political leaders planned or intended. Indeed, in the British case, such an outcome has been actively resisted for decades until very recent times. Positive official and governmental policies obviously assist, but with or without them the networks carry on expanding.

While, at government level, Commonwealth countries may differ and clash, beneath the media radar, the networking process continues – each new connection sparking fresh initiatives and activity, leading to further contacts with yet further networks beyond. Thus, on a 'friend of a friend' basis, entrée to the twenty-first century global system of networks and institutions truly opens up to us.

Chapter Seventeen

Flaws in the Tapestry

'Societies snap when they are bent by forces for which
they are not prepared.'

—Joshua Cooper Ramo[130]

'Great crises come when great new forces are at work
changing fundamental conditions, while powerful
institutions and traditions still hold old systems intact.'

—William Graham Sumner, 1904[131]

IT has been contended in previous chapters that, in contrast to the last century, technology now gives us intellectual mastery of the truths of our universe and the dilemmas of the human condition on a scale and to an extent never before believed possible. This is what Edward O. Wilson, dubbed by some 'the new Darwin', sought to explain about the coming unification and synthesis of all aspects of science and knowledge into a manageable frame.[132] Now it seems possible.

So, is this Gutenberg all over again but on a vastly greater scale? I think it is. A flood of information and connectivity has swept across the simple tableau of free markets and free trade – the dreams of '79 – and turned assumptions and beliefs of that period on their head.

Take assumption *numero uno* of the late 20th century that only in a context of political freedom and the rule of law could the capitalist 'system' work successfully: that capitalism succeeds wherever markets are liberalised, and that this would only be possible under democracy. Wealth, it was firmly asserted, including new wealth, would trickle down. Marx was proclaimed wrong; Fukuyama seemed right; Hayek had been right. The old Left–Right battle of rival economic models was settled, with the liberal, capitalist order the clear winner. It might not be the end of political history but in economic terms it was, it seemed, the clear end of the struggle between state collectivism and market forces operating within the democratic liberal order.

That was 1979 and that was what we believed. What do we make of it forty years later when the world's second largest economy, China, is soaring ahead on different principles? What do we make of it when what we had been persuaded to see as the triumphant capitalist 'system' gave us (in 2008) a financial collapse comparable to the great crash of 1929? And what do we make of it when the prized capitalism 'system', mutating into something very different – perhaps not even a system at all but a vastly complex process – fails to deliver the trickle-down blessings expected of it and loses much of its popular appeal?

Before the onset of turbo-boosted globalisation from the 1990s onwards, some kind of popularised capitalism seemed a reasonable and valid goal. In the early Thatcher days, after the initial wobbles of the first eighteen months, the opportunities for moving along this path and for encouraging the emergence of a benign and socially balanced form of modern capitalism, with the benefits shared widely, markets sensibly regulated and those most vulnerable to free-market upheaval carefully cushioned, seemed attainable. Competition, enterprise and innovation, with the benefits widely shared, had to offer a better future than had the corporate socialist, centralised stagnation and post-war consensus mentality which had blocked everything and damaged everybody.

However, the shift was going to be gradual and moderated – blending the practical with the economically literate, sensibly combining free-market liberalisation with sensitive conservatism, as far as was possible in the rough sea of events.

This was also Margaret Thatcher's original view, contrary to many assertions. In the midst of one long working evening at Flood Street I recall her saying she hoped never to become associated with an 'ism', certainly not with anything that might be called Thatcherism. We would go step by step. And to ensure this went ahead as planned, some of us, led by John Hoskyns, began to put together the pathway document – a map – 'Stepping Stones'.

John Hoskyns was very keen that the 'Stepping Stones' momentum should be kept up. In December 1981, when things were not going brilliantly for the Thatcher administration (to put it as its mildest) he persuaded David Wolfson[133] to make his spacious house at Westwell available for a 'think' weekend at which some of us would give new drive to the grand 'Thatcher revolution'. This was to be the new 'Stepping Stones'. It was attended by Hoskyns, Cecil Parkinson (by then party chairman), Alan Walters, Norman Lamont, Douglas Hague and me. Nigel Lawson had to cancel.

In his superb account, *Just in Time*,[134] (far the best account by someone in the thick of it) Hoskyns describes the two days we spent in considerable comfort at Westwell trying to think ourselves out of a depressing situation and to reignite the government's main themes. According to the opinion polls, the Prime Minister's popularity was at rock bottom, the Tories were generally hated, the economy was still reeling from the 1980–81 oil shock, monetary policy was widely misunderstood and the chances of winning another election, two years ahead, seemed minimal. A lot of discussing and drafting took place and I remember coming away with a feeling, for the first time since 1978, before the election, that some kind of strategic pathway was emerging out of the morass.

The popular legend is that the Falklands War restored Margaret Thatcher's sliding fortunes and put her into winning mode. However, long before the Falklands, there were signs of a change in the public mood. Whether the Westwell gathering made any difference, I have no idea but for the first time in eighteen months it felt that we had regained our balance and knew where we were going, albeit at a gradual pace, ideology-light but building up the common ground in a steady and sensible way. Mouthing free-market generalities and capitalism's virtues was not going to get us through. A new kind of popular capitalism could now be unfolded.

That was not how it turned out, nor was it how the Prime Minister regarded the operation when she learnt about it the following week. She was furious that ministers had been caballing in country places – not so much with the idea as with the fact that she had not been there or been told about it. We all had a blasting.

Nor in the longer term did the Westwell step-by-step approach prevail. Unfortunately for John Hoskyns, and for all of us, politics does not happen in steps; it lurches from one event to another, one new crisis to the next. We were attempting to bring together the methods of the business world, where strategies could be devised and followed and made to work, with the political world where, more like the military at war, strategies did not survive the first encounters with reality. Instead, the best way to proceed with any degree of coherence lay in narrative rather than strategy, a constant weaving of events into purposes – an unending process quite different from those solid one-by-one stepping stones. In politics, the river of events washes half of them away.

Not only was the Falklands episode, with its own trumpets and cheerleaders, about to burst on us but, as time went by in the '80s, the tone of moderation was replaced by a more strident and ideological shrillness which started to pervade the Thatcher narrative. It was this tone, of course, which undermined her in the end and paved the way to the 1997 defeat of the Conservatives, despite John Major's greater emollience. Tony Blair was presented with an open goal.

Even then, in the early Blair years which followed after 1997, the general direction towards market economics seemed right. It was, it seemed, the 'end of history' so confidently spelled out by Francis Fukuyama. Whether over-hyped or not, the 'force' seemed firmly with market liberalisation world-wide. Democracy was about to spread everywhere – even in the crumbling Soviet Union, perhaps even in China. With a Labour Government elected by a large majority still talking of free markets and pressing forward with privatisation plans, there seemed to be no alternative. If there was something that could be called the Thatcher dream, despite its detractors and distorters, this was it.

Looking back one can see it now. One can see how, beneath the surface of this apparent consensus, everything was changing fundamentally. The relatively cautious popular capitalism of early Thatcher was being destroyed by globalisation of a different degree – a hurricane replacing a high wind, bringing not bracing change but violent destruction.

Almost before people grasped what was happening, market liberalisation – which was supposed to work in favour of democracy and a sense of growing fairness – went into reverse gear. Instead of more competition, the system began working in favour of concentrations of power, completely unforeseen, of wild-west investment and banking, and of disruption and an inequality of rewards. As the millennium dawned, monopolies which free markets and free trade were meant to overthrow, were replaced by even bigger global monopolies, anchored at either end of the planet.[135] Forces bigger than governments and bigger than any ideological catechisms were taking over at speeds which very few analysts and policy-makers understood, attacking business, politics, warfare, science and the distribution and use of power itself.

Chapter Eighteen

What Is to Be Done?

THIS book is being written while yet another European Union crisis plays out. It is not the first and won't be the last. The inherent tension between the desire for control, the assertion of identity along with intense local and national loyalties, and the opposite pull of global forces, driven by insatiable consumer demand (with what people across the world in their billions actually want), is nothing new. But what is certainly new in the last decade is the empowerment and amplification of protest with the virulence and intensity that instant, cheap and universal communication now permits.

We saw earlier how the internet's first impact was to mobilise demonstration and protest in de-sovietising Central Europe with a speed and impact that amazed governments. Now we were heading for enraged populism on a scale fifty times more powerful.

Some of us could see the next wave in the EU problem coming a mile off and were convinced that the only way to prepare for it without a real bust-up was to go all out for fundamental EU reform and the reinvention of Europe on more modern, less centralised, less intrusive and more flexible principles (just as all sorts of voices, such as George Soros and numerous European populist leaders, have called for since).

By 2010, at the Foreign and Commonwealth Office, I was making little headway with most officials but I believe William Hague understood the coming danger. But, we were under the shadow of prime ministerial boredom with 'banging on about Europe'. I was repeatedly told that nothing in the way of a radical new European policy could be contemplated or promoted until the 'euro problem' had been solved – which it never will be, since it requires a degree of centralised sovereignty and political integration to which EU member states will never concede and for which Germany will never pay.

I recall thinking with absurd conceit when Cameron rang me in September 2012 that, with my departure, this modest pressure to prepare for a different future for Britain in a different Europe would fall into abeyance and we would drift along until the point of crisis came. Things on this front (the EU), I believed, would go downhill for the government from then on. Sadly, I was right. They did. The crisis came, the fundamental thinking about the EU never started, the experts said it was 'not on' and the issue blew the Cameron administration out of the water.

Nothing is more irritating than people who come along with 'I was right' stories after the event, so I'll leave it there, except to say that all this was set out in my book *Old Links and New Ties*, written in 2013, three years before the final breakaway vote. We could have developed new 'deep and special ties' with the changing EU and 'old friends and new partners' links with the rest of the world (Theresa May's familiar-sounding phrase) without the huge Brexit diversion. Events are now rapidly taking Europe this way (see Chapter Thirteen). However, it was not to be. A more disruptive course was inevitable, amplified to deafening level this time around not by politics but by technology.

The worst advice[136] was from those who insisted to Cameron that the fundamental principles of the old EU model could not be questioned. On the contrary, this was precisely the area of questioning and creative thinking that required a new approach. We can now see how the principles are crumbling, or at least being diluted into vague aspirations, notably the principle of free movement of persons as the pressure mounts from migrants and refugees from Africa, the Levant and Central Asia, and as frontier controls are tightened in almost every member country of the supposed single-market zone.

Free movement in Europe – originally 'of labour' under the Rome Treaty but quietly altered to 'of persons' under the Lisbon Treaty –

has long since gone. Barriers have gone up, borders have been closed, armed guards positioned. The UK should have been in the vanguard, designing new pan-European approaches to managing the refugee/migrant phenomenon in its swelling and mutated form. Instead David Cameron was 'sent in to bat' with a sorry little shopping list of British 'demands', more than half of which were rejected. The scene was well and truly set for the Brexit drama to begin unfolding with new rancour and venom.

Where does this leave us, the last of the Seventy-Niners, as we watch a younger generation flounder? The need to understand the 'large and complex forces' at work on our society, and their true roots, is as great as it was forty or fifty years ago and the means to do so infinitely greater. Yet the absence of a full understanding is as evident now as it was then, perhaps more so since the outside scene has gone into technology-propelled overdrive, unravelling the familiar world order at breakneck speed. Nassim Nicholas Taleb puts it well when he points to the difficulties economists have in escaping the straitjacket of static analysis and understanding that almost everything is moving and that all situations are in a constant state of flexible and interactive adjustment. Statistics and charts are, by definition, conveyors of fixed positions: fixed social patterns, fixed-point business behaviour and activity. What Taleb calls 'ergodicity' means that the probabilities of anything occurring are quite different to the calculated probabilities and certainties embedded in scientific statements and statistical 'evidence'.[137] Ruin is always around the corner, invalidating confident predictions.

If this was important to grasp before the digital age it is now a thousand times more so. Fluidity takes over – in assessments, in any analysis dependent on aggregates, in all concepts of alliance, in almost every judgment based on 'the facts', 'the evidence', the 'figures' and the statistics.

The debate about inequality provides a perfect example of the flaws in static analysis. People and wealth move around. At different stages in a person's life they may either be in the dispossessed category, the angry and resentful middle-income category (the biggest everywhere) or among the tiny top percentage soaked in wealth, whose affairs and lifestyles make the intelligentsia so obsessed about the inequality 'problem' (which is odd when one considers how deeply miserable many of the really rich are). The analysis is static but the real world is fluid and dynamic. Targeted and stereotyped categories and classes, against which measures to reduce inequality are aimed, melt away when lifted from statistics into real life, with all its varieties and unclassifiable eccentricities. Completely unintended targets and groups of people get hurt. The solutions to inequality which looked so good yesterday become counterproductive today and useless tomorrow.

Wealth, Pensions and, above All, Security

Nevertheless, here in Britain an absolute priority is to find new, more effective ways of sharing not only wealth, but the proceeds of the growth of wealth, to every household in the land. A system which simply brings the benefits of growth and expansion to those who already have capital, guaranteeing ever wider disparities in the distribution, of wealth, can no longer be tolerated nor contained within a politically stable and unified society.

This is what some of us have been campaigning for since the 1960s, as described in the previous chapter and in many books, of which Richard Cockett's *Thinking the Unthinkable*[138] is probably the best and most accurate. As he tells, we drew on the work of Louis Kelso, the Californian sage who, in his 1958 book *The Capitalist Manifesto*,[139] described how mass ownership of industry and enterprise could be the best antidote to the swelling and inflationary socialist state and to monopoly-friendly capitalism of the kind which is closing in on us now. The theory that this monopoly concentration of new wealth would trickle down to all was rightly derided but the answer was not to go back to the failed recipes of the state-dominated past but to turn the trickle into a genuine cascade of prosperity and security for almost all. It is possible and necessary.

I have beside me, as I write these paragraphs, Kelso's little green book, *The New Capitalists*,[140] which explains how the benefits of newly-formed wealth can be brought to every household, regardless of whether it already possesses any capital assets – and in doing so cuts clean through the ideologies of Left and Right.[141] This is the great

Lord Carrington. The calming influence. Told Willie Whitelaw to relax at the time of Operation Motorman. But he and Whitelaw were the stabilising influences in the Thatcher Cabinet later on. (Author's Collection)

Technology unravels the World Order, and the Political Order. (WikiCommons)

Tahrir Square 2012. Tyranny is overthrown; power takes to the streets but it does not lead to democracy, or anything like it. In Egypt it led straight to back to military rule – the classic Bonaparte model, but with cell phones and the web added. (WikiCommons)

Digitally organized protest 2018. A thousand towns and villages coordinated but with no leaders. BBC thought it was 'a new type of protest.' Not so. (iStock)

Karl Popper. The voice of warning against 'inevitable' trends, ideology and dogma. (WikiCommons)

Vaclav Havel. The Power of the powerless was the new 20th century message. But has it survived into the digital age? (WikiCommons)

The author with Havel's successor, Vaclav Klaus: the arch-Eurosceptic. But his free market instincts ran up against reality. (Author's collection)

Louis Kelso, who argued that wealth came from capital, not labour. (Wikipedia)

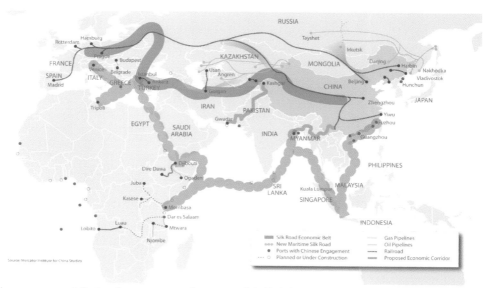

The many new Silk Roads penetrating the West – labelled the Belt and Road Initiative, with the Chinese insisting it was cooperation, not invasion. But what has it done to our Western politics? (Mercator Institute)

One more giant new mega-city: most are in Asia and Decades ahead of the West in both physical and social infrastructure. (iStock)

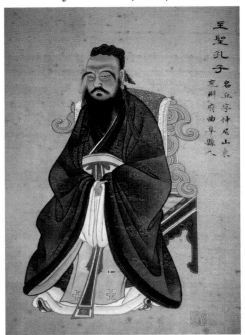

Confucius: Belief still prevails — and spreads — that Government rests on personal authority and virtue rather than law-based and constitutional authority. Can data technology make technocratic government more sensitive and more accountable than democratically elected. governments and parties? (WikiCommons)

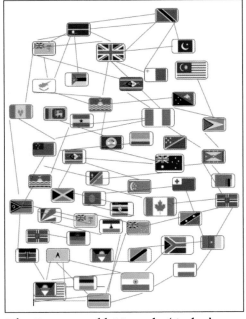

The Commonwealth Network. (Author's collection)

Head of the Commonwealth. Monarch greatly preferred to politicians. (Author's collection)

The Foreign and Commonwealth Office team 2010. Not allowed to 'bang on about Europe'. But with no positive reform strategy in the end it brought the whole administration down. (Author's collection)

The fastest train on earth — due to be in full operation in Japan in the mid-twenties. (Author's collection)

The end of the age-old conflict? Fighting yesterday's battles in tomorrow's world. (Public Domain)

forgotten work of the twentieth century which in time will prove as influential in shaping the world as Marx's *Das Kapital* – perhaps even more so.

What should by now be self-evident is that capitalism in the age of people empowerment needs to find new ways of sharing its benefits more widely. Means of wider capital ownership –not only ownership but participation in the actual growth of new wealth – at present confined to those who have savings already (if they are not too risk-averse) have to be found.

This is sometimes believed to be a new thought, promoted by the staggering sums delivered to certain clever individuals in the globalisation era (truly globalised earnings) versus the relatively modest growth, if any, in wage earnings or middle-class salaries.

In fact, there is nothing new about it all. The idea of wider personal ownership as the central goal of social policy, and of fully completed democracy, has been persistently advanced over the years by a handful of politicians and one or two economists and persistently ignored by almost everyone else. In particular, the academic and intellectual establishment has paid almost no attention to the wider ownership idea or its implications for the structure of society or the role of government.

Yet the notion of widespread personal ownership as a unifying antidote to impersonal collectivism and as an obvious escape route from the class war between wages and capital and from of the excesses of inequality, is far from new. In the 1940s, both Conservative and Liberal leaders in Britain strongly supported a variety of wider ownership ideas. Privatisation certainly widened ownership – although not enough.

The work of Thomas Piketty on this issue[142] – referred to earlier – has been much quoted and lauded – especially his thesis that modern capitalism inevitably and inexorably widens the gap between its ever-richer beneficiaries and the wage-dependent rest.

Missing from Piketty's thesis, and from the views of many others in this field, are the practical means (which he largely skims over) of spreading the ownership and security of capital more equitably in society. Instead of further attacking income with blunt and dubiously effective tax weapons, a much nobler and more practical focus should be on enabling more and more people to share in national wealth and its returns, thus acquiring the dignity, degree of security and, possibly, the sense of social obligation which ownership and earnership, confers.

Piketty half illuminates the dangers but fails to understand the remedies.

The mistake is to believe that we are still in a traditional capitalist age, when in practice, the shift away from formal work and wage structures and towards a more personalised capital-plus-income work pattern is already under way. For example, self-employment is growing at a phenomenal pace in the UK. There is an enormous surge of interest in almost every part of Britain – even including the allegedly 'dead' inner city areas – in small enterprise: how to get it going; how to be part of it; how, in short, to escape the deadweight of sole-income dependence.

Every magazine and newspaper Saturday supplement is now jammed with advice on getting a small enterprise up and running. 'Starting your own business' has long since ceased to be an impossible dream, it has become the subject of the most normal everyday discussion, along with house prices, planning and managing pension savings.

Even sleepy and floundering clearing banks are beginning to be less downright discouraging towards the would-be entrepreneur who, at the outset, has nothing but self-confidence and a few savings as security – though asking for a return of Mr 'Mannering', as the friendly local bank manager[143] may be too much. On the contrary branches seem to be disappearing faster than ever.

Currently, people are saving less in Britain, not more, in sharp contrast to the high-savings economies of Asia, where they spend less time worrying about inequality and more time creating and spreading wealth.

There needs to be a pro-savings, pro-wealth-sharing, cross-party and cross-ideology consensus in favour of the socialisation of capitalism and the universal provision of pension security. This would do more to overcome the bitterness and division of inequalities than any amount of income redistribution.

If across most Western economies, the sheer affordability of welfare state structures is now in question, the chance of reforms and reductions ever being politically manageable will depend upon other imaginative measures to spread capital rather than attack it, and to devise measures to bring the dignity, security and sense of commitment to the community in a way which radical income redistribution can never deliver. The key, so often hidden from those more comfortably provided for, is a feeling of security and the frightening feeling of its absence as age creeps on, family demands increase and earning power dwindles.

In fact, a fairer and less disruptive kind of capitalism has been a constant theme of political speeches, mostly on the Right and centre-Right, for over seventy years. Speeches, yes but not much action. Figures like Anthony Eden and later Harold Macmillan made frequent references to 'popular capitalism' and 'a capital-owning democracy'.

During Ted Heath's premiership some of us argued for the wider ownership cause to be given far greater priority. Heath himself seemed enthusiastic in Opposition, but somehow lost interest as other challenges overwhelmed his premiership. Instead (as recounted in Chapter Eight), he was pushed back onto the ineffectual wealth-disparities consensus, that price caps, incomes policy and income redistribution would do the trick. A dispiriting visit I paid to the then head of the Federation of British Industry (FBI) in the '70s (now the Confederation of British Industry) convinced me of the uphill nature of the task when he told me, politely, that employers felt capital ownership, through shares, etc., was for employers and investors and wages were for workers. Not a glimmer of support there.

Things looked better in 1979 when Margaret Thatcher wholeheartedly backed plans for wider ownership through the sale of council houses on favourable terms. The chief protagonist in her Cabinet was Peter Walker, an immensely energetic minister of centre-Conservative inclinations (then labelled Wet) who interestingly held quite different views to the Prime Minister about public spending, the money supply and other issues usually branded 'right wing'.

The programme of sales was marred by arguments about the proceeds and whether they should go straight back to the Treasury, be used as an excuse to cut central funding of local authorities correspondingly, or permitted to be reinvested in more social housing. Courses one and two prevailed, souring the whole scheme.

Nevertheless, this kind of economic democracy – the socialisation of future wealth – could be seen as a valuable and unifying bridge between the Conservatism of One Nation, described earlier, and the zeal of the free-market aficionados who reigned on the government bench. Here was a common-ground theme, the decisive antidote to the trap of wage-poverty, which combined real ownership by the people, the real spread of the security and dignity of ownership, and the defeat of socialist centralism and fake 'public ownership'. Furthermore, it was a policy which united the Thatcher Cabinet – among, by then, precious few policies with that potential. Today, in an even more divided age, with the contrasts even more vivid, with the concentrations of wealth far greater, and the voices of protest vastly amplified, this kind of resource democracy to help unite and build bridges, at least across the broad centre of politics, is ten times more necessary to bring to reality Theresa May's repeated calls for 'an economy that works for everyone'.

The Hope of '79.

The hope of '79 was that this would be one of the great themes of the Thatcher era, a key part of what we saw as the coming freedom. All through the '70s and as far back as the late '60s, we toiled in Conservative backrooms trying to give momentum and depth to the cause of popular capitalism, wider ownership and capital-owning democracy. We were determined to give it fresh life in the grey atmosphere of socialist – and deeply divided – 1960s and '70s Britain, as the old, failed consensus politics collapsed around us.

Kelso argued that wider ownership of savings in all forms, but particularly of stocks and shares, was not just good labour relations, it was the answer to the paralysing wages-versus-capital conflict, turning earners into owners, making new capitalists by the million and giving dignity, security and status, which sole dependence on the weekly or monthly wage could never ensure. Capital, not labour, he argued, had become the chief source of productivity. For him labour meant subsistence, capital meant affluence – in which everyone in a free society was entitled to share, just as much as, or even more than, the fruits of toil. In effect he was doing nothing less than overturning the labour theory of value, promoted from John Locke onwards and throughout the Enlightenment.

If capital had become the real source of growing productivity then it was wrong that the rewards were to go only to those already holding capital, rather than to wage-earners. If blue-collar workers were due to be replaced by robotic machines and artificial intelligence, then it was wrong, and dangerous, that those who owned the robots and the AI technology should collect all the rewards. They simply had to be shared in the name of common sense and political harmony, if not through direct capital holdings then through savings for pension provision on a far more generous level than skimpy old-age pension provision from a parsimonious state.

Kelso maintained that this was the pathway to genuine public ownership – ownership by the people – as opposed to the bogus 'public' ownership of fat-cat socialist corporatism. It would expand freedom and increase social responsibility at all levels, as well as take steam out of inflationary wage demands and trade union militancy.

All this was music to our ears – and music was what the dismal British economy and British politics badly needed. If it was before its time then, its time has come now.

As the Thatcher revolution dawned, the aim was to marry the wider ownership theme with two other strongly emerging Conservative ambitions – greatly increased support for smaller businesses and privatisation. This added ingredient, it was hoped, would elevate the mere denationalisation of lethargic state enterprises into a popular, wealth-sharing capitalist crusade.

When the opportunity came, did we succeed? Sort of, partially, hesitantly, without follow-through. Not, for sure, during the Heath administration when, after a brief dribble of minor encouragements to wider ownership, the drift back to a thicket of incomes policies and industrial strife soon crowded out most financial and market reforms.[144]

A decade later, with Margaret Thatcher in Downing Street, the big opportunities began to open up again. The obvious manifestation was freedom to buy and own council houses, driven by Peter Walker, while tax changes began to encourage some recovery for SMEs. Then the big tide of privatisations really began, leading in due course to the 'Tell Sid' campaign and the feeling that popular capitalism was at last taking hold.

One of the neatest early privatisations, with the groundwork largely laid by Norman Fowler, was the privatisation of the National Freight Corporation. It dramatically dynamized an inefficient and ramshackle state entity and, more to the point, delivered a nice bundle of shares to 80 per cent of the staff through an employee buy-out scheme. Substantial hidden NFC assets were uncovered – especially real estate (see Chapter Five).

All in all, popular capitalism in Britain moved forward a fraction during the Thatcher era – not nearly as far as some of us wanted and not nearly as a far as the USA, where 40 per cent of the population held shares and was and are kept informed of financial news by intense radio and TV coverage, almost absent in Britain most days on the BBC or other channels.

What does this tell us today? The Thatcher reforms just about survived the Blair years of relative disinterest in popular capital ownership, and some progress has undoubtedly been made over the decades. Traces of the spirit of start-up entrepreneurship and optimism of the Thatcher era are coming back after the grim post-Lehman years. However, something is still seriously missing. Most obviously, the low returns on all forms of lower-risk holdings and assets offer a rotten incentive to savers and the abnormally low interest rate policy, which is bound to come to an end, hangs like a sword of uncertainty over share investment. Soggy management of pension funds, with rip-off charges and commissions, casts another shadow, although recent and proposed pensions reforms will help undo the damage. The total numbers in workplace pension schemes have risen between 2012 to 2019 from less than half to more than three-quarters. This is progress of a kind.[145]

The irony is that when it comes to large-scale progress towards popular capitalism, one needs nowadays to look more to the high-saving Asian societies, with Latin-America and parts of Africa following the same path, to see a culture of widely spread capital ownership truly taking root.

Giving advice to younger generations of leaders can be infuriating, but one piece I have dared to offer is that the butter — when there is some — must be spread to all corners of the toast. Maybe 'tastes like butter' will have to do in the present phase of weak economic growth, but spread it must be, by every conceivable device and incentive, to ensure that as many families in the land as possible have a share in the revived growth of national wealth (with something more than just wages to fall back on), and are stakeholders in the new capitalism of the digitalised age.

The 'Tell Sid' campaign of 1986, which gave special incentives to new and very small shareholders in the privatised British Gas, was a high point of Thatcher-era popular capitalism. But after that, the momentum faded. Both John Moore[146] and Nigel Lawson[147] made repeated pleas for wider capital ownership, for employee share ownership and other schemes to back up millions of households with greater financial security. Not much happened. Yet, with each passing decade, the imperative grows for the evolution of capitalism worldwide and for the avoidance of populist disruptions, to create new global designs combining the best of capitalist wealth creation with the best of wealth-sharing. As world finance has been revolutionised by the turbo-capitalism of the digital era, the need for reform grows more urgent.

One problem is that today's defenders of popular capitalism have made a very poor fist of the task. This is simply because, while their language of defence of capitalism has remained unchanged from Thatcher times, the nature of the capitalist process has evolved almost beyond recognition. They are defending the wrong redoubt. The hopes of ever-rising real wages and trickle-down prosperity which seemed within reach forty years ago, have not been realised. Now, something quite different needs to be defended and reformed.

The plain-to-the-eye facts behind the general Piketty critique, weak though it is in parts, cannot be ignored. The growing concentration of capital in the hands of a tiny minority – who already have more capital than they can ever possibly use – is not the prudent way democratic capitalism should be evolving.

Could it be that capital itself is changing in texture, nature and behaviour? And, as more and more assets assume an intangible character, could this be accelerating the gap between average remuneration and mega-wealth concentrations? The thesis is explored in *Capitalism without Capital*,[148] where it is suggested that when capital is increasingly embedded in software, branding, design and research, rather than solid machinery, the differences of rewards allocated by the system yawn even wider and faster.

The authors' argument is a bit thin but it adds to the evidence that this kind of 'capitalism' is something entirely different to the textbook versions by which so much of politics and economics still seems to be guided.

The lines on which this reform might develop have been available for many decades – certainly since Kelso. Some of us have sought to promote and build on Kelso's ideas under successive governments over the decades but with limited success; they cut right across the ideological divide and bust wide open the post-war Keynesian consensus. Kelso advocated a vastly greater spread, to millions of households and families, not just of capital ownership but of the proceeds of growth in new wealth, instead of seeing it all accrue to the already wealthy.

In a further book in 1986, *Democracy and Economic Power*,[149] Kelso and his partner, Patricia Kelso, set out the detailed means of achieving the capital-spreading goal by a variety of instruments, including generous workplace pensions, ESOPs, CSOPs, GSOPs[150] and a range of other instruments. They also set out the new role of the trade unions in democratising the new capitalism. This would entail both a substantial boost to popular capitalism but also a big increase in new kinds of state intervention – thoroughly unappealing to both old Left and old Right. Perhaps now its time has come.

Again and again these kind of ideas have fallen foul of political shibboleths. For the Left, the Kelso dream was dismissed as a further bonanza for the already rich and the high rollers. For the Right, it looked like a major further incursion by the state in offloading risk onto the taxpayer. It is neither. The unfinished task of statesmen, economists, bankers and social reformers, as technology leaves behind the age of Left and Right, is to enable modern capitalism in all its varied forms across the planet to catch up with the political currents of the digital age and get ahead of populism.

If governments remain inert, or simply too weak to act, or to raise the finance necessary to lift state pensions above their present minimalist levels, as in the UK, then somewhere from within the maelstrom of fintech the driving forces for reformed and popular capitalism could emerge. While politicians will not, or cannot, move forward, networks and algorithms will push ahead, weaving systems together before politics catches up.

An extraordinary feature of the current political debate in the UK (and hardly anywhere else) is the resurgence of attention to Marx's disproven and discredited predictions about the demise of capitalism – as he saw it. In the Cabinet of '79 we thought that was at least one part of the economics of socialism that had been put to rest.

Social democracy, we recognised, for all its blurs and fudges, still had plenty of life in it and demanded plenty of respect, not unassisted by the insights of Keynes. But Marx? Surely that was as dead as the dodo? It turns out we were wrong. Instead it has become a kind of British refuge from the challenges of globalisation and the unfamiliar complexities of the digital age. Yet the real core of Marxism – his belief that there was an inevitable, scientific future which in the end would abolish politics – is surely even less relevant and helpful in shoring up beleaguered democratic power today than it was in the pre-digital age.

In the wider world context, the times call for entirely new economic and diplomatic mindsets. The two are closely linked: the fundamentally revised and greatly widened aims of national economic and social policy, and the fundamental revision of international goals and purposes, which recognises the interaction of alliances, relationships and interests in a deeply networked and connected world, where entirely new patterns of globalisation are forming before our eyes.

One of the people who puts this latter task – the new diplomatic challenge – best is the American thinker Anne-Marie Slaughter, already referred to earlier. In her book *The Chessboard and the Web*[151] she explains how the international system is no longer predominantly a patchwork of competing states but an ever-changing web of intersecting networks and pressures, requiring a new agility – indeed a vastly extended sensitivity – to navigate, and to reconcile with local and nationalist impulses.

As she reminds us, this is far from new. It was opened up for us by Manuel Castells two decades or more ago in his three foresight-laden volumes on the rise of the network society first published in the '90s.[152] My book, *The Edge of Now,* sought to show how the Castells analysis and the magnitude of the changes anticipated would affect our politics and lives in the twenty-first century.

However, even in the electronic age, ideas still take years to trickle down and be 'discovered' as new. And it now requires the genius of figures such as Joshua Cooper Ramo to explain how human beings who are connected all the time need not just Nietzsche's sixth sense but a seventh sense to cope with our new age of constant discussion across the world's communities and peoples, and to understand the fundamental implications of it all.

In his book, *The Seventh Sense,*[153] Ramo describes this new kind of intuitive skill, which he believes is the perception beyond perceptions, the vital fingertip sense, that leaders need to interpret the important strands leading to the future, as distinct from passing fads and fashions. Perhaps he shows a shade of the intolerance (and exuberance) which comes from brilliant surveyors of world trends who have never experienced the endless agonies and impossible dilemmas of government, but his message is crystal clear. He writes:

> At the very early stages of a revolution, most of our leaders are blind. It's not simple technical fluency that eludes them – though this is among the most embarrassing of their deficits, marked by their leaked emails and overheard voice mails. It's certainly true that listening to some of our leaders talk about technology resembles nothing so much as trying to explain Snapchat to your grandparents. But the problem is more profound. Avoiding cyber accidents, controlling the spread of nuclear weapons, handling global warming,

stemming financial crises, restoring equitable growth — all these puzzles yearn to be tackled with a new sensibility. They are produced by new forces, after all. These problems linger not as independent fractures on some solid base that can be easily patched, but rather as markers of connected cracks that are growing over time.[154]

Chapter Nineteen

The New Labyrinth

It is said that a perceptive writer and
commentator must become a foreigner.

—Anon

Pilot Error

'We're not going to make it,' said the man in the seat next to me. The Comet Four was descending smoothly for a night landing at Nairobi airport when there was a loud banging and the aircraft juddered as though the ground had come up too soon to meet us. The engine noise turned to a scream and the plane tilted sharply upwards into the darkness. The oxygen masks came down.

The flight was from Johannesburg. I had been covering rising South African tensions for the *Daily Telegraph* and in the spring of 1971 was moving to East Africa where recent military coups, curiously coinciding in all three countries, Kenya, Uganda and Tanzania, had only just been overcome and reversed. The hope was for a new East African Federation. It never happened.

When we had landed safely it emerged that the pilot had mistaken the lights of Nairobi game park for the airport runway another seven miles ahead (see plate section). The undercarriage was festooned with jungle foliage but by some miracle he had put down in the one flat part of the game park. Surprised but realising his error he had turned on full throttle and pulled sharply off the ground. You could do that in the Comet Four with its four colossal 7,000-pound Rolls-Royce

Avon engines. Another aircraft would have ended in a smouldering pile – along with its occupants. The pilot had just not looked where he was going. He was dismissed.

So also, will today's leaders and governments be dismissed if they don't look more carefully where they are going. There have now been thirty years of globalisation, its forces unifying, fragmenting and transforming the international order. A new wave of globalisation is under way, and probably a new one after that. Whether one is for or against globalisation does not matter. It will happen because it is driven not by governments or by corporations, as demonisers assert, but by demand – by the wish to have the information, communication and control which technology offers. Demand creates supply.

Yet the world seems constantly caught by surprise. Stuff happens, as Donald Rumsfeld ruefully observed when the American-led invasion of Iraq turned from 'mission accomplished' into a blood-soaked mess. Governments, and the armies of experts and advisers who surround them, keep bumping into events that apparently no-one foresaw (although there are always some who did) and being caught badly off balance.

Very few predicted the turmoil into which most countries in the Middle East have now descended, the chaotic turn taken by the wrongly labelled Arab Spring, the sudden mushrooming of the barbarian Islamic State regime, or the rising bitterness and antagonism of Vladimir Putin, in his second phase as Russian President, towards the West. Few foresaw the way in which, in November 2014, the United Kingdom nearly broke apart with Scotland going its separate way (which still might happen).

Back in 2009, governments and the world of finance seemed caught completely unawares at the timing of the euro crisis (although many predicted that it would occur one day – including this author – and that it would be unending, as will be proved). Few foresaw the Lehman bank crisis the year before, which shook the financial world to its foundations – and whose spectre is still with us. And of course, the scale and horror of 9/11 came as a complete surprise.

The sweeping turmoil of the Asian currency crisis at the end of the last century had also erupted with few warnings. Indeed, moving to a larger scale, the information revolution and its profound consequences for every walk of life and for global development, from about 1975 to 1980 and onwards, had very few prophets and continues to take economists, social scientists and all manner of forecasters by surprise as it unfolds in multiple forms. Going a short way forward, Brexit-involved politicians and their expert advisers still argue about hard borders when the technical world foresees customs officers as 'redundant'.[155]

Can we do better? Or do we just shrug our shoulders and wait for the next 'black swan' to come along – the fate so tellingly depicted in Nassim Nicholas Taleb's brilliant theorising? The world mood is very much that way just now, fearing uncertainties on every side, struggling for answers, blind to possibilities, waiting apprehensively for the next crisis to strike from who knows where, listening to a cacophony of contradictory views and predictions about almost everything.

To demand that our leaders and authorities should see around every corner is to ask too much. But to expect a little more illumination from the top, a little more prescience and perspective, a little more consideration of where the world is going, is surely reasonable. More than that, it is becoming the essential quality to enable governments to govern, leaders to lead, decisions to be made, situations to be sustained, and for a general slide towards anarchy and fragmentation of society to be checked.

For the truth is that the old tools and instruments of power and leadership are worn out, most of all in the democracies, less so in the world's autocracies, although they, too, face new challenges. Deference to authority has long since gone. As four-billion-plus people each morning (more than half of humankind) open their laptops, it is certain that everything governments do or say will be challenged and widely disrespected. Even in the most repressive regimes, the power of instantly available, widespread knowledge, opinion and assembled protest makes the most arrogant authorities pause, forcing explanation and hurried changes of direction.

The weapons left to the rulers, and the means of retaining respect, legitimacy and securing compliance, have to be refashioned. Political leaders now live not in the comfortable penthouse floors of lofty hierarchies, but in humbler and more exposed networks, with pressures coming at them from all sides, all the time.

Leadership by assertion and hint of superior knowledge no longer washes. Conviction is not enough to retain followers who insist on transparency and who know instantly, or think they know, as much as their masters. Governments and their leaders who claim to command, and who manage too much then deliver too little, have long since forfeited the right, or the power, to stay in office. Instead, today's leaders will not succeed and hold their constituencies together by promising impossible things, but by seeing a little further ahead, offering guidance and wisdom that provide an extra degree of assurance to their followers in a world of uncertainty. Their task is to piece together and explain events and trends which seem incomprehensible and frightening to most to people. This is the new leadership skill. In its absence old political groupings and parties will fall apart. It is already happening.

Chapter Twenty

The Case for Looking Back

WHAT is the point in looking back? According to Charles Moore, Margaret Thatcher was greatly averse to dwelling on past events. There were always new tasks to be tackled. So, what worthwhile guidance comes to us across the tumultuous decades from that distant May morning gathering forty ago? Locke said that for government to succeed and society to be ordered there had to be 'a bedrock of experience'. So, what lessons for good governance assist us or make for greater wisdom in the entirely changed conditions in which we now live? What is left of the Thatcher dream? Where, if anywhere, is the continuum?

The most positive and obvious element is that there must be an inspiring narrative, a story not just spelled out by words, repeated day after day in fresh and interesting ways, but by actions. The need for this approach in an age of information overload is more crucial to order and stability than ever before, in any nation and certainly in Britain.

A narrative should not be interpreted as some bright slogan dreamed up by a public relations team or phrase-happy speechwriters (even though fifty years ago I was as guilty as anyone of assuming this could be done). A story has to build up with a craftsman's patience, lacquered layer on layer. It has to draw on the deepest understanding of the trends and forces in society and the wider world, and on a fingertip wisdom about the weight they should be given and the manner in which they interrelate – a drawing together of widely different disciplines and developments – Edward Wilson's consilience again, with a touch of Joshua Cooper Ramo's seventh sense. As Henry Kissinger remarked, 'information technology has outstripped strategy and doctrine'. He adds, 'Information at one's fingertips may encourage the mindset of a researcher but may diminish the mindset of a leader.'[156]

The supply lines of successful argument, led by academia, the professions and reflective comment, must go hand in hand with a powerful narrative at the forefront, from which gradual shifts in public opinion can be built up. In the Thatcher case this narrative came very late and slowly. Indeed, in the standard left-wing press and think-tanks and in large areas of university opinion, it never came at all during her time as Prime Minister, as instanced by the refusal of the Oxford academic establishment to give her an honorary degree, seemingly in blank denial of the Thatcher free-market story and her rejection of the corporatist consensus.

But from outside the political, or politically influenced, hothouse, there were enough trends to realise that the era of high state planning was past and that markets were taking centre stage again – not just in Britain and the democracies, but everywhere.

The clearest negative lesson from the Thatcher period is that governments and political parties which rely too much on ideology and theories cannot last. The ideologies crumble in the face of events, the theories are washed away in ceaseless paradox; the practicalities of the Grantham corner shop are just as important as any doctrine or grandiose set of principles, probably more so.

We have entered a completely different world from the one we confronted all that while ago. (Remember the point made in Chapter One that none of the members of the 1979 Cabinet had mobiles, or had even heard of them, although the late and quicksilver-brilliant Ronnie Grierson[157] had a phone in his car by the late '70s, as well as a phone in every room, including the loo – common now, revolutionary then.)

Sceptics will say, 'Ah, but human nature has not changed.' But are we so sure? It can be argued that within the family, between the generations, within the community, within the region, within the nation, the tide of information, and the pattern of low-cost and continuous connectivity have indeed changed some of the most basic patterns of human behaviour and some of the deepest attitudes between one individual and another.

It has long become a cliché that networks are changing the way the world works. They are also change the way our minds work. What John Stuart Mill called the 'inner domain of consciousness', where he saw the true frontier of freedom lay, has been penetrated.

We are now compelled to revisit some of our philosophical fundamentals. For example, the absolutes of 1979 were that democracy, freedom and capitalist free markets were the only possible foundations for economic growth; that free trade and competition, as stipulated by David Ricardo, were the only paths to prosperity; that national competitiveness had to be the aim of policy, otherwise all else would fail. We had it in writing from Von Hayek's *Constitution of Liberty*,[158] from Fukuyama's *End of History and the Last Man*[159] and from the visible failures of the big state era, notably the Soviet Union. Against the crumbling ramparts of the post-war socialist consensus, these ideas were bound to have powerful and penetrating impact and did.

Yet the meaning of these clarion calls, which seemed so clear at the time, has become blurred. So much has happened via randomness and complexity, so much has been unforeseen, wrong-footing gurus, futurologists and highly paid analysts at every stage, that the chain of consequences seems lost.

In between then and today, attempts have been made to explain unlikely, even improbable, events, far outside normal extrapolation, which nevertheless happen, and invalidate all expectations: chaos theory; butterfly economics; Robert Kaplan's 'Coming Anarchy'[160] as the millennium turned, followed by an army of pessimists; the whole scene cleverly repackaged and served up by Nassim Nicholas Taleb in *The Black Swan*.[161]

Think of 9/11, the Arab Spring, Facebook, Instagram (owned by Facebook), Alphabet, Amazon, and all the other developments of recent years, and it may seem fruitless to track the legacies and consequences left by the people looking out at us from that Cabinet photograph forty years ago.

Let us dispose of some distracting diversions – although not too dismissively because they remain current in some circles and are quite interesting. First, is the bottle half full or half empty? Has the state of the world (and of our own little British bit of it) improved over the decades or worsened?

We will get nowhere on this one – except to the point of head-on contradiction between the optimists and the pessimists.

Obviously, it's got better – the bottle is half full. We have Matt Ridley, the 'rational optimist' (the title of his cheering book),[162] to prove it – vast increases in prosperity and living standards for hundreds of millions, huge progress in fighting disease, child mortality dramatically down, and so on. And we have Steven Pinker[163] to tell us that most of the statistics showing downward trends – more crime, more horrors more disasters – point the other way when you come to examine them. Above all, we have the great and late Hans Rosling and his co-authors to tell us 'why things are better than you think'[164] – the book which Bill Gates found so instructive – and to turn many of our perceptions (about the widening gap between rich and poor, for instance) on their heads.

Yet, equally obviously, things have got much worse. Robert Kaplan warned us about the coming anarchy in the twenty-first century and most of the time he has proved deadly right. The collapse of the Soviet imperium lifted the lid on a hundred ethnic and tribal furies. The arrival of the microchip and the information revolution have empowered countless tribes, torn power away from established governments, turbo-boosted markets, enthroned mighty algorithms and corporations who owned them, and e-enabled a rash of violence across the planet.

So, no umpire's decision there. Jury out, and likely to remain out. Utopia, socialist or otherwise indefinitely postponed.

Then there is the globalisation issue. To the world of 1979, the 'new' globalisation looked quite familiar – a massive expansion of world trade, with the usual tirade of warnings and reminders that we had it all before, back at the beginning of the twentieth century. And it came with the same chorus of hopeful guarantees as before – that it meant no more wars – tragically wrong before 1914, and sure to be wrong again.

Now we are in a completely different phase of globalisation from the 1970s and '80s period, or indeed the 1900s phase, with which commentators and historians like to compare the modern situation. What earlier globalisation meant was what it had always meant – a steady expansion of trade between nations in goods, services, commodities and produce of all kinds – in a form which Ricardo[165] would have recognised and which would have pleased him. All sides benefited from the flow. That is what the Ricardian theory said and that is what turned out – until more recently – in practice.

Then came the late twentieth-century globalisation phase, still mostly trade-led and Western-based, bringing with it long supply chains across economies and taking advantage of cheap labour combined with ever easier technology transfers. The positive side was strong world trade growth and, for a time, swelling cross-border financial flows. But, on the negative side, it resulted in lost jobs, industrial disruption and rising divisions between those with the new cosmopolitan skills and those left behind with stagnant or dwindling wages.

These divisions led both to strong political opposition to the globalisation process and to claims that it was in retreat. It is true that world trade growth has faltered while cross-border investment flows have dropped back sharply. But today the scene is totally different again. Globalisation has resumed its march – in some places faster than ever – still demand-driven but in a new form, this time satiated by further technological advances and led largely by China and other Asian powers. Instead of products being made in one place and sold to another, we have the phenomenon of different stages in the production of the same final item being added on from different countries. In effect, products made somewhere are now made everywhere.

Adam Smith's pin-making model, divided, as he explained, into eighteen separate functions, probably now takes place in half a dozen different countries and economies. Add in the raw material sources, the transport, the design process, the packaging, the marketing, the distribution and the back office, the information systems linking it all together – located, possibly, elsewhere again – and we have the effective 'denationalisation' of the industrial production process.

Longer and longer supply chains snake across the globe, across the old trade-bloc zones, across cultures, and across geographical space, with each phase and component part of the process slotting into the next with e-enabled precision.

This is a pattern over which national governments have much less control than they had over trade in the past – a realisation which is slowly dawning on administrators and policy-makers but has not yet reached many. President Trump and his advisers have been formulating policies on the assumption that they are in control of production and trade flows; they are about to discover that they are not. In Europe large sections of the debate about both Brexit and economic reform with the rest of the European Union are carried on in the same way.

No-one puts this better than Richard Baldwin:[166]

> Vast swathes of economic policy are based on the notion that competitiveness is a national feature. In rich nations, policies ranging from education and training (preparing workers for the jobs of tomorrow) to research and development tax breaks (developing the products and processes of the future) are aimed at bolstering national sources of competitiveness. In developing nations, policies ranging from tariff levels (protecting domestic production) to development strategies (moving up the value chain) are founded on the idea that the sources of national competitiveness are national. All these policy presumptions need to be rethought in the light of the new globalisation.

Pause and think about those last words: 'All these policy presumptions need to be rethought.' Baldwin is telling us that most of those slick and certain maxims of long ago are no longer valid nor can they be relied upon. The principles of organisation at the heart of production have changed. Goods are now made in many countries and jurisdictions. Products and services are impossibly intertwined, making the statistical category definitions of 'goods' and 'services 'meaningless – a point completely ignored until very recently by most economists, statisticians and trade analysts. Factories cross borders.

What Baldwin calls a 'denationalisation' of manufacturing has now taken place.

Let us take a typical manufactured retail product, say a modern, state-of-the-art motor mower – design concept, design software, drawing on innovative technology, finance, assembly of materials, new machinery, software to drive the machinery, the range of components, tracking of same, assembly, packaging, marketing, transport, sales. All these stages may take place in different countries, determined by cost calculations (including labour costs), tax and regulation costs, and a general assessment of the political/legal and administrative environments. Note, also, that many of them are services and knowledge inputs rather than hard items.

The distinction between goods and services, lovingly clung to by silo-trapped compilers of economic and industrial statistics, have long since ceased to exist. Some of us have been questioning for years this unrealistic categorisation (see my book, *The Edge of Now*, where the concept of *'mente*facturing' rather than *manu*facturing was introduced). Its recognition by today's commentators, as they struggle to make sense of new trade patterns, is very welcome, even if two decades behind the event.

What, then, is the point of measures and regulations aimed at national competitiveness in one particular product or industry? The benefits or gains almost certainly spread into other economies, job creation and shareholder profits in other societies. The nation's industrial base, its power of attraction for investment and its overall economic performance come to rest not on particular products or industries, but on its skills, its training, its savviness in the provision of infrastructure, the fairness and reliability of its laws and their implementation, the reasonableness of its tax system and in the general 'feel' of welcome and cooperation. That's a million miles away from trying to favour and boost new product areas, and even further from trying to protect existing ones with subsidies and external tariffs.

As Donald Trump is finding out with his steel and aluminium tariffs, these actions cut into modern supply chains at so many unpredictable points and cut across the flow of so many other processes, that the damage to the home economy occurs in a stream of unforeseen ways and vastly outweighs the benefits originally intended.

The focus of industrial policy, indeed the whole focus of national economic policy, therefore has to turn completely away from products and 'winners' and concentrate entirely on skills, on education on agile minds and on the most favourable conditions of innovation and creative activity. Openness, and more openness, is ultimately the only path to prosperity. If trade protection ever worked, which is doubtful, it certainly does not now. The Chinese response is to put up tariffs and tighten quotas against US farm products. Millions of angry farmers may be the best and only way of bringing Trump to understand this new reality.

As Baldwin puts it, we should stop thinking about particular factories or firms as 'the industrial base', and start thinking of services, and the skills and education sector, as the new industrial base. The interest of firms no longer automatically coincides with the interests of nations.

Cities, he adds, are the crucibles for this kind of propagation and growth, which is why city economics and city policy, both national and international, are emerging as the new driving force in economic progress.

Chapter Twenty-one

How to Safeguard
Democracy Now

WE come back to the deeper question – the future of democracy itself. The fundamental assumption of 1979 was that democracies would flourish – meaning countries with fair elections, party systems, parliaments, aspirations to uphold the rule of law, and governments which could be kicked out – whereas autocracies would not and could not.

Yet the glittering success of giant China and tiny Singapore knocks the props of this simplistic view clean away. The gap between the Asian powerhouses and gigantic ultra-modern cities, and the sedate, old Western world is growing daily, not merely in the physical sense that Asia now has better roads, railways, airports and ports, but also in the social sense that better and cleverer systems of welfare support, of housing, of health provision and above all of education are emerging, backed and administered, it seems, by more intelligent design and thought.

This Easternisation process is, again, something which was fully aired way back in the 1990s, when the possibility that such a shift might be happening was very badly received.[167] How could it possibly be, it was demanded, that teeming Asia could be acquiring superior governance forms, and superior social structures to the enlightened West? How could the great lessons of Western enlightenment – for instance David Hume's insistence that a market society went hand-in-glove with liberty – be so rudely, and visibly, challenged?

Yet the Chinese model is large and getting more so, dominating major parts of world trade and development and spreading its presence to every continent. For example, the former British-governed Hong Kong – which Margaret Thatcher reluctantly conceded to China when the lease ended in 1997 – now forms part of a greater Hong Kong-Shenzhen-Macau Bay area with a regional GDP larger than California's, putting it, by size, in the top handful of world economies.

It is possible to argue, in shoulder-shrugging mode, that this Chinese growth model will come to an end because Western-style freedom and democracy will inevitably break out and autocracies must fail.

What seems more likely is that different forms of capitalism will interweave and sometimes merge, interlocking in a web of unparalleled density and complexity, for which no picture frame, no overall theory, no *Wealth of Nations*, no *Das Kapital*, and no *Constitution of Liberty*, and hopefully no *Mein Kampf*, is yet available. Perhaps, even if a definitive tome finally appears, it will already be out of date as technology races on, entering and influencing every sphere of human existence.

The same melding process may now be going on with the concept of democracy itself. In 1979 the question hardly bothered us. It seemed so obvious that democracy meant political freedom under the law, and freedom under the law meant economic growth. Plainly there had to be free elections to elect representatives and governments. Free speech, a free press and scrupulous adherence to the rule of law (with no man, be he so high, above it) summed it up. Around the Thatcher Cabinet table this went almost without saying.

In the background, there was an awareness of Alexis de Tocqueville's warning about 'the tyranny of the majority' which could undermine freedoms (has done so frequently and could do so again), or Walter Lippmann's, that 'confusion between constitutional democracy and the mere will of the majority is the supreme political heresy of our time'.[168]

But nowadays different shades and degrees of 'democracy' have crept into the debate. This is a tricky area to write about, with professional media distorters ready to pounce on any careless wording.

But few authors recently have dealt with the democracy issue more carefully and more deeply than David Runciman in his book *How Democracy Ends*.[169]

Runciman bravely questions Churchill's well-known aphorism about democracy being the worst system except for all the others. He wonders whether this is any longer so, when the tech titans and worldwide connectivity are giving voice to the voiceless on such a massive scale. He argues that this swirling totality of opinion is pulling political parties apart and making orderly democratic government hopelessly unstable.

The UK's constitutional turmoil over its future relations with the European Union, and the apparent inability of conventional democratic institutions to resolve it, would seem to bear out his point.

The accepted democratic model emerging in the twentieth century of one vote for every man and women, regardless of qualifications, was always prone to encourage politicians who offer instant gratification and populist promises and has produced some unhappy outcomes in the modern era. But, empower every voter with mobile connections and computer-driven convening power, and the outcome is uncontrollable volatility with all attempts to adhere to and sustain longer-term policies voted down in favour of immediate benefits and fleeting fashions.

The technology to target individuals personally and to hammer them repeatedly with a persistence unimaginable a few years back, adds further poison to the mix. In these circumstances, other forms of 'democracy' are bound to look temptingly like a better bet for younger and less mature societies, and for the 'illiberal democracies' (viz. Hungary today), or the authoritarian breeds of faux-democracy such as China, or possibly Russia, as examples.

Another author, John Keane, in his massive work *The Life and Death of Democracy*,[170] identifies a new phase which he calls 'monitory democracy'. He describes a world in which 'the rules of representation, the processes of accountability and the degree of public participation are applied to a much wider range of settings than ever before'.

The 'much wider range of settings' factor is, of course, the hyper-connectivity of the digital age, which enters every sphere of existence and which allows the formation of opinions and views, and organisation in advancing them, on a scale and with a speed unimaginable a few decades ago.

John Keane's 2009 forecast has already come about, as the old institutions of the twentieth century, both national and multinational, struggle to connect with a wider and more informed public than ever before. At the United Nations, in the World Trade Organization, in the Bretton Woods institutions, in NATO, in the EU and in the Commonwealth, this struggle is now seen as the greatest, challenge – almost an existential one. Political parties, parliaments and governments all face the same bewildering and intensive pressures where manageable inertia and more restrained forms of representation prevailed before.

The confidence and superior certainty that the Westminster model of representative government has always offered as the gold standard in democratic systems, has long since evaporated. In its place we now have illiberal democracies, majoritarian democracies, democratic elections producing one-party tyrannies. Hereditary rulers and autocrats have no difficulty in arguing that, with the advent of the communications revolution, they are now in closer touch daily, even hourly, with 'the people' and with civil society in all its manifestations, than they were through old-style parliamentary institutions.

Visiting the former ruler of Qatar, Sheikh Hamad bin Khalifa Al Thani, soon after the Iraq invasion, I spoke to him about the dire threats that had rumbled out of Washington about 'draining the Middle East swamp' and the need to spread democracy. The Sheikh, who, like most Arab rulers, had opposed the invasion idea from the start, looked both pained and puzzled. Either side of him sat brothers, sons, daughters and relatives. 'But we *are* a democracy,' he said, spreading his arms out to those either side of him. 'We are closer to our people than many in the West.' I was the one lost for a response. Was it the usual Westminster uproar at Prime Minister's Questions, or the Sheikh's weekly *diwan,* or open-door session, to which almost anyone, suitably checked at the door, apparently had access, which was more democratic. I was not at all sure.

There are more volumes waiting to be written – maybe as wide-ranging as David Runciman's or John Keane's – to add to a stream of works from both sides of the Atlantic on the changing shape of democracies everywhere.[171] Democracies now are greatly impacted by the internet and the communications revolution, and the ocean of fake and genuine information in which free and rational debate suffocates. Public opinion, with its outriders of opinion polls, angry newspaper columns, blog-based organisations and rallies of mutually reinforcing views (and, of course, tweets – the chosen method of Donald Trump) becomes increasingly strident and demanding, yet harder and harder to assess. The ground is shifting so fast that too few politicians have caught up with the new methods required to create this magic state of being 'in touch', which almost all political institutions are accused of failing to achieve.

Returning to the Foreign and Commonwealth Office in 2010, after more than twenty years outside government, I found a surprising change from the routines of earlier times. With my own department (Energy) under Margaret Thatcher three decades earlier, the pattern had been to gather the departmental ministers first thing in the morning, at least twice a week, to discuss and decide our policy and our stances in relation to on-going events, pressures, crises opportunities, and so on. Later in the day we would talk with press officers, advisers, spin and media experts, parliamentary private secretaries and other parliamentary contacts, to work out how best to present and promote what we had earlier decided.

By 2010 the process had been reversed. At the FCO it was the press, publicity and spin experts who went in first in the morning, to advise the Secretary of State. They ascertained what 'the public' was thinking, what the media claimed they were thinking and what the polls reflected, and the ministers and officials were called in later to respond accordingly.

One had to assume that this change – in the almost three decades between my stints in government – was what being 'a listening government' had come to mean, in the age of a communications revolution; bringing 'public opinion' into policy-making and diplomacy. If so, one can only wish ministers good luck. But, it seemed to me then, and seems even more so now, that there are two fundamental flaws in the approach.

First, 'public opinion' is composed of a now vastly amplified cacophony of different views and opinions, and a fragmented mosaic of lobbies and interests. Secondly, it is highly volatile and can flip from week to week and from issue to issue and fashion to fashion, making any policies based on, or adapted, to what is believed to be 'public opinion' extremely hazardous and almost certain to be wrong-footed.

Some publicly asserted views, observed and recorded as being held consistently and persistently over long periods, can obviously be the foundations for government measures and programmes. But the sorting out and filtration of deeper and more enduring attitudes from transient flushes of enthusiasm and passion, requires the maintenance of trust on a sustained scale between rulers and ruled – a skill not within every government's grasp, and often not within the grasp of advisers, the media or the opinion pollsters either.

Pity the rulers who follow slavishly what they deem to be public opinion, only to see it vaporise and leave them without cause or support. In his book, *Diplomacy*,[172] Henry Kissinger wrote a telling passage about Napoleon III. Kissinger avers that Napoleon – guided by his desire to impress the public – conducted his foreign policy, 'in the style of modern political leaders who measure their success by the reaction of the television evening news'. Kissinger adds, 'The public does not in the long run respect leaders who mirror its own insecurities.' Fickle French public sentiment left Napoleon III as a refugee, living in exile in Chislehurst.

The new dilemma of democracy is simply this: Democratic systems which cannot deliver 'quality' government are now in acute danger. Democracies which crumble into wrangling political process, which confuse politics with good government, will be neither sustained nor tolerated in the age of continuous mass connection. In the digital era, somewhere between the indecision and incompetent short-termism that now grips traditional democracy, and the authoritarian insensitivity of technocratic government, lies a pathway that minimises the flaws and maximises the benefits of both.

David Runciman's view is that democracy is going through 'a mid-life' crisis'. Note that he is not predicting the imminent expiry of democracy but explaining perceptively *how* it could crumble.

Could the democratic process in fact be saved by advances in the very technologies that now seem to abuse, distort and undermine it? Perhaps the social media could help drain away some of the very poison and hatreds it has spawned, and which would otherwise spill out into open anarchy and violence . And if the ideological warriors of the past would put aside their outdated weaponry, irrelevant clashes and false dreams of yesterday, and focus instead on this greatest of all challenges, ways might yet be found to make the communications revolution the friend, rather than the destroyer, of stable and trustworthy government.

Is that facile hope, clutching at straws, or an attainable goal?

Chapter Twenty-two

Conclusions, Answers, Lessons, Hopes

THIS is where the chain of ideas, the path of pressures, the sequence of events, leads so far, where we pause on a continuing journey and review the arguments and contentions of the preceding pages. We have waded through the past in order to find some sort of footing for the future.

Clearly, the national bargain in a restless age has to be rewritten: Internally, the populist impulse, now vastly magnified by technology, has to be handled but not succumbed to, and faith restored in democratic and parliamentary politics. To meet doubts, both deep within society and about the nation's purpose and direction, requires re-articulation in the language and context of the age. Externally, the rules and techniques of a new international order, neither loftily supranational, nor narrow and selfish, have to be learnt and practised.

As the current political turmoil persists the cry goes up in Britain for strong leadership, with Margaret Thatcher's name inevitably being invoked. Oh yes, you hear it said, she would surely have settled things by now.

But would she, and could she have? Remember that Margaret Thatcher had supreme contempt for referendums, so she would not have been in the position of her beleaguered successors anyway. But, that aside, the answer is still is mostly, no, simply because circumstances over the four decades past have altered almost beyond recognition.

In some key respects the lessons of her times could be of real assistance to the new Johnson government. To these I will come in a moment. First, though, the differences – there is an obvious and fundamental one: Thatcher had a solid parliamentary majority, modest at first but much bigger later on, and Theresa May did not – basic arithmetic from which many of May's problems arose. In the unfolding digital age, public opinion is bound to be splintered into a thousand shards. It could not be otherwise. And splintered opinion is bound to deliver splintered politics and splintered parties.

Thatcher could be sure of getting her way in the Commons. May has been a general almost without troops, relying on rapid day-to-day manoeuvres and surprise tactics, so as not to be cornered.

The parliamentary majority gave Margaret Thatcher her authority and dominance. It allowed her to be sharp, to the point of rudeness, to all and sundry around the Cabinet table. Not for her the calm and balanced summing up after hearing all viewpoints. On the contrary, the Thatcher style was to begin with her own emphatic opinion then see who was unwise or daring enough to disagree.

One can argue as to whether this approach was strength or dominance, and whether it gave her successive and growing Commons majorities, or whether the majorities begat the growing dominance. Either way, this was her authority and she certainly used it.

Another obvious point is that the two Prime Ministers presided at different junctures in history. The Thatcher Cabinet assembled on that late Spring morning in 1979 sensed that they (we) were on the cusp. There were to be bitter disputes about precisely which way to go, and how fast. Heads would roll and doubters depart, as we saw in Chapter Three. But the era of state economic mastery was plainly coming to an end and an era of market liberation was beginning. Indeed, beneath the frothing surface of politics it was already well under way.

Even more significantly, the international context was far simpler and far less unstable. In 1979 the US supremacy, or primacy as some called it, still held, almost unquestioned and supported strongly by Britain and the rest of Western Europe. The close and good relations between Margaret Thatcher and Ronald Reagan both symbolised and strengthened it. As the first cracks appeared in the Soviet empire, the sense of free-world victory was to grow. China was just emerging from internal turmoil, the Indian giant still asleep, South Africa still gripped by apartheid, the European Community beginning to irritate but liveable with, at least for the time being. The rise of Asia, the post-Western world and the turbo-boosting of global capitalism as the digital age clicked in, all lay ahead, mostly out of sight.

By speeches, by asides, by argument, by explanation, by insistence, Margaret Thatcher began to establish in the public mind that someone of conviction was in charge of the nation's direction and that this in the minds of many, if not all, fitted in with history and destiny. Her message was certain to infuriate some (and still does), and the Falklands victory clearly bolstered her appeal and helped towards a second victory at the polls in 1983, but even before then, there were signs that opinions about her and her government were beginning to turn from outright hostility to a grudging respect.

If there is a major missing leadership element in the Brexit-obsessed scene, it has been the perception – or sense – that the movement by Britain to a new European relationship is an advance, not a surrender, nor a defeat, so long as it is sensibly and gradually managed; that we are in line both with our historical European role *and* with an era of global revolution at an even bigger turning point than the one faced forty years ago.

It is the absence of this wider contextual frame – this intuitive association of Brexit not with retreat and a return to the past but with the practical way nations and societies are going to secure their health and wealth in the digital age – which leaves the scene so wide open for facile talk of Britain becoming a vassal or a colony (implying, laughably, that the EU is an empire), and that 'ever closer union' is the 'role model for the future', when it is anything but.

Of course, it may no longer be possible in the information age to sustain a convincing narrative at all. Every attempt is bound to be torn to pieces in a billion tweets and blogs. Most reasonable folk marvel marvelled at Theresa May's resilience under incredible pressure, even while constantly questioning what she stood for. Strong leadership in the sense of Thatcher-like dominance may simply not be have been available to her. Perhaps resilience and courage are the best survival qualities left to democratic leaders against the populist storm. Nor is a leadership 'vision' necessarily what a divided and troubled nation any longer needs – see, for example, Archie Brown's telling book, *The Myth of the Strong Leader*,[173] where he rightly cautions against confusing good leadership with 'the overmighty power of overweening individuals' – at least in the democracies, and at least in peacetime.

Brown questions the notion of one single person as leader being empowered to take decisions, impose his or her views on a nation or society, and demonstrate 'strength' when so many other qualities are needed to guide a government and steer a nation:

> There are many qualities desirable in a political leader that should matter more than the criterion of strength … These include integrity, intelligence, articulateness, collegiality, shrewd judgment, a questioning mind, willingness to seek disparate views, ability to absorb information, flexibility, good memory, courage, vision, empathy and boundless vision. … Those who deserve the greatest respect are frequently not the most domineering.

Amen to that. Margaret Thatcher possessed many of these qualities, but certainly not all. To believe otherwise would be to draw the wrong lessons and legacies from her example and her times.

Today there are other forms of leadership strength which the changed world demands. Deploying them could yet convince the divided public, all sides in the Westminster hothouse and even the lofty Eurocrats in Brussels, that a British path forward is at last on offer, compromise though it may be, and that it is in everybody's interests to buy into it.

From the age of Thatcher to the digital age – with its insistent compression of time, its new centres of power, its changed America from the one that seemed so solid and immutable forty years ago, its unnerving uncertainties and its enormous possibilities – the messages and lessons come across the years. They are not all clear because the past has been distorted in a thousand ways and the present is not yet fully understood. Intuition may be the vital extra leadership quality needed to decode them. The age of the servant-leader may truly have arrived.

So we come back to Joshua Cooper Ramo's 'seventh sense' and the connected and growing cracks. The central question elbows itself forward through the jostling crowd of issues: What can possibly check and repair these 'connected cracks' before they spread to the point of social disintegration, anarchic politics and international breakdown in the environment of rules and reason?

The answers – no, that's too bold – the beginnings of constructive response lie both within and without: deep within the community structure and the pattern of daily life and order; far outside in the shifting, churning pattern of international relations. Each plays upon the other.

Some have argued that, from 1979 and earlier, the start along the path to popular sharing of wealth and ownership was one of the right ways forward to societal reform, even though it faltered and could not keep up with the pace of fundamental change occurring in the capitalist system – or changed capitalist process, as this book has preferred to call it.

Obviously, too, if the phrase 'a system that works for everyone' is to be anything more than incantation, there has to be a halt to the divisive behaviour of the corporate sector. A business world in which CEOs pay themselves (or are awarded by timid remuneration committees and supine auditors) salaries at 231 times the average pay of their employees, plainly does not work for everyone. Nor does it begin to motivate wage-earners, or create any sense of shared identity and purpose. This is 'strategy' which not only weakens performance but, in anything but the shortest of short terms, shafts investors and shareholders to the heart. Just as some of the old ideological 'differences' do not really exist, so the 'difference' for a firm between ethical policy and shareholder value no longer exists in practice. Trust and common endeavour are woven into a firm's workforce and its success path; the two cannot be separated. The corporate past is littered with the corpses of businesses that missed out on this inevitable merger of business interests, or went after the quick buck and paid fat dividends to momentarily happy stockholders, chief executives very much included.

Sharing wealth accumulation is now a central concern, more than ever because personal survival – the management of daily life with all its problems – has to be underpinned by more than wage dependence and benevolent authority, and because the digital revolution has made a different lifestyle both possible and necessary for most human beings (although obviously still not all).

The esteem, dignity, sense of fairness and, above all, sense of security, which personal ownership brings to every family is exactly matched by the power and control of life which the computer brings to the individual. Thomas Friedman's 'the power of one' has arrived.[174] Madeleine Albright had a similar phrase when she noted that technology has given every individual their own echo chamber. Everywhere, the binding links that held societies together within states are under new strain, and everywhere the binding links which held states together are under intense new strain. The two conditions are one.

External Bonds

We have entered a new cycle in international history. The 1979 world view of the Atlantic Alliance and the special relationship, seemingly so solid then, has been overtaken by the surging rise of other powers, lifted by the phenomenon of instant communication, pioneered, ironically, in America, but seized and built upon with Asiatic vigour.

Throughout the Thatcher period, the growing awareness that pushing nations together and building trade blocs was not the way forward, undoubtedly planted the seed which grew years later into Brexit. The sense of nationhood was rekindled by Thatcher and her team after years of talk about Britain's 'inevitable' decline. The need to fill out that story and reconcile it with the demands of an interdependent and hyper-connected world remains as urgent as ever.

Today's world of networks, and the rising power and influence of China, were not yet on the horizon in 1979, nor the potential for Britain in a changing Commonwealth. But the sense that markets needed to be liberated from state domination and that the balance between state collectivism and market power had to be shifted to a sensible degree, was right for the time and remains completely valid today, even when the talk now is for a resurgence of state power and state intervention.

But the preceding chapters have sought to demonstrate that the settlement between government and governed, between the frame of authority and order, and the impulse and flow of personal power and creativity, no longer turns on the old divisions in political debate or the clash of ideologies or economic philosophies. The new networks of the planet have their own logic and their own momentum. They and their algorithms will apportion power and influence, change fates, determine destinies and shape lives.

Finally, the democratic case has to be defended anew. What could be safely and comfortably assumed forty years ago – democracy was winning out after the dark totalitarianism of the twentieth century – can no longer be assumed. The difference now is that the democracy to be defended has changed its character and needs a different kind of defence – as does the free-market system.

More than ever, it now needs to be acknowledged that democracy is not just about votes and elections, let alone referenda. More than ever, it depends on restraint and on the moderating voice of those in positions of influence and power at all levels in society. For democracy to work there has to be democratic man and democratic women. More than ever it depends on avoidance of majoritarian intolerance, respect for minority views and a high degree of civility and patience.[175] More than ever, it depends on a fair and undistorted election of a parliamentary assembly which can be trusted to address complex issues wisely and sustain a capable and efficient executive administration (a notable lack in Britain at the time of writing). More than ever, it depends on awareness of the corrupting and narrowing influence of the algorithms which allow each one of us to be repeatedly targeted, with devastating polarising and 'silo' effects on public debate and the international climate.

Maybe courtesy, absent as of now from the unrestrained and poison-filled online political debate, will make a return as the great moderating force in our societies.

There is much disruption ahead. In the worst case, rival world models could collide violently with catastrophic results. In a less bad case they could be woven together and work to reinforce each other. The clash of civilisations is possible[176] though not inevitable.

This book offers a more hopeful story – that the raucous ideologues will see that their day is over and their relevance to the human condition past, that technology can be mastered, culture clashes averted and bridges built between the past and the future, with foundations resting on structures and designs which last and withstand all stresses.

In Conclusion

I have always written about what really matters to me and my starting point has always been what I know, and my experience of the world from several different standpoints and through many, many stages.

Many of the ideas this book has elaborated on arose in my earlier writings. In *Old Links and New Ties*, published well before the Brexit era, I argued that, with power moving to Asia and to the people, the UK urgently need to reposition itself in the networked world, finding new friends (and markets) and acting with new élan and agility.

Further back, in 2000, in *The Edge of Now*, I tried to show that the age of networks was going to weaken governments and empower non-state actors. I foresaw a new age of e-enabled and electronically organised protest. I tried to balance the benefits of this, in terms of liberalisation from an overbearing state apparatus, against the dangers of too much disorder and loss of central authority. I probably came out too optimistically for the former, the freedom from too much state authority, and gave too little weight to the dangers of populist fragmentation and volatile chaos making steady and firm governance nearly impossible. In the event, we now have more of the latter than the former.

For example, look no further than the way in which the Arab Spring turned to Arab winter then Arab nightmare. Eighteen years later, BBC correspondents have just been discovering what they term 'a new age of digital protest' (slow learners, they), as demonstrated by France's *gilets jaunes*, leaderless yet coordinating their street barricades and car-burning in a thousand French towns and villages.

* * * * *

In this book I have focused on three episodes in the last half century: the age of Thatcher, the roots of market liberalisation, and the succeeding digital revolution which has overturned nearly all assumptions.

This is the fifth book I have written arguing – in suitably revised and updated form each time as conditions change – that:

[] The age of hyper-connectivity, driven by new technology at breakneck pace, has empowered populism as never before in centuries past, with tremendous, and not fully understood, impact on both the internal stability of nations and the pattern of international relations. Both must be managed with new imagination, be responded to and, yet, be contained.

[] Political parties are essential to democratic stability, but parties clinging to the old ideologies will crumble – and are already doing so. The doctrines of yesterday do not , and cannot, fit the parties of today and tomorrow.

[] Globalisation, constantly changing its form, is here to stay and grow, regardless of what governments may wish or do. It is an embedded and evolving part of the free human condition, and not, as Marx would have it, a mere bolted-on system of capitalist production which can be discarded and replaced with some other arrangement of human affairs.

[] Trying to defend a static capitalist model, which scarcely exists any longer, is a hopeless endeavour. Technology has blown away the arguments of the past. There are new world financial conditions to be explained, reformed and interpreted. There is also the ghost of rational 'economic man' to be exorcised from governance and policy (and from underlying economic theorising). For a start, economic theorists need the voice of rational women as well. But perhaps the assumption of 'rationality' itself is too narrow? A fuller account of social and non-economic motivations might provide a better guide to understanding how economies work and how democracies are going to work.

[] One domestic political imperative in order to head off anarchy and social breakdown is to find ways of sharing the growth of capitalism's wealth on a massive scale and refresh the democratic process in totally changed conditions of understanding and communication. Genuinely secure provision for every family is the absolute. Wages and welfare benefits are not enough to do this. State pensions fall well short of old-age dignity. Shares for millions of households in society's growing wealth must supplement income and savings and ensure that old age ceases to be an oncoming time of fear.

[] Britain has now to find a new position. What should have been obvious long before Brexit is now ten times more so. It has to play the network game and the soft power game with agility and skill in a transformed international system, using its links with the vast Commonwealth network – the 'mother of all networks' – in particular, but also consolidating all parts of the British Isles as a force in international affairs.

[] Britain should cease hanging onto America's coattails, or those of any posturing alliance claiming 'world leadership'. An entirely new network and system of security has emerged into which individual nations need to be integrated. And a network world has no hierarchy of nations, and no dominant superpower.

The process of forming a government on a firm party basis, assembling a cabinet, holding it in a reasonable degree of unity, and placing it at the fountainhead of a story of national purpose and direction which inspires trust and loyalty, has become progressively more difficult over the four decades – and is going to get more difficult still. In Britain, the two main parties, Labour and Conservative, both of venerable vintage , are bound to continue crumbling, unless and until they can shed their past baggage.

One reason for this is because the task of directing an informed, connected, digitalised nation has become vastly more complex. Big failures in computerised programmes designed to exert central control over the nation have become a regular feature of Whitehall departmental government. Public opinion has become far more informed, far better equipped to track and monitor every move of the administration, on a screen of almost total transparency, and yet at the same time far more volatile and fragmented. These are conditions in which even a strongly entrenched administration with a clear democratic mandate, such as the Thatcher Government of '79, would have found it harder and harder to govern and to make the necessary difficult and unavoidable choices.

It is going to be an increasing challenge even to secure that mandate. Under Western systems of democracy there must be a choice, an alternative government. This means that an administration must be strong enough to radiate authority on behalf of the state and yet at the same time resilient enough to live with, and accept, sharp opposition, as a constitutional necessity.

But I have sought in this book to identify a deeper reason still. The puzzled world is now looking to its leaders not just for debates of economic theology but for some form of renewed moral framework. The seven strategic priorities above require enormous strength of will to pursue and complete, but they need a wider context. Economic advance is only a means to an end. The central story of this book has been to explain how governments and the voices of authority need to find new themes just when they have become weaker and their capacities increasingly limited. Their power has drained away to the street, to the locality, to markets and to the global leviathans of technology.

What would have been formidable policy shifts in the glad confident morn of 1979, with a potentially strong Cabinet and leader, and a strong story for its day, are now a hundred times more difficult in the political conditions created by the connectivity age, by an empowered public and by a new international politics, which could be the biggest influence of all on our society and nation.

Judged beside this scene of global upheaval and turmoil, the Brexit saga is for Britain a vexing but lesser issue, but one which must be sensibly settled. It will take years to disentangle patterns of government which, over four decades, have grown together and twisted around each other like two separate but deeply intertwined climbing plants. It would have been infinitely better to have pushed forward the reconstruction of the EU to meet modern conditions from inside the tent, but the exit route was chosen. The task remains to settle amicably and constructively our proper regional role in the European constellation – a neighbourhood in which Britain has played a decisive role for over a thousand years, and for the health and stability of which it continues to have a major responsibility, beside that of being a good neighbour. That is going to take years of unwinding and stitching together again in a new tapestry.

Some of these initiatives may have started in the period between writing these words and publication, but will not have finished. The conflict between identity and higher cooperation, between the local and the global, between own control and total connection, is now on a rising curve of intensity. Old and manageable differences become new unmanageable fissures. New tensions inevitably make analysis look dated. I will just have to ask indulgence for an unavoidable deficiency.

There are right and wrong lessons to be drawn from the Cabinet of 1979, from what followed that first gathering and the roots from which it drew. One is that it was reforming but not transforming. There was no 'unbridled free-market' revolution, either to be hailed or denounced. This kind of polarised picture should be expunged from political memories, although it lingers on, distorting our grasp of present-day realities.

Above all, the onward rush of modern technology, in all its awesome power to change everything, has no Left or Right dimension. The caps of capitalism and socialism simply no longer fit. The ideological roots of the debates of those times, deep as they lie in the decades before 1979, do not connect with the great challenges and issues of today. The lingering perceptions, the language of the old political spectrum, the tired mindsets, the numerous threads still tie us to a different past. It is time the threads were cut, the ties broken.

John Maynard Keynes once observed that his quarrel was not so much with those who disagreed with his economic arguments as with those who refused to see the significance of what was actually happening in the world around them.

It is hard not to feel the same today. If this volume lifts even a corner of the curtain on how we adapt to an entirely new cycle in the history of international affairs and in our own national fortunes, then it will have done its small bit.

Chapter Twenty-three

Afterthoughts: On the Head of a Dictator, the Power of Us and Catching Up

'How do you live in an age of bewilderment where the old stories have collapsed, and no new story has yet emerged to replace them?

— Yuval Noah Harari[177]

The Head of a Dictator

It was a grisly object. I held in my hands the severed head of Oliver Cromwell, John Milton's 'chief of men',[178] Lord Protector of the Commonwealth of England, Scotland and Ireland 'and the Dominions and Territories thereunto belonging'. Years later it was to receive a decent burial at an unmarked spot within Sidney Sussex College, Cambridge. But at this time – it was the summer of 1947 – it was still in the possession of Canon Horace Wilkinson who kept it in the hall of his Woodbridge house in Suffolk, in a chest, not large, say thirty inches long and twenty deep. Inside were folds of maroon silk, and in the middle of them lay the head – which the canon Canon lifted out and placed in my hands.[179]

It had a wooden spike through it – the original top of the traitor's pole – tipped with metal just poking out of the top of the skull, traces of gingery hair (at some stage in its history it had become pickled) and axe marks where the head had been roughly hacked off the disinterred body by a furious mob. Two teeth remained in the leathery mouth, and blackened skin.

It was the head that never wore a crown. And it was the head of a man who removed a Parliament by force. (Could that happen again? Surely not). But the greatest idea from within it lives on and thrives, although in a totally new form. His dream was of the great and strong Commonwealth, not just of England but of the British Isles and beyond. It was a vision which, despite its blemishes, raised England's prestige to unprecedented heights. Antonia Fraser's glorious biography[180] tells us that his temper was short and he felt empowered by divine providence. Yet he was able to inspire and attract loyalty for his purposes — at least for a good while — to an amazing degree across a whole nation.

Today's reality is a vast Commonwealth network encompassing almost a third of the human race and creating a network of culture, language, habits and outlooks, no longer Anglocentric, yet with roots going back to the Commonwealth of England, Scotland and Ireland — notwithstanding the bloody Cromwellian legacy on Irish soil.

This book has been less about parties and politics and more about the ebb and flow of ideas and modern Britain's prospects in a completely transformed international landscape — a landscape of networks and connections of a new kind; an altered world from the one confronting those figures in that front cover photograph, the class and Cabinet of '79. Of this new world it has been argued that the modern Commonwealth network is a major component — not the only new network by far, and not the only new live-grid of soft power, but for Britain a treasure and an asset, to be cherished and respected.

Of course, this Commonwealth is an entirely different construct not only from Cromwell's seventeenth-century creation but also from the British Commonwealth and Empire of the twentieth century, and indeed from the 'modern' Commonwealth which came into being in 1949. Yet the Cromwellian idea of unity, welding the British Isles into a united kingdom, still has a flicker of resonance, a flicker which could grow into a strong light if the Irish Question can finally be put to bed and replaced by an Irish-British partnership solidly based on mutual respect, and if Scotland can settle for power and prosperity alongside, rather than separated from England, and if a wise balance of devolved powers and shared prosperity can be achieved with the Welsh principality and all the regions – 'ifs' indeed, but none beyond the possible.

In contrast to 1979, it is undeniable that the hegemony of the West is now over. The very nature of relationships between states has been altered, with much of the economic analysis and theorising underpinning the old order ceasing to be relevant or to explain what is happening.

The Power of Us

An irrevocable shift in the distribution of power and influence across the planet has now occurred and a new constellation of nations, powers, influences and forces has emerged. Even what it means to be a democratic state has changed in the instant communication age.

Networks introduce an entirely different dimension into the foreign policy picture. Contacts and culture at non-governmental levels become infinitely more important and influential. International *involvement* becomes a better description of a nation's overseas relationships than foreign policy, allowing a nation or state to shape and keep modifying its relations with others, and with great global trends, with far greater latitude and flexibility than was available in the age of fixed alliances and bloc entanglements.

In the British case, relations with our European Continental neighbours will, of course, be close and can and ought to become both comfortable and, in a broad sense, settled. But they are already a shrinking part of the new picture (despite their intensely divisive nature within the UK, shredding the body politic to ribbons and straining the founding assumptions of parliamentary democracy). This is hardly surprising when, according to the International Monetary Fund, the EU's share of world output, once over 30 per cent, had fallen to 17 per cent by 2017, and the Eurozone's share to an even smaller 11.9 per cent.

The bigger part of commerce and international business of all kinds is being filled by a latticework – a vast new weave of connections –

between Britain and the cities and powers of Asia, Africa and Latin America, and between Britain and the scores of small nations who populate the global network and who command a new degree of respect, understanding and friendship.

From the diplomatic angle, the essential point to grasp is that the peoples of the Commonwealth are not foreigners, they are family. The governments of Commonwealth states may be unfriendly at time, critical, awkward, even hostile, but these are family matters, not foreign policy matters. The difference is crucial because the handling of family matters requires a quite different approach to the handling of matters than with either neighbours or strangers.

The new network world that has emerged is neither Anglocentric, nor Eurocentric, nor even Atlantic-centric. In truth a vast global *bouleversement* is taking place. The developing nations and communities are fast becoming the developed. The poor are becoming the less indebted while the rich, the so-called 'advanced' nations, are mired deeper in debt than ever before in history. The savings of the east and the south are coming to the rescue of the north and the west. The so-called backward states turn out to be forward – in some cases ahead of the West technologically. The small are setting the pace for the big – as David Lloyd George (the Welsh Wizard) – once said they always have done. Small is becoming more beautiful. Power is slipping away to the powerless. Václav Havel's dazzling insight becomes the new reality.

Parts of official government circles and policy establishments may not have understood what has happened, and old perceptions left over from the 1980s and 1990s may linger on. But outside government, the peoples, the communities, businesses, professions and civil society organisations certainly have. Governments may have their disputes and differences, but outside government, away from officialdom, the intertwinement links every thread of international life. The preceding pages have sought to show how this altered world is driven increasingly by what has come to be called soft power.[181] It used to be said that trade follows the flag. But that is no longer the case. Trade – and investment – follows the patient cultivation of linkages between peoples, cultures and markets, layer upon layer. It is the new skill, the exercising and deployment of soft power, which trade now follows.[182]

The statistical trends (where they can be extracted and relied upon) concerned with trade growth, capital movements, educational linkages and social and professional activities confirm this to be so. With or without the blessings of authorities, the everyday world is being woven together as never before.

But this is precisely where wrong geo-political conclusions get drawn. What doomsayers forecast is a continuing amalgamation of old nation states into bigger and bigger units. In this prediction, these respected voices are at one with both the founders and the latter-day leaders of the European Union, who sincerely believe that big is best and that Europe must be propelled into some form of superpower status to compete with and face up to the other super blocs of the world. Yet here, in this insistent view that bigger is always better, we have the real blindness to the paradox of the digital world.

This book attests to the world moving in an entirely different direction. Massive technological forces are coming over the horizon which will work decisively the opposite way: localising instead of centralising and exerting immense centrifugal pressures on all societies.

Proof of this lies in the visible break-up of states, whether in political discord or outright violence, in turn eroding the rules-based order built up over seventy years since 1945. New forces have altered the place and power of the main international players and the multinational institutions of the past. Impatient electorates, overloaded with information, have decreasing time for international responsibilities and compromises, or for the plight of other nations, pressing weakened governments into ever more inward-looking policies of instant gratification.

It should be no surprise that Francis Fukuyama's latest book takes us far away from economic issues, and his earlier theses, to the small but furious world of identity politics, where social media and the power of clustering give the demands of every category, cause and campaign, however selfish and however narrow, a new thrust and political priority.[183]

The sequence is direct and obvious, yet often overlooked. Ever more empowered lobbies organise with increasing thoroughness and effect, courtesy the Web, to scare nervous and yet vote-needy politicians and weak governments into meeting their demands for recognition and support, regardless of any wider or longer-term considerations. The new political punch comes upward from constituencies and silos based on sects, races, tribes, religious coteries, clubs, ethnicity, gender, sexuality and from the discordant clatter of shifting and fragmented , but ever more amplified, opinion which the digital age has wrought. And , always, the force of it turns attention inwards, towards satisfying immediate close-to-home demands. International dangers or duties inevitably go to the bottom of the pile.

Both deep within societies and between societies, trust has faltered, leaving the darkest global challenges unattended. The catalogue is huge, but begins with such things as resumed nuclear weapons proliferation and weapons competition; unpoliced cyber banditry, accompanied by the fatal trust-destroyer, fake news; treaties violated; loss of control over chemical and biological horrors; failure to form a common international approach to mass migration, to climate threats and a world on the move; and, e-enabled religious and doctrinal extremism unleashed. The identity scramble hardly stops to glance at these questions, except in the case of global warming, and even there, more by demands than by actual personal sacrifice.

* * * * *

Through these past chapters it has been argued that to step into the next stage there must, above all, be a unifying sense of nation, a focus for patriotism. We cannot hope to speak or act with confidence in the transformed international milieu until we have mastered and restrained our own internal demons or begun sewing the fragments together again. The age of hierarchy has gone for good. It must be replaced by leadership with the stance and tone of servanthood in a society of unstoppable grassroots empowerment, classlessness and transparency.

In the British case, the repair and popularisation of the ever-changing capitalist process is very far from completion: The unity and purpose of the United Kingdom must be restored and put beyond question, the closeness with Ireland must be taken to a new phase.

In the digital age, the communications revolution and the networks in which Britain now has to operate, have replaced the old international and mostly Western patterns of power, and have put China, and indeed most of Asia, now to the fore. This is a world where we need new friends and new forms of relationship: The Commonwealth family gives Britain enduring advantage to survive and prosper in these novel global conditions.

None of this work is completed, most of it is very much in progress, some of the work has not even begun. Nevertheless, the journey continues.

Catching Up

A phrase familiar in Asian commentary around the turn of the century was that the rising nations of the Asian region had to 'catch up'. Catching up meant aiming for the standards set by Western powers, in economic weight, inventiveness, and the values and the political freedom which had given Europe then America three centuries of dominance.

There is now just one big difference. Catching up is still the theme but it is in Western, not Eastern, voices, and British voices in particular, that the phrase needs to be heard. It is becoming the urgent goal which British leaders, as well as other European leaders, should now be setting before their peoples.

The paths of '79 on which we set out so full of hope, have mostly petered out or been blocked. The arrival in office of the '79 Cabinet marked a sort-of end and a sort-of beginning. What ended was the collectivist consensus which had governed Britain since 1945. What was beginning was an unravelling of the corporatist state and its power centres. Beginning, too, were first new moves towards popular capitalism. But these moves faltered and other far bigger forces of change swept in, unleashed and uncontrolled. Ahead lay incurable divisions in both the major political parties, Conservative and Labour, on which twentieth-century political stability had rested.

Ahead, too, lay a totally transformed international milieu, with America no longer its bedrock — a world of networks of which the governments of the '70s and '80s knew nothing. And ahead lay a new and threatening instability in the democratic process as it had been practised for a century before.

In a changed, noisy democracy public forum we have to take on new obligations and fight for democracy in new ways. And in a heavily altered international order we have to shoulder new kinds of collective security. With these obligations Europe, alone, cannot begin to cope. Even NATO, the vessel of Atlantic security, is not strong enough to encompass the ubiquitous threats of cyber-attack against which nations are largely undefended and which threaten cities and communities almost to the same existential degree as nuclear weapons.

In one key aspect in particular we should feel fortified by that group which stares out at us across the gap of forty years. The undeniable gift of the Thatcher era was to give a confused and troubled nation a renewal of confidence and a sense of national purpose — at least for a while.

Now, all that is left behind. At each bend in the road an entirely new vista and an entirely new range of challenges open up of which, often much too slowly, we become aware, but which in the end we have to face. We cannot afford to neglect the lessons of recent history, even when the conditions and circumstances our predecessors faced were fundamentally different. But we must make sure the lessons are the right ones, the relevant ones and the true ones. So far, we have not done too well.

Appendix I

A Chequered Career –
Author's Note

1954–56 Second Lieutenant, Coldstream Guards

1959–60 Economic section of the Treasury

1960–64 *Daily Telegraph* feature and leader writer

1961–64 Parliamentary candidate for Dudley and Stourbridge

1962 Joint Secretary, the UK European Movement

1962–63 Chairman of the Bow Group

1963–64 Editor of *Crossbow*

1964–66 Director of the Conservative Political Centre

1966–70 Director of the Public Sector Research Unit (PSRU)

1966–97 MP for Guildford

1966–2010 Occasional columnist, *Wall Street Journal*

1970–71 Lord Commissioner of the Treasury

1970–72 Parliamentary Secretary, the Civil Service Department

1971–72 Parliamentary Secretary, Department of Employment

1972–73 Parliamentary Secretary, Northern Ireland Office

1973–74 Minister of State, Northern Ireland Office

1974 Minister of State, Department of Energy

1974–77 Opposition spokesman on Treasury and Financial Affairs

1975–80 Trustee of the Federal Trust

1976–79 Adviser to Wood Mackenzie

1976–79 Adviser to Merch, Sharpe and Dohm

1977–79 Opposition spokesman on Home Affairs

1978–79 Head of speech-writing team for Margaret Thatcher

1979 Privy Counsellor

1979–81 Secretary of State for Energy

1981–83 Secretary of State for Transport

1983–85 Visiting Fellow, Policy Studies Institute

1983–86 Consultant to Savory Milln plc

1983–2001 Visiting Fellow, Nuffield College, Oxford

1983–2010 and 2013–★ Columnist, the *Japan Times*

1984–89 Consultant to Coopers & Lybrand

1987–96 Member of the International Advisory Board of Swiss Bank
  Corporation

1987–97 Chairman of the Commons Foreign Affairs Committee

1989–1997 Chairman UK-Japan 2000 Group

1990–96 Non-Executive Director Trafalgar House plc

1992–94 Member of the Giscard d'Estaing-Helmut Schmidt Committee for Monetary Union (UK representative with Lord
  Callaghan)

1993–2004 Non-Executive Director Monks Investment Trust

1994–97 Non-Executive Director Jardine Insurance Brokers plc

1996–2000 Advisory Director, UBS-Warburg

1997 Created a Life Peer

1998–2000 Chairman of the House of Lords Sub-Committee on
  European Foreign and Security Policy

1998–2000 Governor of Sadler's Wells Foundation

2000–03 Non-Executive Director John Laing plc

2000–2010 Occasional op-ed columnist, *International Herald Tribune*

2000–2010 Trustee of Shakespeare's Globe Theatre

2001–2010 Conservative Foreign Affairs Spokesman, House of Lords

2001–2011 and 2013–★ European Consultant, Japan Central Railway
  Co.

2002–2010 Deputy Opposition Leader, House of Lords

2003–2010 and 2012–★ Member of the Financial Advisory Board to
  The Kuwait Investment Authority

2003–11 and 2013–★ European Consultant Mitsubishi Electric, Europe
  BV

2003–2012 President of the British Institute of Energy Economists

2004–★ Chairman of the Windsor Energy Group

2008–2010 Trustee of the Duke of Edinburgh's Commonwealth Conference

2009–2010 Vice-President of the Middle East Association

2009-2010 Vice-President of the Conservative Middle East Association

2009–2010 Chairman of the UK-Azerbaijan Business Council

2009–★ Vice-Chairman of the Asia-Pacific CEO Association

2010 Minister of State, FCO, and Minister for the Commonwealth

2013–14 Chairman of the Lords Ad-Hoc Committee on Soft Power

2014–★ President of the Royal Commonwealth Society and The Council of Commonwealth Societies

2016–2019 Chairman of the Lords International Relations Committee

2018–★ Member of the High Level Group on Commonwealth Governance

Author of eight books and twelve pamphlets

Appendix II

The Times: Mr Howell's Account of the Whitelaw Years in Belfast

The Policies Which Prepared the Ground for Trust in Ulster

Published Monday 10 February 1975

The Whitelaw period of government in Northern Ireland began on March 30, 1972, when the Northern Ireland (temporary provisions) Act became law. It ended, strictly speaking, with the departure of Mr Whitelaw, to take up the post of Secretary of State for Employment on December 2, 1973.

In fact, the Sunningdale Agreement reached on December 9, 1973, and the final handing over of the wide range of powers in the domestic, economic and social field to the new power-sharing executive at midnight on December 31, must be regarded as the terminating events of this particular episode in Irish history.

It is, of course too early to make judgments – although this has not prevented some from doing so. But myths and legends about events as dramatic as those of the Whitelaw period take root as quickly as weeds unless dug out early. It may, therefore, be no bad thing to begin putting on record a few notes and reasonably fresh recollections of what went on at that time even if one cannot at this stage go very deep and even if the events with which we grappled are still working themselves through and look like doing so for a long time to come.

David Windlesham, who was my colleague in Northern Ireland for most of the period, set out in a lecture to the new University of Ulster in April 1973 a lucid account of the way in which we sought to carry out governmental duties. His account brings home effectively the operational atmosphere in which the Whitelaw administration did its work: the hurtling back-and-forth between Stormont Castle and Westminster; the constant demands, day and night, of the security situation in Northern Ireland; the tasks of civilian administration, often hopelessly intertwined with the violence, as in the case of housing, for example; the vast legislative programme at the Westminster end; the overriding need to make progress with our strategic objectives; and – to survive at all – the daily or even hourly need to hold the balance and prevent the landslide – either way – to civil collapse and massacre.

To make all this work, to build a going concern upon the bitter and uneasy situation prevailing in Belfast immediately after the dissolution of the Stormont parliament, required both the personality of Whitelaw and the brilliance of Whitehall's most able official. It also required calmness of nerve and complete loyalty from the Northern Ireland Civil Service, the ongoing administrative corpus, and this too was forthcoming.

It was clear to us from the start if terrorism must be checked at all that it could not be done while violence had widespread political support; while there was an open border and while an ambivalent attitude to IRA terrorism prevailed the other side of it; while outside world opinion had a distorted hostile opinion of British policy; while arms and succour poured in; while a large proportion of the Roman Catholic minority saw no chance of ever being involved in their own government; while it was still widely believed that civil rights were being denied; while areas of Northern Ireland are not even under British military, let alone civilian control; while the economic and social fabric of Northern Ireland was under threat.

I do not think there was ever a moment when it was possible, or even useful, to set down a list of all our objectives within our broad aim. It was not that kind of life, and Willie Whitelaw was not a man for ponderous analytical papers usually arriving for discussion days after the relevant events have passed.

We did have one 'think' weekend at Chequers, which the PM kindly lent us, and this helped clear our minds on the broad framework and timetable. But if we had ever set down a comprehensive list of all the things we sought to do, I suppose it would look something like this:

- To isolate the violent men and women for political support and having isolated them, to destroy them.
- To take and keep control of the no-go areas and to reintroduce (or introduce in some cases) regular law enforcement.
- To win back the bulk of the Catholic population to the path of politics and the politics of hope.
- To do so without provoking Loyalist fears to boiling point.
- To build up, by every means available, a band of moderate opinion drawn from both sides (meaning roughly, those who understood that we could never go back to the old Protestant hegemony but that United Ireland could not be achieved by the violence and certainly not in the foreseeable future by any means – and that it was more important to deal with the possibilities of the present that the impossibilities of a remote future).
- To show that it was possible to set up government again in Northern Ireland which could contain both Catholics and Protestants in fair proportions.
- To strengthen and improve the entire economic and social infrastructure of the Province in *all* areas.
- To legislate into being a new Assembly and new government from it which would satisfy the principles above.
- To do all this while holding the bipartisan line at Westminster.
- To move opinion in Dublin to a far more sympathetic and cooperative position.
- To shift world opinion into a more realistic understanding of the dilemmas.

It would be hard to think of anyone better suited to the daunting task of recreating the moderate centre ground in Ulster and gradually isolating the exponents of violent methods than Willie Whitelaw.

It is difficult to recall now, thinking back, how remote and almost unattainable the goal seemed of bringing ourselves into any kind of working relationship with either the SDLP leaders on one side, or Brian Faulkner and the 'dispossessed' Unionists on the other, let alone bringing them together.

'Difficult' because these were people who later on one came to admire immensely, who worked in the closest relationship with Willie Whitelaw and other British ministers, and who grew into each other's confidence in a way which, even now, cannot all have been destroyed.

Balance

In the early days the arrival of Brian Faulkner to see the Secretary of State at Stormont Castle was an event marking a major advance out of the uneasy post-Stormont situation vis-à-vis the former Unionist ministers.

Soon it would all be off again then on, then off, as some furious row blew up – over housing, over policing, over harassment, over the Army pressure in certain schools, over the alleged behaviour of some new regiment, over detention, over an accidental shooting.

On the Protestant side a different but equally volatile catalogue would be ground out – not enough being done against lawlessness, not enough troops, harassment (again) – in one case from the very regiment which had aroused Catholic complaints, which seemed to be nobody's friend and was probably getting it just about right – housing, the border, the plebiscite, local planning, and most often of all the 'frustration' of the loyalist people.

Seen in this context of the essential balance, by far the two most sensitive and critical acts in the early days were the taking out of the no-go area – Operation Motorman – and the Secretary of State's controversial meeting with Provisional IRA leaders in London.

The former ran the obvious risk that if the operation led to substantial bloodshed it would drive the Catholic community more firmly into the arms of the gunmen. Yet it had to be done, and the

Bloody Friday massacre – in which ten civilians and three soldiers died on July 21 in Belfast – gave the final pretext, if indeed that was needed, for moving.

The meeting some weeks earlier with the Provisional leaders, I believe, also had to be, unpleasant though Willie Whitelaw found it. The danger again, was driving a frightened Protestant community into the hands of its extreme elements. The gain, and the reason why it had to be a stage along the critical path, lay in the need to establish in Catholic minds that everything had been tried – truce, meeting, every effort – and that these were people beyond reason, beyond politics, beyond decency, existing not for political ideals but for the sake of violence itself.

The meeting was bitter and acrimonious and from then on it was inevitable that the so-called truce meant nothing.

That Mr Whitelaw tried this path helped, I believe, in showing the Catholic community that true interests lay not with the IRA but with the SDLP and its courageous leaders.

It had to be gone through, though the price paid in Protestant suspicion was heavy, in turn demanding compensating measures.

The danger point of autumn, 1972, was the two nights of rioting, October 11 and 12, led by the UDA, under Mr Tommy Herron, and accompanied by threats from Mr Billy Hull of the Loyalist Association of Workers, to halt the power stations. There were bitter charges of harassment by British troops, fears that the longed-for plebiscite would not take place, frustration at IRA violence, an accumulation of pent-up and understandable feelings.

At the beginning of the second night of rioting Mr Herron (later murdered) was brought to see me at Stormont Castle. There was to be no negotiation with him (he had just held a press conference and 'declared war' on the British Army) but there had to be some understanding and sympathetic comprehension of his followers' feelings. This was given. The army had a further meeting with him the following day and, handling the tense situation with its usual skill, appeared to satisfy him and his followers. Next day Mr Hull went on holiday and all was well. We were back from the precipice again.

From the end of 1972 to the late summer of 1973, the pattern of violence changed and declined. Policies began to break through. Local elections were held, then Assembly elections. The moderate ground was growing firmer and bigger – readier to bear the weight of a new Assembly and a new Executive.

All these efforts, all the endless patient diplomacy by Willie Whitelaw, reached its culminating phase in the Stormont Castle talks between three of the Assembly parties, Official Unionist, SDLP and Alliance, which began on October 5 1973, under the Secretary of State's chairmanship. The talks continued for just under seven weeks. They were historic in the sense that those around the table, Catholic and Protestant, had not sat down together, certainly not to hammer out detailed issues, in living memory. The chairmanship of these marathon sessions constitutes one of the major feats of diplomatic skill in the history of Britain and Ireland.

At several points during the seven weeks, the project seemed hopeless.

Years of mistrust, not only between the two sides, but also of the British Government, had to be worn down. The positions were apparently irreconcilable. Subcommittees under junior ministers met some mornings to reach common ground on seemingly less contentious issues like economic official policy. Even here, argument hovered just below flashpoint on questions like housing as we sought to work out agreed positions. The fact that we were also, in effect, constructing an economic and social 'coalition' programme to satisfy both socialist (SDLP) and Unionist (economically centre-right) aspirations seemed a minor challenge compared with the sheer suspicion and fear that the two sides had for each other at their first encounter.

But in the main meetings the atmosphere was steadily improving. The moments of tension were fewer. In between highly personal attacks jokes were beginning to appear. On the night of November 21 the final critical point was reached with a debate over the way in which the posts on the Executive should be shared. The Unionists had to have a simple level majority, or the package was unsaleable to their followers. The SDLP had to have, with the Alliance Party, at least equal strength, otherwise the party would reject it. Alliance had to have two places, otherwise it would pull out.

Out of this impossible arithmetic, Mr Whitelaw deftly drew an answer. At 9pm on Tuesday, November 21, all seemed lost. An hour later, after numerous adjournments, caucuses, visits to the Secretary of State, withdrawal to other rooms and further visits, it had all become possible. The numbers were agreed, giving the Unionists six places, SDLP four and Alliance one, with other posts outside the Executive. The political basis for recovery had begun to emerge.

The Sunningdale Agreement followed inevitably from the ties formed over the weeks of Stormont Castle talks. It has been much reviled since as inflexible and failing to take full account of the weight of loyalist opinion and of loyalist fears about the Council of Ireland. If one regards the Sunningdale Agreement as the last final and formal word on an Irish settlement, this view is probably correct, though lamentable because the fears are groundless. But they existed, do exist and have to be taken into account.

There was, of course, nothing new about this – as Willie Whitelaw and those who served with him, and as his immediate successor, Francis Pym, well knew. The management of the Northern Ireland situation required constant temperature-taking constant attention to loyalist sensibilities and suspicions. Perhaps Sunningdale was a shade too grand an occasion, too intergovernmental, too polished to fit into this pattern of constant shift and change as one struggled to maintain an equilibrium. But this is taking us into things that came later.

At the end of 1973 the incredible been achieved on the political front – a government commanding wide support had been established. And on the security front there had been definite progress, although all was far from satisfactory. But the daily shoot-outs in the streets of Belfast were a thing of the past, so it seemed. The level of bombings was down.

We were through the appalling assassination phase. There was a basis for hope.

Indeed, in the first weeks of 1974 there were grounds for claiming that, in a limited sense, the Whitelaw period has succeeded. If by 'succeeded' one means setting oneself certain objectives in a certain timescale, then reaching more than half of them, then the word is as justified as it is about everything in Ulster. On January 1, the new

Northern Ireland executive came into being after a brief ceremony. But more than the creation of a new government there was the creation of a new setting.

The attitude in Dublin changed to one of active and positive help. World opinion had been vastly altered. The men of violence had been politically isolated. The trust in political processes of large sections of the Catholic population had been won. The economy, far from being torn apart, prospered mightily and registered one of the fastest growth rates in Europe. The appalling housing problems at Belfast, and elsewhere, were beginning to be contained. Unemployment was lower than for many years. This was indeed something on which to build.

But fantasies, and their skilled promoters, bedevilled Mr Whitelaw's task throughout. Perhaps the cruellest and yet most understandable fantasy was that military victory was obtainable.

Why could not the terrorists be crushed by all-out effort. Why, went the cry, did the army have one hand tied behind its back?

If there been no political strategy; if there have been unlimited troops; if there had been readiness to accept the casualties both among the civilian population and the troops not in hundreds but in thousands; if there had been a willingness to plunge into all-out war against the Catholic minority, then I suppose this line, characterised as the 'Get in' approach, as against 'Get out', could have been followed. But that was not the policy. The Whitelaw approach, supported by the army in general and by most thinking commanders, was to lower the temperature, not to raise it, among the Catholic population.

Fantasies

To be sure, once the terrorists could be isolated from politics, once doors were closed to them, they could be struck at with the same ferocity as they themselves are ready to use. One of the outcomes of a longer life of the power-sharing Executive might have been precisely that it would have established a situation in which Catholics would be prepared to put up with far more troop activity and more searches and would supply far more information once they had *their* government, or part of a government, at Stormont Castle.

Another fantasy, which seems to be growing in Britain, is that we can pull down the shutters on Ulster and get out. It is the parallel and companion of the view held in some circles in Northern Ireland that if the British went, the Ulster people would manage. IRA and loyalists would come together in an independent Ulster, friendly with, but joined neither to Britain nor the Republic.

The delusion here is complete. If Iceland, with a far smaller population, if Luxembourg ... of course, of course. But who would rule? it would be the old problem, magnified by fright to scales of slaughter and terror which would at last bring about the Civil War, on a Spanish Civil War scale of deaths which commentators have been asserting is around every corner.

Behind the pathetic, sometimes even endearing, fantasies, the reality sits. There is only one forward path. One place it does *not* lead to is to truces and deals with professional murderers – whose very reason for existence is violence, based on money and publicity on a scale beyond their wildest dreams.

That course had to be tried – once – but the lessons from it were well learnt by the bulk of the Catholic population and it should not have been tried again.

No, the only way forward is to isolate and defeat terror. And that can only be done if minority and majority trust can somehow be united in one administration at Stormont Castle. One way or another, we had to live with the inherent ambiguities of Northern Ireland.

Men who dream of a united Ireland – one day – will have to sit down again with men who insist it must never happen, and both have to put their dreams aside and deal with the problems this week and next, this year, next year, sometime, instead of with the contradictory politics of never.

Of course, this does not mean adhering to every letter of the Sunningdale Agreement. There was and must always be, room for manoeuvre. If the loyalists could have accepted even that, how welcome they would have been at the Sunningdale conference, instead of handing in petitions at the door of the Civil Service College.

The Whitelaw period showed it could be done. The spirit was and is there. For reasons outside this story, the January 1 Executive was never given a chance. Its test of strength came when it was scarcely weaned, and it crumpled. But what was achieved can be achieved again, where such brave men are involved and where such sturdy people, Catholic and Protestant, are involved.

For just a moment there came together in Ulster the right Englishman, the right Irishmen, the right Ulstermen in common achievement. It did not last, but it was no fantasy. It will turn this way again. —*David Howell*

Bibliography

Agar, Herbert. *A Time of Greatness*. Little, Brown, 1942

Agar, Herbert. *The Perils of Democracy*. Bodley Head, 1965

Aitken, Jonathan. *Margaret Thatcher: Power and Personality*. Bloomsbury, 2013

Baldwin, Richard. *The Great Convergence*. Harvard University Press, 2016

Bannister, Robert C. (ed.). *On Liberty, Society and Politics: The Essential Essays of William Graham Sumner*. Liberty Fund, 1992

Blackstone, Tessa; Plowden, William. *Inside the Think-Tank*. William Heinemann, 1988

Bloomfield, Ken. *Stormont in Crisis*. Blackstaff Press, 1994

Brown, Archie. *The Myth of the Strong Leader: Political Leadership in the Modern Age*. The Bodley Head, 2015

Cartledge, Paul. *Democracy: A Life*. Oxford University Press, 2016

Castells, Manuel. *Information Age* trilogy. Blackwell 1996, 1997, 1998

Churchill, Winston S. *Thoughts and Adventures*. Thornton Butterworth, 1932

Cockett, Richard. *Thinking the Unthinkable: Think-tanks and the Economic Counter-revolution, 1931–83*. HarperCollins, 1994

Collier, Paul. *The Future of Capitalism: Facing the New Anxieties*. Penguin, 2018

Coyle, Diane. *GDP: A Brief but Affectionate History*. Princeton University Press, 2014

Erhard, Ludwig. *Prosperity Through Competition*. Thames and Hudson, 1958

Ferguson, Niall; Zakaria, Fareed. *The End of the Liberal Order?* Oneworld Publications, 2017

Ferguson, Niall. *The Square and the Tower*. Penguin Books, 2018

Fitzgibbons, Jonathan. *Cromwell's Head*. The National Archives, 2008

Fraser, Antonia. *Cromwell, Our Chief of Men*. Weidenfeld & Nicolson, 1973

Friedman, Thomas L. *The Lexus and the Olive Tree: Understanding Globalization*. Farrar, Straus and Giroux, 1999

Friedman, Thomas L. *The World is Flat*. Penguin Books, 2007

Friedman, Thomas L. *Thank you for Being Late*. Penguin Books, 2017

Fukuyama, Francis. *The End of History and the Last Man*. Free Press, 1992

Fukuyama, Francis. *Identity: The Demand for Dignity and the Politics of Resentment*. Farrar, Straus and Giroux, 2018

Gilmour, Ian. *Dancing with Dogma*. Simon & Schuster, 1992

Harari, Yuval Noah. *Sapiens*. Vintage Books, 2016

Harari, Yuval Noah. *Homo Deus*. Vintage Books, 2017

Harari, Yuval Noah. *21 Lessons for the 21st Century*. Vintage Books, 2018

Haskel, Jonathan; Westlake, Stian. *Capitalism without Capital: The Rise of the Intangible Economy*. Princeton University Press, 2017

Havel, Václav. *Living in Truth*. Amazon Books, 1986

Heath, Edward. *The Course of My Life: The Autobiography of Edward Heath*. Hodder & Stoughton, 1998

Heclo, Hugh; Wildavsky, Aaron. *The Private Government of Public Money*. Pan Macmillan, 1974

Hennessey, Thomas. *The First Northern Ireland Peace Process: Power-sharing, Sunningdale and the IRA Ceasefires 1972–76*. Palgrave Macmillan, 2015

Hoskyns, John. *Just in Time: Inside the Thatcher Revolution*. Aurum Press, 2000

Howell, David. *The Edge of Now*. Pan Macmillan, 2000

Howell, David. *Old Links & New Ties: Power and Persuasion in an Age of Networks*. I.B. Tauris, 2013

Huntingdon, Sam. *The Clash of Civilizations and the Remaking of the World Order*. Simon & Schuster, 2011

Jacques, Martin. *When China Rules the World: The End of the Western World and the Birth of a New Global Order*. Penguin Putnam, 2009

Keane, John. *The Life and Death of Democracy*. Simon & Schuster, 2009

Kelso, Louis O.; Adler, Mortimer J. *The Capitalist Manifesto*. Random House, 1958

Kelso, Louis O.; Adler, Mortimer J. *The New Capitalists: A Proposal to Free Economic Growth from the Slavery of Savings.* Random House, 1961

Kelso, Louis O.; Kelso, Patricia Hetter. *Democracy and Economic Power: Extending the ESOP Revolution.* Ballinger, 1986

Khanna, Parag. *Connectography: Mapping the Future of Global Civilization.* Random House, 2016

Khanna, Parag. *The Future is Asian.* Weidenfeld and Nicolson, 2019

Kissinger, Henry. *Diplomacy.* Simon & Schuster, 1994

Kissinger, Henry. *World Order: Reflections on the Character of Nations and the Course of History.* Allen Lane, 2014

Lawson, Nigel. *The View From No.11.* Bantam Press, 1992

Levitsky, Steven; Ziblatt, Daniel. *How Democracies Die.* Viking, 2018

Luttwak, Edward. *Turbo Capitalism.* HarperCollins, 1999

Marx, Karl; Engels, Friedrich. *Correspondence 1846–95*, Martin Lawrence, 1934

Moore, Charles. *Margaret Thatcher: The Authorised Biography, Vols. 1 & 2*, Allen Lane, 2013

Piketty, Thomas; (Goldhammer, Arthur. English translator). *Capital in the Twenty-first Century.* Belknap/Harvard University Press, 2014

Pilling, David. *The Growth Delusion.* Bloomsbury, 2018

Pinker, Steven. *Enlightenment Now: The Case for Reason, Science, Humanism, and Progress.* Viking, 2018

Popper, Karl. *The Poverty of Historicism.* Routledge, 1957

Prestowitz, Clyde. *Three Billon New Capitalists.* Basic Books, 2006

Rajan, Raghuram. *The Third Pillar: The Revival of Community in a Polarized World.* HarperCollins, 2019

Ramo, Joshua Cooper. *The Seventh Sense: Power, Fortune and Survival in the Age of Networks.* Little, Brown, 2016

Ridley, Matt. *The Rational Optimist: How Prosperity Evolves.* Harper, 2010

Rosling, Hans; Rosling, Ola; Rosling Rönnlund, Anna. *Factfulness: Ten Reasons We're Wrong about the World.* Sceptre, 2018

Runciman, David. *How Democracy Ends.* Profile Books, 2018

Schlesinger Jr., Arthur M. *The Vital Center: The Politics of Freedom.* Houghton Mifflin, 1949

Sellar, W.C.; Yeatman, R.J. *1066 And All That.* Methuen Publishing, 1930

Slaughter, Anne-Marie. *The Chessboard and the Web*. Yale University Press, 2017

Smith, Adam. *The Wealth of Nations*. W. Strahan and T. Cadell, 1776

Stuenkel, Oliver. *Post-Western World*. Polity Press, 2016

Taleb, Nassim Nicholas. *The Black Swan*. Random House, 2007

Taleb, Nassim Nicholas. *Skin in the Game*. Allen Lane, 2018

Trevelyan, G.M. *English Social History*. Longmans Green, 1951

Tuchman, Barbara W. *The March of Folly*. Alfred A. Knopf, 1984

Von Hayek, Friedrich A. *The Constitution of Liberty*. Routledge and Kegan Paul, 1960

Wells, H.G. *A Short History of the World*. Cassell & Co., 1922

Wilson, Edward O. *Consilience: The Unity of Knowledge*. Alfred A. Knopf, 1998

Young, Kenneth. *Arthur James Balfour*. HarperCollins, 1963

Endnotes

Introduction

1　https://www.newstatesman.com/politics/uk/2018/08/rabbi-jonathan-sacks-hate-begins-jews-never-ends-jews

2　Winston S. Churchill, *Thoughts and Adventures* (Thornton Butterworth, 1932)

3　Herbert Agar, *A Time of Greatness* (Little, Brown 1942)

4　A noble exception is Richard Cockett's book, *Thinking the Unthinkable* (HarperCollins, 1994).

5　BBC Radio 4, 7 September 2018.

6　*Financial Times* interview, 8 September 2018.

7　Prophetic words from Madeleine Albright.

8　Parag Khanna, *The Future is Asian* (Weidenfeld and Nicolson, 2019)

9　Paul Collier, *The Future of Capitalism: Facing the New Anxieties* (Penguin, 2018), p. 6.

10　Raghuram Rajan, *The Third Pillar: The Revival of Community in a Polarized World* (HarperCollins, 2019)

11　Francis Fukuyama, *The End of History and the Last Man* (Free Press, 1992)

12　Latest estimates claim that 6-billion people now have mobiles – seven-eighths of the entire human race.

13　Niall Ferguson and Fareed Zakaria, *The End of the Liberal Order?* (Oneworld Publications, 2017)

14　David Runciman, *How Democracy Ends* (Profile Books, 2018). See also p. 164 ff.

15 Pages of UK legislation created per year: 1979, 7,500 pages; 1991 10,000 pages. See House of Commons Briefing Paper CBP 2017, April 2017.
16 Parag Khanna again, *The Future is Asian* (2019)
17 Dr Andreas Dombret, Deutsche Bundesbank Communication Director, at the London School of Economics, 18 February 2018.
18 Charles Moore, *Margaret Thatcher: The Authorised Biography* (Allen Lane, 2013)
19 Jonathan Aitken, *Margaret Thatcher: Power and Personality* (Bloomsbury, 2013)

PART ONE: Origins

Chapter One The Crossroads Cabinet
20 Pierre Trudeau, Valéry Giscard d'Estaing, Francesco Cossiga, Helmut Schmidt, Margaret Thatcher, Jimmy Carter, Roy Jenkins (EU Commission President). The Japanese Prime Minister Masayoshi Ōhira died of a heart attack a week before the summit.
21 Otto Friedrich Wilhelm von der Wenge Graf Lambsdorff.
22 The 'by invitation' label was a formality. In practice, Michael Jopling, the Chief Whip (entitled Parliamentary Secretary to the Treasury), and Norman Fowler, the Minister of Transport, were automatic and, in the Chief Whip's case, essential attendees like everyone else.
23 Moore, *The Authorised Biography*, Vol. 1, p. 432
24 1926–2018. MP for Horncastle and Father of the House until his retirement in 2015.

Chapter Two The Wind Changes
25 See in many of his writings, but especially in his books *Thank You for Being Late* (Penguin Books, 2017) and *The World is Flat* (Penguin Books, 2007).
26 Edward Luttwak, *Turbo Capitalism* (HarperCollins, 1999)
27 Clyde Prestowitz, *Three Billon New Capitalists* (Basic Books, 2006)
28 Nigel Lawson, *The View From No.11* (Bantam Press, 1992), p. 86.
29 The phrase comes from Robert Skidelsky's Lecture to the London School of Economics, September 2018.

Chapter Three The Seventy-Niners
30 Jonathan Aitken, *Margaret Thatcher*, p. 253.

31 Hamish Gray, Lord Gray of Contin (1927–2006). MP for Ross and Cromarty.

32 This reality makes nonsense of the narrow 2 per cent target for military spending, much trumpeted in NATO circles. Effective defence and security need far larger resources. Note that in 1964 the outgoing Conservative Government was spending, on then definitions, 7.2 per cent of GNP.

33 Norman St John Stevas, Baron St John of Fawsley (1929–2012). Leader of the House of Commons in Mrs Thatcher's first administration, 1979–81.

Chapter Four The Tigress Emerges

34 See details in Chapters Five and Six.

35 The Rt. Hon. Ernest Marples, house-building and road-building minister under Harold Macmillan, but left out of the shadow team by Ted Heath, of whom he was a vociferous critic. He was credited with being the driving force behind achieving the target of 300,000 new houses a year under Macmillan. In fact, 373,000 were built in 1963, while, in 1964, 434,000 houses were under construction when the Tories left office.

36 Ian Gilmour, *Dancing with Dogma* (Simon & Schuster, 1992)

Chapter Five Manoeuvres at Court

37 Peter Walker, later Lord Walker of Worcester, was a political phenomenon. He had been the youngest member of Ted Heath's Cabinet and now served first as Agriculture Minister, then as Energy Secretary, under Mrs Thatcher – who did not much like him (he was allied to the Wets) but did respect him.

38 Hugh Fraser, MP for Stone from 1945, and for Stafford and Stone from 1950, until his early death in 1984, Secretary of State for Air – when we wisely had such a post – 1962–64, and first husband of Lady Antonia Fraser.

39 Subsequently killed in a motor accident.

40 Particularly unexpected at the BBC. Travelling up to the BBC Shepherd's Bush centre from Guildford on election night 1970, we found a man up a ladder working on their giant swingometer. It was painted to allow for a maximum of a 40-seat majority on the Tory side and about 80 on the Labour side. My swing of 6.2 per cent at Guildford – the first result of the evening – indicated (at that stage) a Tory majority far higher than anything on the clock

face of the swingometer – at least 70. So new numbers were being hurriedly painted in and there were some quite long BBC faces all around.

41 Quoted in Herbert Agar's prescient monograph, *The Perils of Democracy* (Bodley Head, 1965). Agar also authored the slim volume, *A Time for Greatness* (Little, Brown, 1942), published in the darkest days of World War II. Margaret Thatcher said it was the most inspiring book she had ever read.

42 H.G. Wells, *A Short History of the World* (Cassell & Co., 1922)

43 Pepper was a partner in the stockbroking firm W. Greenwell and a strong influence over Mrs Thatcher.

44 This is supported both by Adrian Williamson in his massively thorough (and expensive) analysis of the origins and development of Conservative economic policy under Thatcher, and also by Nigel Lawson in *The View From No.11* (Bantam Press, 1992).

45 Interviewed on BBC TV Channel 4, February 1985, by Peter Jay. Are there echoes here of Karl Marx writing '... all I know is that I am not a Marxist', from Marx and Engels *Correspondence 1846–95* (Martin Lawrence, 1934).

46 Chancellor of the Exchequer, 1983–89.

47 *The View From No.11*, p. 70.

48 *Ibid.*, p. 989.

49 Chair of the US Federal Reserve 2006–14, succeeding Alan Greenspan.

50 Brookings Institute paper, 'Why the Fed needs a new monetary policy framework', June 2018.

51 As observed in Sellar and Yeatman's *1066 And All That* (Methuen Publishing, 1930), the Irish keep changing the question!

52 Institute of Economic Affairs.

53 Centre for Policy Research.

54 On my second day in the Department of Energy, officials informed me that the European Commission was objecting doggedly to subsidies and state aids to UK suppliers of equipment to the booming North Sea oil industry, put in place by my energetic (and distinctly Eurosceptic) predecessor, Tony Benn. The only solution, they advised, was to fly at once to Brussels and encounter the relevant commissioner face to face. This I did. The commissioner relented and we got away with it. However, the episode left no doubt as to who was in charge.

55 In Margaret Thatcher's actual Bruges Speech words, the EU was 'the greatest folly of the modern era' and the UK's part in it was 'a political error of historic magnitude'.

56 *The End of History and the Last Man* (Free Press, 1992)

57 Yuval Noah Harari, *21 Lessons for the 21st Century* (Vintage Books, 2018), author also of *Sapiens* (2016) and *Homo Deus* (2017).

58 Richard Baldwin, *The Great Convergence* (Harvard University Press, 2016)

59 Immuta Inc., Maryland, USA.

60 Hans Rosling, Ola Rosling, Anna Rosling Rönnlund, *Factfulness: Ten Reasons We're Wrong about the World* (Sceptre, 2018), p. 27.

61 Rosling is supported by the latest UN figures reporting that, if the poverty level is set at $1.90 a day, in 1990 35.5 per cent of world population were living beneath it. In 2013 the figure was 10.9 per cent. Rosling thinks that it was 6 per cent in 2018. Still, a terrible blight and source of suffering for those affected, but a fundamentally different picture from the 'developing world' generality that still governs much of world debate and thinking.

62 See David Pilling's masterpiece of GDP disaggregation in *The Growth Delusion* (Bloomsbury, 2018).

63 *GDP: A brief but Affectionate History* (Princeton University Press, 2014)

Chapter Six Origins and Fears

64 Barbara W. Tuchman, *The March of Folly* (Alfred A. Knopf, 1984)

65 See also the reported Thatcher remark that her greatest political achievement was New Labour.

66 Except that it wasn't. On second and third and fourth readings, people began to row back. On the very first page of the introduction to the fourth edition of *The Wealth of Nations*, readers are warned about 'the mad attempt to derive every consequence from the truth which does most to discredit them', 'them' being economists.

67 See, for example, Karl Popper's *The Poverty of Historicism*.

68 Although it turns out this was mainly due to the quirk of a statistical change in the measurement of Italian GDP.

69 Margaret Thatcher, remarks on becoming Prime Minister, 4 May 1979: 'Where there is discord, may we bring harmony. Where there is error, may we bring truth. Where there is doubt, may we bring faith. And where there is despair, may we bring hope.'

70   Anne-Marie Slaughter, *The Chessboard and the Web* (Yale University Press, 2017)
71   Parag Khanna, *Connectography: Mapping the Future of Global Civilization* (Random House, 2016)
72   *The Great Convergence* (Harvard University Press, 2016)
73   Oliver Stuenkel, *Post-Western World* (Polity Press, 2016)
74   G.M. Trevelyan, *English Social History* (Longmans Green, 1951)

Chapter Seven Unspinning the Past

75   Quoted by Sir Max Hastings in *The Times*, 17 August 2018.
76   Opening words of Friedrich A. von Hayek's *The Constitution of Liberty* (Routledge and Kegan Paul, 1960).
77   Nassim Nicholas Taleb, *The Black Swan* (Random House, 2007)
78   See *The Square and the Tower* (Penguin Books, 2018) where Ferguson argues with his usual brilliance that they have.

PART TWO Roots and False Dawns

Chapter Eight Roots of the Revolution

79   Resale Price Maintenance had allowed UK manufacturers and suppliers to set the retail price of their goods, thus effectively blocking price competition and discount wars.
80   In the 1950s and '60s these extravaganzas – to mark the 'coming out' of debutante daughters – were part of a right of passage. The archaic system was closed down in 1975.
81   My father was a retired territorial soldier. After three years in the desert war, a year in Italy and a year in Churchill's War Rooms, he was demobbed, with a grateful government giving him a green tweed jacket, a pair grey flannel trousers and a brown trilby hat. There was no pension attached. He died leaving £1,000. My mother inherited £20,000 in 1947. I went to Eton with the help of an Essex County Scholarship. Does that make me a toff?
82   The John Vassall affair, which had broken in 1962 but rocked on through the early '60s, involved a low-level admiralty official who had been blackmailed over his homosexual tendencies by Moscow into serving as a Soviet spy. Innuendos flew around, in a world with very different attitudes from today, including unsubstantiated claims about improper closeness to a government minister – who had to resign.

83 Ludwig Erhard, *Prosperity Through Competition* (Thames and Hudson, 1958)

84 William Rees-Mogg, then editor of *The Times*. Nigel Lawson, star city editor of the new *Sunday Telegraph* and subsequently editor of the *Spectator* – before moving into politics. Andrew Shonfield, Left inclined but brilliant and scintillating director of Chatham House, and an author.

85 It was, literally, a black-covered volume, compiled with the help of a team of specially selected businessmen and drafted by Mark Schreiber and me, entitled 'Preparation for Government: Urgent Action Dossier'.

86 For a time it was believed that, by an odd coincidence, this was a popular and inspiring mistress at my own prep school. But this may have been a case of confused identities.

87 The massive Victorian and very stately Cheshire home of the Bromley-Davenports.

88 Henry Brandon, much celebrated *Sunday Times* Washington correspondent. William Clark, at this time vice-president of the World Bank, former foreign correspondent of *The Observer*, press adviser to Anthony Eden, founder of the Overseas Development Institute – and often referred to as the man who knew everyone.

89 Now Lord Marlesford.

Chapter Nine Heath and Hopes

90 Famous for its annual theatricals, directed by Peter Daubeny, and inducing at least half a dozen MPs to take to the chorus line. There was a 100-seat theatre in one of the wings.

91 Sir Hamilton Kerr MP (Cambridge), Sir John Foster MP (Northwich) and Sir Harmar Nicholls MP (Peterborough) were frequent guests at Capesthorne.

92 The ancient 'seat' of the Home family.

93 See David Howell, *The Edge of Now* (Pan Macmillan, 2000) and again in *Old Links & New Ties* (I.B Tauris, 2013).

94 Madron and Nancy Joan Seligman, Ted's oldest and most loyal friends. Later Madron served for some years as an enthusiastic MEP.

95 Not to be confused with the dour Gordon Brown, Prime Minister some four decades later. George Brown was extremely affable and friendly to all and sundry, regardless of party affiliation (as was his equally warm and friendly brother, Ron Brown MP).

96 Basil de Ferranti – a fascinating mixture of innovator/inventor, playboy. Briefly an MP and junior minister and heir, with his elder brother Sebastian, to the Ferranti fortune and business – at one stage one of Britain's most successful electrical and electronic names and pioneer of semi-conductor and microchip technology in the UK. Their business acumen did not quite match their innovative style and Ferranti collapsed in the '90s in a mire of fraud and mismanagement.

97 Kenneth Young, *Arthur James Balfour* (HarperCollins, 1963)

Chapter Ten Wrong from the Start

98 The full story of the new central staff we longed for, eventually emerging as the CPRS, is best set out in Tessa Blackstone's and William Plowden's *Inside the Think-Tank* (William Heinemann, 1988).

99 The CSD had been set up a few months earlier, following the recommendations of the Fulton Report on Reform of the Civil Service. I was its first junior minister, the overseeing Cabinet minister being Earl Jellicoe, a man of endless charm and friendliness, with an impressive war record. He was also Leader of the House of Lords, although confiding in me that he could not really understand Ted Heath or what he was about. Its first home was at the back of the Treasury building overlooking St James's Park. However, after a year we moved to the newly done-up Old Admiralty across Horse Guards Parade.

Chapter Eleven A Diversion: What If?

100 Hugh Heclo and Aaron Wildavsky, *The Private Government of Public Money* (Pan Macmillan, 1974)

101 Richard Cockett, *Thinking the Unthinkable* (HarperCollins, 1994)

102 Edward Heath, *The Course of My Life: The Autobiography of Edward Heath* (Hodder & Stoughton, 1998)

Chapter Twelve A Tale of Two Roles

103 Nassim Nicholas Taleb, *Skin in the Game* (Allen Lane, 2018)

104 *The Authorised Biography* (Allen Lane, 2013)

105 In 2012, the Labour Party leader, Ed Miliband, attempted to steal Conservative clothes and brand Labour the party of One Nation, as inspired by Benjamin Disraeli. It did him no good. Labour lost in the subsequent election (2015).

Chapter Thirteen Ireland, Europe and the Eternal Question

106 Together with the full flowering of the Scottish grievance culture.

107 Ken Bloomfield, *Stormont in Crisis* (Blackstaff Press, 1994)

108 Thomas Hennessey *The First Northern Ireland Peace Process: Power-sharing, Sunningdale and the IRA Ceasefires 1972–76* (Palgrave Macmillan, 2015)

109 An officer serving with the Secret Intelligence Service (MI6).

PART THREE The Inheritance

Chapter Fourteen Technology Unravels the Global Order

110 Most recent examples of this phenomenon include the violent Paris riots against President Macron and his fuel tax impositions in December 2018. This event was described by the BBC's Paris correspondent as 'a novel form of digitally based protest'. Why it should be 'novel' when it has been the most obvious driver of organised protest almost everywhere for all of 30 years past is something the BBC would have to explain.

111 Archie Brown, *The Myth of the Strong Leader: Political Leadership in the Modern Age* (The Bodley Head, 2015)

112 The escape from Communism in 1969/70 involved only one student death – a tragedy of course but gentle as compared with the numerous fatalities at the time of the crushed Prague Spring uprising and the immolation of Jan Palach of 1969.

113 Václav Havel, *Living in Truth* (Amazon Books, 1986)

114 And subsequently highly effective chairman of The National Trust.

115 Martin Jacques, *When China Rules the World: The End of the Western World and the Birth of a New Global Order* (Penguin Putnam, 2009)

Chapter Fifteen Asian Reset

116 David Howell, *The Edge of Now: New Questions for Democracy in the Network Age* (Pan MacMillan, 2000)

117 *Factfulness* (Sceptre, 2018)

118 Xi Jinping. Speech on 40th anniversary of China's reform, 18 December 2018.

119 To some of these, Britain is already reaching out, such as the new Asian Infrastructure and Development Bank (AIIB) and the Mark Two Trans-Pacific Partnership, now called The Comprehensive

and Progressive Agreement (CPTPP) – and to the Commonwealth network belatedly, after years of neglect. However, now along come the Shanghai Cooperation Organization (SCO),The Eurasian Economic Union (EAEU), the newly formed ASEAN Economic Community, the Pacific Partnership, a much stronger African Union, and several others – while, through most of the regions and countries covered by these associations, China plans to thread its various Belt and Road structures, underpinned by an investment programme of a trillion dollars.

120 FCO official response to the Lords International Relations Committee Report, 'UK foreign policy in a shifting world order', 18 December 2018.

121 China's largest nuclear power construction company, CGN, already finances 40 per cent of Britain's newest large nuclear station project at Hinkley Point, is ready to build its own-managed new station at Bradwell in Essex, is bidding to be part of the joint venture at Sizewell C in Suffolk and has its eye on projects at Wylfa in North Wales and Moorside in Lancashire, where Japanese companies have pulled out.

122 Germany's attempted, and vastly expensive, energy transformation has been a saga of unintended consequences. Closing down nuclear power, and heavily subsidising wind and solar power, has perversely led first to increased coal-burning, with higher carbon emissions, then to big new demands for gas which will be met mostly by Russia. The outcome: Europe's most expensive energy, increased Russian gas reliance and rising emissions.

Chapter Sixteen The Mother of All Networks

123 The Queen's Christmas Broadcast, 2009.

124 Thanks largely to the personal initiative and insistence of Lord Marland, chairman of the Commonwealth Enterprise and Investment Council.

125 If I may indulge in a literary 'selfie' – the title of a book I wrote in 2013 – *Old Links & New Ties: Power and Persuasion in an Age of Networks* (I.B. Tauris, 2013).

126 Itself under dire current threat from President Trump's apparent dislike of multilateral institutions.

127 McKinsey Global Institute, 'Globalization in Transition: the Future of Trade and Value Chains', January 2018.

128 China has opened numerous Confucius Institutes across the world. Analysts estimate that there is an annual Chinese budget for 'external propaganda' in the region of $10-billion. The USA spends less than a tenth of that on 'public diplomacy', aka soft power. The UK 'soft power' budget about a fiftieth. Note also that in China 'propaganda' is not considered a bad or loaded word.

129 Formerly called just the Trans-Pacific Partnership, until America walked out on it. Now consisting of Japan, Canada, Mexico, Australia, Peru and New Zealand. Recently, Shinzō Abe, the Japanese Prime Minister, has stated that the UK would be welcomed 'with open arms' to join.

Chapter Seventeen Flaws in the Tapestry

130 Joshua Cooper Ramo, *The Seventh Sense* (Little, Brown, 2016), p. 304.

131 Robert C. Bannister (ed.), *On Liberty, Society and Politics: The Essential Essays* of *William Graham Sumner* (Liberty Fund, 1992)

132 Edward O. Wilson, *Consilience: The Unity of Knowledge* (Alfred A. Knopf, 1998)

133 Later Lord Wolfson of Sunningdale

134 John Hoskyns, *Just in Time: Inside the Thatcher Revolution* (Aurum Press, 2000)

135 China-based Baidu, Tencent and Alibaba may now be bigger than Google, Facebook, Instagram and the rest, and certainly will be if policies in Western countries succeed in breaking up these near-monopolies, thus leaving the field more open than ever for the global advance of the Chinese giants. In the end East and West will have to cooperate or see the algorithmic jungle take over.

Chapter Eighteen What Is to Be Done?

136 The second worst advice was, of course, to promise a referendum. George Osborne tried desperately to dissuade David Cameron from holding it. He warned that it would split the Conservative Party down the middle. It has done so. Third worst was to hold it in the summer of 2016 instead of waiting until the end of 2017. A year later both the costs of staying in an increasingly dysfunctional EU and the cost of leaving would have made for a far more informed debate.

137 Nassim Nicolas Taleb, *Skin in The Game* (Allen Lane, 2018)

138 Cockett (HarperCollins, 1994)

139 Louis O. Kelso and Mortimer J. Adler, *The Capitalist Manifesto* (Random House, 1958)

140 Louis O. Kelso and Mortimer J. Adler, *The New Capitalists: A Proposal to Free Economic Growth from the Slavery of Savings* (Random House, 1961)

141 Amplified and deepened a decade later in his subsequent book *Democracy and Economic Power.*

142 Thomas Piketty (English translation by Arthur Goldhammer), *Capital in the Twenty-first Century,* (Belknap/Harvard University Press, 2014)

143 As in *Dad's Army.*

144 Thomas Cook and the Carlisle Breweries marked the dismal sum of 'back to the people' privatisation during the Heath administration.

145 Torsten Bell, director of the Resolution Foundation think-tank.

146 Secretary of State for Social Services – an impossibly large portfolio which finally wore down his health.

147 Chancellor of the Exchequer, 1983–89.

148 Jonathan Haskel and Stian Westlake, *Capitalism without Capital: The Rise of the Intangible Economy* (Princeton University Press, 2017)

149 Louis O. Kelso and Patricia Hetter Kelso, *Democracy and Economic Power: Extending the ESOP Revolution* (Ballinger, 1986)

150 Employee Stock Ownership Plans; Company Share Option Plans; Generalized System of Preferences.

151 Anne-Marie Slaughter (Yale University Press, 2017)

152 Manuel Castells, *Information Age* trilogy (Blackwell 1996, 1997, 1998)

153 Joshua Cooper Ramo (Little, Brown, 2016)

154 *Ibid.*

Chapter Nineteen The New Labyrinth

155 Daniel Kroening, professor of computer science, Oxford University, from *The Times* 26 October 2017.

Chapter Twenty The Case for Looking Back

156 Henry Kissinger, *World Order: Reflections on the Character of Nations and the Course of History* (Allen Lane, 2014)

157 Sir Ronald Grierson 1921–2014. Banker and public servant. Described by the *Daily Telegraph* as an 'international networker *par excellence*'. As a director or Warburgs he managed to give two lunches a day. An exhilarating friend.

158 Von Hayek (Routledge and Kegan Paul, 1960)

159 Fukuyama (Free Press, 1992)

160 Robert D. Kaplan, 'The Coming Anarchy: How Scarcity, Crime, Overpopulation, Tribalism and Disease are Rapidly Destroying the Social Fabric of Our Planet' (The Atlantic Monthly, February 1994)

161 Taleb (Random House, 2007)

162 Matt Ridley, *The Rational Optimist: How Prosperity Evolves* (Harper, 2010)

163 Steven Pinker, *Enlightenment Now: The Case for Reason, Science, Humanism, and Progress* (Viking, 2018)

164 *Factfulness* (Sceptre, 2018)

165 David Ricardo (1772–1823), political economist.

166 *The Great Convergence* (Harvard University Press, 2016)

Chapter Twenty-one How to Safeguard Democracy Now

167 *The Times*'s columnists were particularly snooty and dismissive.

168 Quoted in Herbert Agar's *Time for Greatness* q.v.

169 Runciman (Profile Books, 2018)

170 John Keane, *The Life and Death of Democracy* (Simon & Schuster, 2009)

171 *Viz*: Steven Levitsky and Daniel Ziblatt, *How Democracies Die* (Viking, 2018), or Paul Cartledge, *Democracy: A Life* (Oxford University Press, 2016).

172 Henry Kissinger, *Diplomacy* (Simon & Schuster, 1994)

Chapter Twenty-two Conclusions, Answers, Lessons, Hopes

173 Brown (The Bodley Head, 2015)

174 See Thomas L. Friedman, *The Lexus and the Olive Tree: Understanding Globalization* (Farrar, Straus and Giroux, 1999), on 'the little guys' – and many other of his works.

175 These points, too, draw on Herbert Agar's superb *The Perils of Democracy*.

176 Sam Huntingdon's book and theme. See *The Clash of Civilizations and the Remaking of the World Order* (Simon & Schuster, 2011).

Chapter Twenty-three Afterthoughts: On the Head of a Dictator, the Power of Us and Catching Up

177 *21 Lessons for the 21st Century* (Vintage Books, 2018)

178 John Milton (1608–74), Sonnet 16: 'Cromwell, our chief of men, who through a cloud'.

179 For the best account of the long history of how this came to be and how scientific proof confirmed that this was genuinely the head of the Lord Protector, see Jonathan Fitzgibbons's book, *Cromwell's Head* (The National Archives, 2008).

180 Antonia Fraser, *Cromwell, Our Chief of Men* (Weidenfeld & Nicolson, 1973)

181 Thanks to the persuasive analysis of Joseph Nye. See the seminal Lords' report of March 2014, 'Persuasion and Power in the Modern World', House of Lords, Paper 150.

182 Remembering that soft power and hard power are now merging into one stream of influence and projection as 'smart power'. Just as the right soft power narrative can win battles, so strong military forces are now part of the armoury of persuasion.

183 Francis Fukuyama, *Identity: The Demand for Dignity and the Politics of Resentment* (Farrar, Straus and Giroux, 2018)

Index

Note: The following abbreviation has been used – *n* = note